Heroes of the Nations

EDITED BY

Evelyn Abbott, M.A.

FELLOW OF BALLIOL COLLEGE, OXFORD

FACTA DUCIS VIVENT, OPEROSAQUE
GLORIA RERUM. — OVID, IN LIVIAM, 265.

THE HERO'S DEEDS AND HARD-WON
FAME SHALL LIVE.

SALADIN

THE CITADEL OF CAIRO, EAST ANGLE

Frontispiece.

SALADIN

AND THE FALL OF THE KINGDOM OF JERUSALEM

BY

STANLEY LANE-POOLE, M.A.

AUTHOR OF THE " LIFE OF STRATFORD CANNING," " THE ART OF THE SARACENS "
" CAIRO," " STUDIES IN A MOSQUE," " THE MOORS IN SPAIN "
" TURKEY," " THE BARBARY CORSAIRS " ETC.

———

G. P. PUTNAM'S SONS

NEW YORK   LONDON
27 WEST TWENTY-THIRD STREET   24 BEDFORD STREET, STRAND

The Knickerbocker Press

1898

PREFACE.

SALADIN is one of the few Oriental Personages who need no introduction to English readers. Sir Walter Scott has performed that friendly office with the warmth and insight of appreciative genius. It was Saladin's good fortune to attract the notice not only of the great romancer, but also of King Richard, and to this accident he partly owes the result that, instead of remaining a dry historical expression, under the Arabic style of "*el-Melik en-Nasir Salah-ed-din Yusuf ibn Ayyub*," he has become, by the abbreviated name of "Saladin," that familiar and amiable companion which is called a household word. The idea, it is true, is vague and romantic. The *Talisman* has given us a noble portrait of the Sultan whose chivalry and generosity excited the admiration of the Crusaders, but the reader is left in uncertainty as to the history and achievements of the hero, and what he is told in those fascinating pages is not always strictly authentic. On the historical relation of the novel to which Saladin owes so much of his fame something is said at the end of this book. The present biography, the first that has been written in English, aspires to fill in, from contemporary sources, the details of the picture.

It is singular that, so far as English literature is concerned, the character and history of Saladin should have been suffered to remain where Scott left them seventy years ago, and that no complete Life of the celebrated adversary of Richard Cœur de Lion should have been written in our language. The materials are abundant, even exhaustive, so far as eastern scholars understood biography. We must not expect the personal details which delight the student of "interviews" : there were no illustrated papers in Saladin's time. But for the essential facts of his life and the qualities of his nature we have the best possible evidence, rich in extent and faithful in detail. The writers of the two chief Arabic records had excellent opportunities of ascertaining the truth, and both were men of learning and high character. Baha-ed-din, who was only seven years younger than Saladin, though he survived him by forty, was an Arab of the celebrated tribe of Asad, born at Mosil on the Tigris in 1145. He went through the arduous course of study by which Moslems in those days qualified themselves for the judicial office of Kady. In the famous Nizamiya college at Baghdad, founded by the great Vezir Nizam-el-mulk, the friend and schoolfellow of the astronomer-poet Omar Khayyam, Baha-ed-din attended the lectures of the most dis-tinguished professors of the day, men who had wandered, like our own medieval scholars, from uni-versity to university, from Spanish Cordova to Tatar Samarkand, teaching and learning as they went. He became a professor himself at his native city of Mosil, and his wisdom and judgment so commended him to the Atabeg or ruler of Mesopotamia that he chose him repeatedly to be his ambassador in grave political emergencies.

Baha-ed-din was at Mosil when Saladin twice laid siege to it in 1182 and 1185 ; he went on an embassy to Damascus in 1184, when Saladin was so much impressed by his ability that he offered him a judgeship, which was loyally declined by the envoy ; but they met again at Harran in the spring of 1186, when Baha-ed-din assisted in drawing up a treaty of peace between his sovereign and Saladin. After making the pilgrimage to Mekka, and to Jerusalem, then newly recovered from the Christians, he visited the Sultan once more, and from that time forth he seldom left his side. Entering his service on 28th June, 1188, he was present throughout his subsequent campaigns, witnessed the siege of Acre from the beginning to the end, accompanied him as he harassed Richard's march down the coast, took a prominent part in the engagements at Jaffa in 1192, and was at Saladin's bedside during his fatal illness. After the Sultan's death, he accepted the high dignity of judge of Aleppo, and there he devoted his zeal and his savings to founding colleges and training doctors to be learned in the law. One of his pupils has left a touching description of the venerable Kady, as he knew him, when a heated alcove and heavy furs could not warm the chilled blood of 85 ; but the old scholar still loved to teach the students who came to him after Friday prayers, when he could no longer

go to the mosque, and when even in his private de-
votions he could scarcely keep his feet. " He
drooped like an unfledged bird for weakness," says
his biographer, and in 1234 he died, twoscore years
after the events he related in his Life of his master.

For the last five years of Saladin's career, Baha-ed-
din is an incomparable authority, an eye-witness of
what passed, and an intimate friend and counsellor
of the Sultan. For the earlier periods he is less accurate and much less detailed ; but even here he is
able to record several important transactions at first
hand, and his familiar intercourse with Saladin and
his officers and kinsmen must have supplied him with
much of his information. He writes, it is true, as an
avowed panegyrist, but though in his eyes the King
can do no wrong, he is so frank and guileless in his
narrative, and so obviously writes exactly what he
saw and thought, that the biography has not suffered
by the writer's hero-worship. It bears the unmistak-
able stamp of truth, and its personal bias and oriental
hyperbolism are easily discounted. As our sole first-
hand witness to the negotiations between Richard I.
and Saladin, Baha-ed-din's simple veracity is especially a quality of importance.

If Baha-ed-din is an avowed hero-worshipper, in the
other prime authority we find a useful corrective to
undue admiration. Ibn-el-Athir had every political
reason to decry the supplanter of his local lords, and
his annals contain criticism of Saladin's generalship
and one or two graver accusations. Ibn-el-Athir, who
was also an Arab, of the tribe of Sheyban, was fifteen
years younger than Baha-ed-din, and was born in 1160

at Jezirat-ibn-Omar on the Tigris, over which city his father was Waly or prefect. The historian spent most of his life in laborious study at Mosil, where his brother was a distinguished councillor of the Atabeg who ruled Mesopotamia. Another brother held a post in Saladin's chancery. Ibn-el-Athir, like Baha-ed-din, was present when Saladin besieged Mosil in 1185, and he accompanied the contingent which the Mesopotamian princes afterwards sent to join the Sultan's army in his north Syrian campaign of 1188; he was also a traveller, and in his journeys to Damascus, Jerusalem, and Aleppo, he had means of verifying his information. His *History of the Atabegs of Mosil*, completed in 1211, is as much a panegyric as Baha-ed-din's biography of Saladin, but it is a panegyric of Saladin's enemies; its author can never forgive him for supplanting the dynasty of the Atabegs in Syria, and making even the great lord of Mosil his vassal. Thus, if anything can be urged in disparagement of Saladin, we may be sure that Ibn-el-Athir will not pass it over. Yet, with this natural bias in favour of his family's old masters and benefactors, he is not usually unfair. He recognises Saladin's great services to Islam, and in his later work, the *Kamil*, or *Perfection of History*, which is brought up to within three years of his death in 1233, he shows a more impartial spirit than in his special eulogy of the Atabegs of Mosil.

These two historians must be the prime authorities for a Life of Saladin; but there are others of great value for particular portions or aspects of his career. Of these Imad-ed-din of Ispahan, generally

known as el-Katib, "the Scribe," Saladin's chief
secretary or chancellor for the Syrian provinces, is of
the first importance ; but unfortunately only a small
part of his work has been printed. He was with his
master at the siege of Acre, and his writings, despite
their intolerable rhetoric, have the merit of first-
hand documents. The *Autobiography* of Osama, an
Arab prince and poet, of the castle of Sheyzar on the
Orontes, who witnessed the greater part of the Crusading period from his birth in 1095 to his death in
1188, presents a vivid picture of the times ; but although in his old age he lived for some years at
Damascus in frequent intercourse with Saladin, his
reminiscences in this regard are disappointing : the
old Arab was too full of himself to give much space
to the sayings and doings of others. Ibn-Khallikan,
the assiduous biographer of eminent men, and Abu-
Shama, the author of *The Two Gardens*, were neither
of them contemporaries ; but both knew people who
knew Saladin, and their writings sometimes supply
what was missing, or amplify what was meagre, in
the contemporary records.

Among the Christian chroniclers we are fortunate
in the presence in Palestine of the incomparable Archbishop William of Tyre, whose *Historia*, far trans-
cending in vividness, grasp and learning all Latin or
Arabic annals of the time, deals with the events in
the East from 1144 to 1183 from personal knowledge. The Archbishop left no successor of his own
calibre, and that he should not have lived to carry
his history ten years further, to the end of the Third
Crusade, is a loss which every student of the period,

and not least the biographer of Saladin, must lament. The various continuators of his work cannot lay claim to his great qualities as an historian, but their merits are not to be undervalued, and the *Chronicle* of Ernoul in particular supplies valuable contemporary evidence. Ernoul was squire to Balian of Ibelin, who played a prominent part in the Holy War and was frequently in personal relations with Saladin ; and the squire doubtless attended his master to the memorable field of Hittin and afterwards in the defence of Jerusalem. Ernoul's narrative, which is full of vivid personal touches, is thus extremely valuable as representing the Christian side of events which the Arabic writers describe from a Mohammedan point of view. It is also useful, in a less degree, in checking the exuberant Ricardolatry of the *Itinerarium Regis Ricardi*, which forms our fullest authority for the Third Crusade, and, despite its exaggerations and party spirit, is a marvellously graphic recital of the achievements of the English hero.

These then are the chief sources from which the present Life of Saladin is drawn. They are nearly all contemporary, and a large part of the story is told by actual eye-witnesses, whilst in no instance has an authority been relied upon who was more than one generation removed from the events he relates. References to these sources are given when a statement seemed to require authentication, and in the later chapters, when it is important to distinguish the testimony of Christian from that of Moslem witnesses, such footnotes are frequent; but in the earlier

part, where nearly everything rests upon the authority of Ibn-el-Athir and Baha-ed-din, references
are given only when there is a serious discrepancy
between the two. In an historical study founded
upon original research such verification is, of course,
essential ; but where none is given, some confidence,
it is hoped, will be placed in the biographer. There
is not a line in this volume that cannot be substan-
tiated by practically contemporary evidence.

It has been remarked as strange that such abundant
materials should not long ago have been utilised in
an exhaustive Life of Saladin, but it would not be
fair to ignore the admirable labours of M. Marin,
"un écrivain aussi connu par la douceur de ses
mœurs que par l'étendue de ses lumières et l'élé-
gance de sa plume." M. Louis-François-Claude
Marin was born in Provence, where he eventually
held the posts of Censeur Royal et de la police, and
Sécrétaire général de la Librairie et des Académies
de Marseille et Nancy. In 1758 he published in two
charmingly printed duodecimo volumes an *Histoire
de Saladin, Sulthan d'Egypte et de Syrie* (Paris, chez
Tilliard, Libraire, Quai des Augustins, à l'Image
Saint Benôit). The book appears to be almost unknown, or it would surely have found a translator.
At once scholarly, philosophic, and written with that
light touch by which the French, preëminently, are
able to carry off the ponderous effect of real learning, M. Marin's biography has only to be read to be
admired. He made a full use of the Crusading
chronicles, and of Schultens' edition of Baha-ed-din,
and he consulted Ibn-el-Athir's *Atabegs* in an Arabic

manuscript at Paris. So far as his contemporary
materials go, he is excellent; but he relied overmuch
on later writers, and on unequal though learned com-
pilations such as Herbelot's *Bibliothèque Orientale ;*
and of course a great deal has been discovered and
published since his time. Still, considering his necessary limitations, he achieved a remarkable success,
and the only serious fault to be found with his manner of dealing with such authorities as he was able
to use is a tendency to read more "between the
lines" than the text really justifies. M. Marin employed what is called "the historical imagination"
over freely, and despite his frequent references to
original sources one can detect a personal equation
which has to be eliminated. It is much more interesting to give oneself a free hand in writing history,
but the temptation must be subdued and the letter
of the text must be respected.

Some authors, in treating of the history of Mesopotamia, have thought it necessary to prepare their
readers by beginning at the Flood. M. Marin considered that his Life of Saladin demanded an introduction which went back to Mohammed and the first
preaching of Islam. I have not tried the patience
of the reader quite so severely, but without some account of the course of history in western Asia during the eleventh and twelfth centuries, the political
situation in which Saladin began his career would
be unintelligible. Especially important is the position achieved by his great forerunner, Zengy, the
conqueror of Edessa, whose unfulfilled ambitions
prepared the way for the imperial realisations of

Saladin. The introductory chapters, however, have been reduced to as small a compass as possible.

Oriental names are naturally a stumbling-block to western readers, and the use of accents, long marks, dots, and the like, does not seem to be of much assistance to the unlearned. In the present work, therefore, the names are written as simply as possible, and the reader is only asked to pronounce the vowels after the Italian manner. Those who are curious as to the more precise transliteration will consult the index, where every name is furnished with the proper accents and distinguishing marks, and can be at once converted by the scholar into the Arabic character. In the text, the article *el* is generally omitted before the well-known names of towns, such as el-Mosil, er-Ramla, and western names are given when familiar, as in the case of ʿEdessa (for er-Ruha), Aleppo (for Halab), and Cairo (for el-Kahira). When a town has two names, one used by the Arabs, the other by the "Franks" or Crusaders, both are given on its first occurrence, and Crusading names are retained so long as the place remained in the hands of the Crusaders.

Tables of contemporary sovereigns and princes in western Asia, of Saladin's family, and of the chief Crusading houses, will help the reader to understand the political situation. The maps are based upon the "Survey of Western Palestine," Thuillier and Rey's "North Syria," and the Arab geographers. Much assistance has been derived from Mr. Guy Le Strange's valuable work on *Palestine under the Moslems ;* the notes contributed by Gen.

Sir Charles Wilson and Lieut.-Col. Conder, R.E., to the Palestine Pilgrims' Text Society's translation of Baha-ed-din have been consulted; but the text of that work, not being directly translated from the Arabic, has not been cited. The author is specially indebted to Mr. T. A. Archer, not only for ready help in any difficulty that arose in connexion with the Crusading chronicles, but also for permission to quote his translation of parts of the *Itinerary of King Richard*, originally published in his fascinating little book, *The Crusade of Richard I.*, in the series of " English History from Contemporary Writers," edited by Professor York Powell. His thanks are also due to Mr. E. B. Knobel, late President of the Royal Astronomical Society, for kindly investigating the chronology of the eclipses recorded in the course of Saladin's campaigns, and to the editor of the *Quarterly Review* for permission to reprint part of an article on " The Age of Saladin."

SALADIN.

ADDENDA AND ERRATA.

Page XIII. Add to preface :

M. Paul Casanova has kindly permitted the reproduction of three
of the photographs which illustrate his valuable *Histoire et description de la Citadelle du Caire ;* to Dr. F. J. Mackinnon is due the
illustration of the tomb of Saladin at Damascus, as restored in Ottoman times. The author is also obliged to the Council of the Royal
Institute of British Architects for the use of two views of the Omayyad Mosque of Damascus, before the fire, from sketches by Mr. R.
Phenè Spiers, F.S.A.

Page XXI. Line 3 from bottom *for* Crusades *read* Crusade.

"   XXIII. Line 9, *for* Yuluk Arstan *read* Yūluk Arstān.

"   "   " 11, *for* Harran *read* Harrān.

"   "   " 13, *for* Mesud, Atabeg *read* Mes'ūd, Atābeg.

"   24. Line 11 from bottom, *for* Tripoli *read* Tripolis.

"   54. First line from bottom, *for* Khanum *read* Khatun.

"   73. Fifteenth line from bottom, *for* noli *read* nolo.

"   84. Tenth line from bottom, *for* Tripoli *read* Tripolis.

"   98. Title beneath coin, *for* Nug-ed-din *read* Nur-ed-din.

"   134. Eleventh line from bottom, *for* Whose sister was his
own wife, *read* With whom he was nearly connected.

"   159. Ninth line from bottom, Dele comma after " skin of
water."

"   238. Fourth line from bottom, *for* Salahed-Dunya *read*
Salah-ed-Dunya.

"   404. Left hand column, *for* Asākir *read* 'Asākir.

"   404. Left hand column, *for* 'Asimat *read* 'Aṣimat.

"   404. Right hand column, *for* Azāz *read* 'Azāz.

"   404. Right hand column, *for* Bab-el-'Imady *read* Bab el-
'Imādy.

"   408. Left hand column, *for* Ibn-Asākir *read* Ibn-'Asākir.

"   408. Right hand column, *for* Jurdik *read* Jūrdīk.

"   409. Right hand column, lines 15 to 18 from bottom, *for*
Sultan and Sultans *read* Sulṭān and Sulṭāns.

"   510. Left hand column, line 21, *for* " de Balafré " *read* " le
Balafré."

"   412. Left hand column 19 from top, *for* Dārmū *read* Dārūm.

"   412. Right hand column, lines 3, 5, 7, *for* Azāz *read* 'Azāz.

"   314. Left hand column, line 16 from bottom, *for* Sumeysaṭ
read Sumeysāṭ.

"   414. Right hand column, *for* Siffīn *read* Ṣiffīn.

PRINCIPAL AUTHORITIES.

Ibn-el-Athīr (1160–1233), *el-Bāhir :* History of the Atābegs of el-Mōsil, written in 1211 (*Recueil des historiens des Croisades : historiens orientaux*, tome ii., 2, Paris, 1876).

Ibn-el-Athīr (1160–1233), *el-Kāmil fi-t-tarīkh :* General History, written up to 1231 (ed. Tornberg, 14 vols., Leyden, 1866–76 ; *Recueil*, tome i., 1872 ; tome ii., 1, 1887).

Bahā-ed-dīn, Ibn-Sheddād (1145–1234), *en-Nawādir es-Sultanīya wa-l-Mahāsin el-Yūsufīya :* Life of Saladin (ed. Schultens, Leyden, 1732 ; *Recueil*, tome iii., 1884 ; and Palestine Pilgrims' Text Society, ed. Sir C. W. Wilson, K.C.B., R.E., 1897).

Ibn-Khallikān (1211–1282), *Wefayāt el-Aᶜyān :* Biographical Dictionary (trans. de Slane, 4 vols., Paris, 1843–71).

Osāma ibn Munkidh (1095–1188), *Kitāb el-Iᶜtibār ;* Autobiography (ed. and trans. H. Derenbourg, 2 vols., Paris, 1886–93).

ᶜImād-ed-dīn el-Kātib (1125–1201), *el-Feth el-Kussy* (ed. Landberg, vol. i., Leyden, 1888).

Abu-Shāma (ob. 1267), *Kitāb er-Rōdateyn :* History of Nūr-ed-dīn and Saladin (2 vols., Cairo, 1870–71).

William of Tyre (*c.* 1137–1185), *Historia rerum in partibus transmarinis gestarum* (*Recueil : historiens occidentaux*, tome i., Paris, 1844).

Ernoul (fl. 1187), *Chronique* (ed. Mas Latrie, Paris, 1871).

Itinerarium Peregrinorum et Gesta Regis Ricardi (1190–92) (ed. Stubbs, Rolls Series, vol. xxxviii. a, London, 1864).

Archer, T. A., *The Crusade of Richard I.* (London, 1888).

Le Strange, Guy, *Palestine under the Moslems* (Palestine Exploration Fund, 1890).

Rey, E., *Les colonies franques de Syrie* (Paris, 1883).

Other works are also referred to in the footnotes.

CONTENTS.

PART I.—INTRODUCTORY.

CHAPTER I.

CHAPTER II.

CHAPTER III.

CHAPTER IV.

PART II.—EGYPT, *1138–1174.*

PART III.—EMPIRE, *1174–1186.*

PART IV.—THE HOLY WAR, *1187-1191.*

ILLUSTRATIONS.

---

* Nos. 2, 3, 4, 5, 6, and 10 represent paintings on glass windows, now demolished, at the abbey of St. Denys, executed by order of Abbot Suger in the middle of the twelfth century, and are valuable as contemporary attempts to depict Crusaders and Saracens in their armour. They are reproduced from Montfaucon's *Monuments de la Monarchie Française*, Tome I., pl. LI.–LIV.

† Reproduced from Archer's *Crusades of Richard I.*

‡ Reproduced from the *Journal of the Royal Institute of British Architects*.

PAGE

* Reproduced from Lane-Poole's *Cairo.*

† Reproduced from Lane-Poole's *Art of the Saracens.*

‡ Reproduced from G. Paris' *Guillaume de Tyr.*

§ Reproduced from *Mémoires publiés par les Membres de la Mission Archéologique Française au Caire.*

PAGE

---

* Reproduced from the *Journal of the Royal Institute of British
Architects.*

† Reproduced from G. Rey's *Monuments de L'Architecture Mili-
taire des Croisés.*

✦ Reproduced from G. Paris' *Guillaume de Tyr.*

PAGE

NOTE.—The head- and tail-pieces not described above
consist of Kufic inscriptions and arabesques not later than
the thirteenth century.

MAPS AND PLANS.

* Reproduced from Lelewel's *Géographie du Moyen Age.*
† Reproduced from Archer's *Crusades.*
‡ Reproduced from C. Oman's *Art of War.*

SALADIN.

PART I.

INTRODUCTORY.

MINE EYES HAVE SEEN THE DAYS OF HIS MAJESTY,
KING STRONG TO AID ; THE SUM OF PIETY,
BANE OF THE CRUCIFIX-IDOLATRY,
BANNERET OF RIGHT AND GENEROSITY,

SALĀH-ED-DĪN,

LORD OF ISLĀM AND MUSLIMĪN,
SAVING GOD'S HOUSE FROM THE NAZARENE,
SERVING THE HOLY PLACES TWIN,
VICTORIOUS YŪSUF, SON OF AYYŪB, OF SHADHY'S KIN:
GOD WATER HIS GRAVE WITH SHOWERS OF CLEMENCY,
AND GRANT HIM IN MERCY'S HOME THE MEED OF CONSTANCY.

BAHĀ-ED-DĪN

THE LIFE OF SALADIN.

CHAPTER I.

SALADIN'S WORLD.

IN the year 1132 a broken army, flying before its
pursuers, reached the left bank of the Tigris.
On the other side, upon a steep cliff, stood the
impregnable Fortress of Tekrit, defended landwards
by a deep moat and accessible only by secret steps
cut in the rock and leading from the heart of the
citadel to the water's edge. The one hope of the
fugitives was to attain the refuge of the castle, and
their fate turned upon the disposition of its warden.
Happily he chose the friendly part, and provided a
ferry by which they crossed to safety. The ferry
boats of the Tigris made the fortunes of the house of
Saladin. The flying leader who owed his life to
their timely succour was Zengy, the powerful lord of
Mosil; and in later days, when triumph returned to
his standards, he did not forget the debt he owed
Tekrit, but, ever mindful of past services, carried its

3

warden onward and upward on the wave of his
progress. This warden was Saladin's father.

Ayyub (in English plain Job), surnamed after the
fashion of the Saracens Nejm-ed-din, or "Star of
the Faith," the fortunate commandant at this critical moment, although an oriental and a Mohammedan, belonged to the same great Aryan stock as
ourselves, being neither Arab nor Turk, but a Kurd
of the Rawadiya clan, born at their village of Ajda-
nakan near Dawin in Armenia. From time immemorial the Kurds have led the same wild pastoral
life in the mountain tracts between Persia and Asia
Minor. In their clannishness, their love of thieving,
their fine chivalrous sense of honour and hospitality,
and their unquestioned courage, they resembled the
Arabs of the "Days of Ignorance" before Islam, or
the Highland Scots before the reforms of Marshal
Wade. They have ever been a gallant and warlike
people, impervious as a rule to civilisation and difficult for strangers to manage, but possessed of
many rude virtues. At least, they gave birth to
Saladin. Of his more distant forefathers nothing
is known. His family is becomingly described by
his biographers as "one of the most eminent and
respectable in Dawin," but even if true this is at
most a provincial and limited distinction. Dawin,
formerly called Dabil, was the capital of Inner or
Northern Armenia in the tenth century, long before
Tiflis attained to its greater importance. It was
a large walled city, the residence of the governor
of the province, and its inhabitants were chiefly
Christians, who carried on a rich trade in the goats'-

hair clothes and rugs which they wove and dyed
with the brilliant crimson of the kirmiz worm. Jews,
Magians, and Christians dwelt there in peace under
their Mohammedan conquerors, and the Armenian
Church stood beside the Mosque where Moslems
prayed.

But Dawin was already in its decline when
Saladin's grandfather, Shadhy, son of Marwan, inherited the family position of "eminence and respect-
ability"; and having a large number of sons he
resolved to seek careers for them in the more stir-
ring life of Baghdad, where the courts of the Caliph
and the Sultan offered prizes to the ambitious.
Shadhy is but a name; nothing is known of his
character or history, except that he had a close
friend in the Greek Bihruz, who rose from slavery
at Dawin to high office at the Persian court, became
the tutor of Seljuk princes, and was rewarded with
the important government of the city of Baghdad.
To this old friend Shadhy resorted, and Bihruz out
of his large patronage presented his comrade's son
Ayyub to the post of commandant of the castle of
Tekrit. Probably the whole family accompanied
the fortunate nominee; certainly Shadhy and his
son Shirkuh joined Ayyub; and if the last justified
his patron's trust by the wisdom and prudence of
his rule, Shirkuh, ever hasty and passionate, wrecked,
as it seemed, the good fortune of the family by an
act of chivalrous homicide: he killed a scoundrel
to avenge a woman's wrong. Bihruz was already
annoyed at the escape of Zengy, whom he did not
love; and he was not inclined to overlook the

violence of Shirkuh. The brothers were commanded
to seek employment elsewhere. They departed
from Tekrit, oppressed with a sense of misfortune,
and drew a sinister omen from the fact that on the
very night of their flitting a son had been born to
Ayyub. Never, surely, was augury worse interpreted; for the infant whose first cries disturbed
the preparations of the journey that night in the
castle of Tekrit in the year of Grace 1138, was
Yusuf, afterwards renowned in East and West under
his surname of " Honour of the Faith," *Salah-ed-din*,
or, as we write it, SALADIN.*

Before attempting to relate whither Ayyub carried
the baby Saladin, or what befell them, we must
glance briefly at the political conditions in which
the future leader of the Saracens would have to
shape his career. The eastern world of that day
was widely different from the old empire of the
Caliphate; it had vitally changed even in the life-
time of Saladin's father. The flaming zeal which
had at first carried the armies of Islam, like a rushing prairie fire, from their ancient Arabian muster-
ground to the desert of Sind in the east and the
surge of the Atlantic on the west, had not availed
to keep together, in a well-knit organisation, the
vast empire so suddenly, so amazingly, acquired.
The Caliphate lasted indeed for over six hundred
years, but it retained its imperial sway for scarcely

---

* The Mohammedan year, 532, in which Saladin was born, cor-
responds to the interval between 19 Sept. 1137, and 8 Sept. 1138.
The month of Saladin's birth is not recorded, and he may of course
have been born in 1137.

a third of that time. In the seventh century, the soldiers of the Arabian Prophet had rapidly subdued Egypt, Syria, Persia, and even the country beyond the Oxus, and early in the eighth they rounded off their conquest of the Barbary coast by the annexation of Spain. Such an empire, composed of contentious and rival races, and extending over remotely distant provinces, could not long be held in strict subjection to a central government issuing its patents of command from Damascus or Baghdad. The provincial proconsul of the Mohammedan system was even more apt to acquire virtual independence than his Roman prototype. The very idea of the Caliphate, which was as much an ecclesiastical as an administrative authority, encouraged the local governors to assume powers which were not irreconcilable with the homage due to a spiritual chief; and the religious schisms of Islam, especially the strange and fanatical devotion inspired by the persecuted lineage of Aly, led by a different road to the dismemberment of the state.

Already in the ninth century the extremities of the Mohammedan empire were in the hands of rulers who either repudiated the authority of the Abbasid Caliph of Baghdad, or at least tendered him, as Commander of the Faithful, a purely conventional homage. The Caliph's writ—or its Arabic equivalent,—even in the days of "the good Harun er-Rashid," did not run in Spain or Morocco, and met but a qualified respect in Tunis. Egypt on the one hand, and north-east Persia on the other, soon followed the lead of the extreme west, and by

the middle of the tenth century the temporal power
of the Caliph hardly extended beyond the walls of
his own palace, within which his authority was
grievously shackled by the guard of mercenaries
whom he had imprudently imported in self-defence.
This state of papal impotence continued with little
change until the extinction of the Baghdad Caliphate by the Mongols in 1258. Now and again, by
the weakness of their neighbours or the personal
ascendency of an individual Caliph, the Abbasids
temporarily recovered a part of their territorial
power in the valley of the Tigris and Euphrates ;
yet even then, although the Caliph had a larger
army and possessed a wider dominion than his predecessor had enjoyed, his authority was restricted
to a narrow territory in Mesopotamia, and his influence, save as pontiff of Islam, was almost a negligi-
ble quantity in Saladin's political world.

This political world was practically bounded by
the Tigris on the east and the Libyan desert on the
west. For a century and a half before Saladin
began to mix in affairs of state, Egypt had been
ruled by the Fatimid Caliphs, a schismatic dynasty
claiming spiritual supremacy by right of descent
from Aly the son-in-law of the Prophet Mohammed,
and repudiating all recognition of the Abbasid Caliphate of Baghdad. Still more nearly affecting the
politics of the Crusades was the situation in Syria
and Mesopotamia. The whole of these districts,
from the mountains of Kurdistan to the Lebanon,
are in race and politics allied with Arabia. Large
tribes of Arabs were settled from early times in the

fertile valleys of Mesopotamia, where their names are still preserved in the geographical divisions. Bedawy tribes wandered annually from Arabia to the pasture lands of the Euphrates, as they wander to this day: and many clans were and are still permanently settled in all parts of Syria. The decay of the Caliphate naturally encouraged the foundation of Arab kingdoms in the regions dominated by Arab tribes, and in the tenth and eleventh centuries the greater part of Syria and Mesopotamia owned their supremacy; but by the twelfth these had all passed away. The Arabs remained in their wonted seats, and camped over all the country to the upper valleys of Diyar-Bekr, as they do now; but they no longer ruled the lands where they pastured their flocks. The supremacy of the Arab in those regions was over for ever, and the rule of the Turk had begun.

The Turks who swept over Persia, Mesopotamia, and Syria in the course of the eleventh century were led by the descendants of Seljuk, a Turkman chieftain from the steppes beyond the Oxus. In a rapid series of campaigns they first overran the greater part of Persia; other Turkish tribes then came to swell their armies; and the whole of western Asia, from the borders of Afghanistan to the frontier of the Greek empire and the confines of Egypt, was gradually united under Seljuk rule. Persians, Arabs, and Kurds alike bowed before the overwhelming wave of conquest. But wide as was their dominion, the significance of the Seljuk invasion lies deeper than mere territorial expansion. Their advent formed an epoch in Mohammedan history by creating a revival of the Moslem faith.

"At the time of their appearance the Empire of the Caliphate had vanished. What had once been a realm united under a sole Mohammedan ruler was now a collection of scattered dynasties, not one of which, save perhaps the Fatimids of Egypt (and they were schismatics), was capable of imperial sway. The prevalence of schism increased the disunion of the various provinces of the vanished empire. A drastic remedy was needed, and it was found in the invasion of the Turks. These rude nomads, unspoilt by town life and civilised indifference to religion, embraced Islam with all the fervour of their uncouth souls. They came to the rescue of a dying State, and revived it. They swarmed over Persia, Mesopotamia, Syria, and Asia Minor, devastating the country, and exterminating every dynasty that existed there; and, as the result, they once more reunited Mohammedan Asia, from the western frontier of Afghanistan to the Mediterranean, under one sovereign; they put a new life into the expiring zeal of the Moslems, drove back the re-encroaching Byzantines, and bred up a generation of fanatical Mohammedan warriors to whom, more than to anything else, the Crusaders owed their repeated failure." *

Melik Shah, the noblest of the Seljuk emperors, was one of those rulers who possess the power of imposing their minds upon their age. To belong to his household, to hold his commands, was not merely an honour and a privilege; it was also an apprenticeship in principles. In serving the Sultan,

* S. Lane-Poole, *The Mohammedan Dynasties*, 149, 150.

one grew like him ; and a standard of conduct was thus set up, modelled upon the life of the royal master, the pattern and exemplar of the age. It is recorded by an Arab historian that a chief or governor was esteemed by public opinion in accordance with the degree in which he conformed to the Sultan's example ; and the standard thus adopted formed no ignoble ideal of a prince's duties. Justice was the first aim of Melik Shah ; his chief effort was to promote his people's prosperity. Bridges, canals, and caravanserais bore witness to his encouragement of commerce and inter-communication throughout his dominions. The roads were safe, and it is stated that a pair of travellers could journey without an escort from Merv to Damascus. Generous and brave, just and conscientious, he fulfilled the ideal of a Moslem Prince, and his example impressed itself far and wide upon the minds of his followers.

Great as he was in character and statesmanship, Melik Shah owed much of his principles and his successful organisation to the still wiser man who filled the highest office in the realm. Nizam-el-mulk stands among the great statesmen of history. His Mohammedan eulogists dwell fondly upon his spiritual virtues, and recount with unction how he could repeat the entire Koran by heart at the age of twelve ; but the supreme testimony to his ability is seen in the prosperity and progress of the great empire for nearly a third of a century committed to his charge. His capacity for affairs was joined to a profound knowledge of jurisprudence and an en-

lightened support of learning and science. He it
was who encouraged Omar Khayyam in his astronomical researches,—less famous to-day but certainly not
less important than his well-known *Quatrains*,—and
founded the famous Nizamiya college at Baghdad.
And it was he who in his *Treatise on the Principles
of Government*,* drawn up at the bidding of Melik
Shah and adopted by the Sultan as his code, set
forth an ideal conception of kingship that embodies
an uncompromising doctrine of Divine Right. The
sovereign, he holds, is without doubt God's anointed ;
but the doctrine is tempered with a stern insistence
upon the king's responsibility to God for every
detail of his conduct towards the subjects entrusted
to his protection. Παντὶ δὲ ᾧ ἐδόθη πολὺ, πολὺ
ζητηθήσεται παρ' αὐτοῦ, "For unto whomsoever
much is given, of him shall be much required," is the
Vezir's principle, as it was of a greater Teacher before
him, and his ideal of a true monarch savours of a
counsel of perfection. He defines the character of
a king by a quotation from an old Persian anecdote :

"He must subdue hatred, envy, pride, anger, lust,
greed, false hopes, disputatiousness, lying, avarice, malice, violence, selfishness, impulsiveness, ingratitude, and
frivolity ; he must possess the qualities of modesty,
equability of temper, gentleness, clemency, humility,
generosity, staunchness, patience, gratitude, pity, love of
knowledge, and justice."

One weighty judgment, it is alleged, is of more serv-

* Published by M. Schefer with the title of *Siasset Nameh*, Paris,
1893.

ice to a king than a mighty army. He is cautioned
to avoid favouritism and disproportionate rewards,
to eschew excess in wine and unkingly levity,
and recommended to be strict in fasting, prayer,
almsgiving, and all religious exercises. In every
circumstance he is to " observe the mean "; for
the Prophet of Islam said, unconsciously quoting
Aristotle, that in all things "the mean" is to be
followed.

The most striking feature in the system of government outlined by Nizam-el-mulk is his constant insistence on the duties of the sovereign towards his
subjects, and the elaborate checks suggested for the
detection and punishment of official corruption and
oppression. Twice a week the Sultan was obliged
to hold public audience, when anybody, however
humble and unknown, might come to present his
grievances and demand justice. The Sultan must
hear these petitions himself, without any go-between,
listen patiently, and decide each case in accordance
with equity. Various precautions are recommended
to ensure the free access of the subject to the king.
The example is cited of a Persian sovereign who
held audience on horseback in the middle of a plain,
so that all might see and approach him, when the
obstacles of " gates, barriers, vestibules, passages,
curtains, and jealous chamberlains " were thus removed. Another king made all petitioners wear
red dresses, so that he might distinguish and take
them aside for private audience; and the example
is approved of a Samanid prince who sat alone and
unattended all night during heavy snow, in the mid-

dle of the great square of Bokhara, on the chance
that some oppressed subject, who might have been
turned away by his chamberlains, should see him
and come for redress.

Extraordinary pains were to be taken lest the
maladministration of local governors should escape
detection :

" When an officer is appointed to a post, let him be
benevolent to God's creatures. One must not exact
from them more than is right, and one should demand
it with gentleness and consideration. Taxes should
never be claimed before the fixed legal day, else the
people, under pressure of need will sell their goods at
half-price, and become ruined and dispersed."

Constant inspection of the tax-gatherers and other
officials is recommended, and severe punishment is
to be meted out to the unjust. " Spies," he says,
" must perpetually traverse the roads of the various
provinces, disguised as merchants, dervishes, etc., and
send in reports of what they hear, so that nothing
that passes shall remain unknown." Another precaution was to change all tax-gatherers and agents
every two or three years, so that they should not
become rooted and overbearing in their posts.
Further, inspectors of high character, above suspicion, paid by the treasury and not by local taxation, were appointed to watch the whole empire ;
" the advantages which their uprightness brings will
repay an hundredfold their salaries." A prompt and
regular system of post-messengers maintained rapid
communications between the inspectors and the cent

ral government. Finally, the good behaviour of vassal chiefs was ensured by their sending hostages, relieved every year, to the imperial court, where no fewer than five hundred were constantly detained.

These provisions for just administration and frequent inspection were all the more necessary in an empire which was founded upon a military organisation, wherein the government was vested in the hands of foreigners. The Seljuk power rested on an army composed, to a great extent, of hired or purchased soldiers, and officered by slaves of the royal household. Freemen were not to be trusted with high commands, at least in distant provinces; native Persians and Arabs could not, as a rule, be expected to work loyally for their Turkish conquerors; and it was safer to rely on the fidelity of slaves brought up at the court, in close relations of personal devotion to the Seljuk princes. These white slaves or *mamluks*, natives for the most part of Kipchak and Tartary, formed the bodyguard of the Sultan, filled the chief offices of the court and camp, and rising step by step, according to their personal merits and graces, eventually won freedom and power. They were rewarded by grants of castles, cities, and even provinces, which they held of their master the Sultan on condition of military service. The whole empire was organised on this feudal basis, which seems to have been usual among the Turks, and which was inherited from the Seljuks and carried into Egypt by Saladin, where it was for centuries maintained by the Mamluk Sultans. The greater part of Persia, Mesopotamia, and Syria was parcelled out in military fiefs, and governed by

Seljuk captains—quondam slaves in the mamluk bodyguard—who held them in fee simple by letters patent, revocable at the Sultan's will, and who levied and lived on the land tax, on the sole condition of furnishing troops at the Sultan's call.

The greater feudatories in turn let out portions of their fiefs to sub-vassals, who were bound to furnish troops to their overlord, just as he was required to bring his retainers to the support of his sovereign. We read of a primitive method of summoning the military contingents, by sending an arrow round from camp to camp, or village to village, as a signal for assembly. After a campaign the feudal troops were dismissed to their homes, whither they always retired during the winter, under an engagement to join the colours in the spring. In the interval a general was obliged to be content with his own immediate followers, his bodyguard, and any mercenaries who could be induced to remain in the field. Saladin, as will be seen, invariably observed this custom. When living on their lands, the vassals were only allowed to collect the legal tax, amounting apparently to about one-tenth of the produce, and were straitly enjoined not to oppress the people or seize their goods. " The land and its inhabitants are the Sultan's," wrote the great Vezir, " and the feudal lords and governors are but as a guard set for their protection." No doubt, so long as the Seljuk empire held together, the omnipresent spy kept license and corruption at bay; but when there was no supreme government, during the troublous times that preceded the establishment of Nur-ed-din's and Saladin's organised rule, much mis-

ery, instead of " protection," must have come in the
train of feudalism. We read constantly of the barons
or emirs setting forth on the war path, followed by
their retainers, and such a party was as likely as not
to meet a rival troop somewhere along the rugged
tracks of Mesopotamia, with the usual result of a
skirmish, perhaps a victory, and then slaughter and
pillage. The life of the shepherd, the husbandman,
and the trader, must have been sufficiently exciting,
and not a little precarious, in the midst of the valorous activity of neighbouring chiefs; and the equita-
ble precepts of Melik Shah and his wise Vezir must
often have been forgotten in the flush of victory.

The Arab chronicler, however, prone as he is to
dwell upon feats of arms, never quite overlooks the
condition of the peaceful population; and it is worth
noticing that in signalising the virtues of a great lord
he puts prominently forward the justice and mildness
he displayed towards his subjects. The " Gyrfalcon "
(Ak-Sunkur) of Mosil is held up to admiration as a
wise ruler and protector of his people.* Perfect justice reigned throughout his dominions; the markets
were cheap; the roads absolutely safe; and order
prevailed in all parts. His policy was to make the
district pay for its own misdeeds, so that if a caravan
were plundered, the nearest villages had to make
good the loss, and the whole population thus became
a universal police for the traveller's protection. It
is recorded of this good governor that he never broke
his word, and the same might be said of more Moslem than Christian leaders of the Crusading epoch.

---

* Ibn-el-Athir, *Atabegs*, 29, 30.

2

The example of a just and virtuous chief naturally inspires emulation among his retainers, and it is not difficult, in many instances, to trace the effects of such influences. The constant endeavour of a great baron was to surround himself with a loyal body of retainers and minor feudatories, who could be trusted to support his arms, extend his dominions, and carry out his policy in the management of their domains. Upon their loyalty depended the succession of his family. When a baron died, his vassals and mamluks would rally round his heir, obtain for him the succession in the fief, and uphold him on the throne. No feeble ruler, however, had a chance in that strenuous age ; he must be strong in war and firm in peace. It sometimes happened that an emir failed to satisfy the demands or retain the loyalty of his followers, who would then transfer their services to a more popular master.

In spite of its military character and the truculence of many of its leaders, nothing is more remarkable in Seljuk civilisation than the high importance attached to education and learning. Although colleges existed before in Mohammedan countries, we must ascribe to Seljuk patronage, above all to the influence of Nizam-el-mulk, the great improvements in educational provision in the East during the eleventh and twelfth centuries. The celebrated Nizamiya *medresa* or university at Baghdad, founded by the Vezir himself, was the focus from which radiated an enthusiasm for learning all over Persia, Syria, and Egypt, where it met a kindred stream of erudition issuing from the Azhar university of Cairo. To found a college was

as much a pious act among Seljuk princes, as to
build a mosque or conquer a city from the "infidels."
The same spirit led the great vassals and the numerous dynasties that sprang up on the decay of the
Seljuk power, to devote particular attention to questions of education, and by Saladin's time Damascus,
Aleppo, Baalbekk, Emesa, Mosil, Baghdad, Cairo,
and other cities, had become so many foci of learned
energy. Professors travelled from college to college,
just as our own medieval scholars wandered from
university to university. Many of these learned
men and ministers of state (the two were frequently
united) were descendants or household officers of
Seljuk Sultans. The Atabeg Zengy of Mosil, with
all his vast energy and military talent, could scarcely
have held the reins of his wide empire without the
aid of his Vezir and right-hand-man Jemal-ed-din,
surnamed el-Jawad, "the Bountiful," whose grandfather had been keeper of the coursing leopards in
Sultan Melik Shah's hunting stables. So ably did
he administer the several governments successively
committed to his charge, and so charming were his
manners and conversation, that Zengy received him
into the intimacy of his friendship and advanced him
to the post of Inspector-General of his principality
and President of the Divan or Council of State.
His salary was a tenth of the produce of the soil
and he spent his wealth in boundless charity ; minis-
tered lavishly to the necessities of the pilgrims at
Mekka and Medina ; built aqueducts and restored
mosques ; and kept a gigantic roll of pensioners.
When he died, "the air resounded with the lament-

ations" of widows and orphans and of the countless
poor who had hailed him benefactor.*

The ranks of the wise and learned were recruited
from all parts of the Moslem world. Professors from
Nishapur delighted audiences at Damascus. Persian
mystics like es-Suhrawardy met traditioners like Ibn-
Asakir, whose funeral Saladin himself attended in
1176. In the same year there arrived at Cairo a
stranger from Xativa in distant Andalusia, drawn
eastward by the fame of the revival of learning ; it
was Ibn-Firro, who had composed a massy poem of
1173 verses upon the *variæ lectiones* in the Koran,
simply "for the greater glory of God." This marvel
of erudition modestly confessed that his memory
was burdened with enough sciences to break down a
camel. Nevertheless, when it came to lecturing to
his crowded audiences, he never uttered a superfluous
word. It was no wonder that the Kady el-Fadil,
chief judge and governor of Egypt under Saladin,
lodged him in his own house and buried him in his
private mausoleum. The presence of such philosophers tempered with cool wisdom the impetuous
fire of the predatory chiefs. Many of the great
soldiers of that age delighted in the society of men
of culture ; and though the victorious Atabeg might
exclaim that to him "the clash of arms was dearer
far than the music of sweet singers, and to try conclusions with a worthy foe a greater delight than to
toy with a mistress," yet he loved the company of
his wise counsellor el-Jawad. His successor Nur-ed-
din was devoted to the society of the learned, and

---

* Ibn-Khallikan, iii. 295–9.

poets and men of letters gathered round his Court ;
whilst Saladin took a peculiar pleasure in the conversation of grave theologians and solemn jurists.
The most bloodthirsty baron of them all could not
do without his poet and historian. It was the same
in later centuries with the Mamluk Sultans of Egypt.
Barbarous and savage as they seemed, prone to deeds
of blood and treachery, they loved the arts, encouraged *belles-lettres*, and made Cairo beautiful with
their exquisite architecture. It would seem that in
the East, at all events, violence may go hand in hand
with taste and culture, and it was not Saul alone
whose moody fits were relieved by the music of
sweet singers.

The effects of the Seljuk domination reached far
and wide ; but the dynasty itself was shortlived.
Less than half a century after they had entered
Persia as conquerors, the vast fabric they had auda-
ciously planned and splendidly maintained split up
into fragments. Three Seljuk emperors in succession held their immense dominions under their
personal rule without fear of rivalry or revolt ; but
when Melík Shah died in 1092, civil war broke out
between his sons, and the empire was divided.
Seljuks continued to rule at Nishapur, Ispahan, and
Kirman ; Seljuks at Damascus and Aleppo ; Seljuks
in Anatolia : but they were divided planks of the
mightly bole, unable long to resist the forces which
pressed upon them from within and without. Their
overthrow was the inevitable consequence of their
feudal organisation ; they were hoist with their own
petard. The slaves whom they imported for their

defence became their destroyers, and the great fiefs that they had constructed for the protection of the empire proved to be its chief danger. The prime defect of European feudalism was equally conspicuous in the Seljuk system. The slave owed his master service, the vassal was bound to his overlord, but the service and loyalty did not extend beyond the immediate superior. If a chief vassal found himself strong enough to rebel against his overlord, his retainers, sub-vassals, and slaves followed him; they owed no service to the overlord. Nor was there any equivalent to a direct oath of allegiance to the sovereign, though one sometimes finds the sentiment of loyalty that induced sub-vassals to leave a rebellious overlord and go over to the side of the Crown. As the sovereign power grew weaker, this sentiment ceased to operate, and the great feudatories were able to found independent kingdoms of their own with the full concurrence of their vassals. When the empire became divided against itself, the captains who had fought its battles and reaped its rewards became independent princes; the mamluks who had won victories for their emperors became regents or governors (Atabegs) of their emperors' heirs; and the delegated function was presently exchanged for the full rights of sovereignty and the transmission of hereditary kingship.

The twelfth century saw the greater part of the Seljuk empire in the hands of petty sovereigns who had risen from the ranks of the mamluks and converted their fiefs into independent states. In Persia, and beyond the Oxus, a cupbearer and a *major domo* had founded powerful dynasties; and the slaves of these slaves, a generation of "gentlemen's gentlemen," had established minor principalities on the skirts of their masters' dominions. In this way a slave became regent over his master's heir and on his death assumed regal powers at Damascus; thus Zengy, founder of the long line of Atabegs of Mosil, was the son of one of Melik Shah's slaves; and the Ortukids and other local dynasts of Mesopotamia traced their fortunes to a similar source. However servile in origin, the pedigree carried with it no sense of ignominy. In the East a slave is often held to be better than a son, and to have been the slave of Melik Shah constituted a special title to respect. The great slave vassals of the Seljuks were as proud and honourable as any Bastard of medieval aristocracy; and when they in turn assumed kingly powers, they inherited and transmitted to their lineage the high traditions of their former lords. The Atabegs of Syria and Mesopotamia carried on the civilising work begun by the wise Vezir of Melik Shah. The work was interrupted, indeed, by internal feuds, but its chief hindrance during the twelfth century came from the Crusades.

CHAPTER II.

THE FIRST CRUSADE.

1098.

MELIK SHAH, the great Seljuk Sultan, died in 1092, and civil war immediately broke out between his sons. Four years later, the First Crusade began its eastward march; in 1098 the great cities of Edessa and Antioch and many fortresses were taken; in 1099 the Christians regained possession of Jerusalem itself. In the next few years the greater part of Palestine and the coast of Syria, Tortosa, Acre, Tripoli, and Sidon (1110), fell into the hands of the Crusaders, and the conquest of Tyre in 1124 marked the apogee of their power. This rapid triumph was due partly to the physical superiority and personal courage of the men of the North, but even more to the lack of any organised resistance. Nizam-el-mulk had died before his master, and there was no statesman competent to arrange the differences between the emperor's heirs. Whilst the Seljuk princes were casting away their crown in fratricidal strife, the great vassals,

24

STORMING OF ANTIOCH, 1098.

(FROM A PAINTED WINDOW AT ST. DENYS, 12TH CENTURY.)

though on the road to independence, had not yet learned their power: all were struggling for pieces of the broken diadem, each was jealous of his neighbour, but none was yet bold enough to lead. The founders of dynasties were in the field, but the dynasties were not yet founded. The Seljuk authority was still nominally supreme in Mesopotamia and northern Syria, and the numerous governors of cities and wardens of forts were only beginning to find out that the Seljuk authority was but the echo of a sonorous name, and that dominion was within the reach of the strongest.

It was a time of uncertainty and hesitation—of amazed attendance upon the dying struggles of a mighty empire; an interregnum of chaos until the new forces should have gathered their strength ; in short, it was the precise moment when a successful invasion from Europe was possible. A generation earlier, the Seljuk power was inexpugnable. A generation later, a Zengy or a Nur-ed-din, firmly established in the Syrian seats of the Seljuks, would probably have driven the invaders into the sea. A lucky star led the preachers of the First Crusade to seize an opportunity of which they hardly realised the significance. Peter the Hermit and Urban II. chose the auspicious moment with a sagacity as unerring as if they had made a profound study of Asiatic politics. The Crusades penetrated like a wedge between the old wood and the new, and for a while seemed to cleave the trunk of Mohammedan empire into splinters.

Seven years before the birth of Saladin, when

Fulk of Anjou ascended the throne of Jerusalem in 1131, the Latin Kingdom was still in its zenith. Syria and Upper Mesopotamia lay at the feet of the Crusaders, whose almost daily raids reached from Maridin and Amid in Diyar-Bekr to el-Arish and "the brook of Egypt." Yet the country was not really subdued. The Crusaders contented themselves with a partial occupation, and whilst they held the coast lands and many fortresses in the interior, as far as the Jordan and Lebanon, they did not seriously set about a thorough conquest. The great cities, Aleppo, Damascus, Hamah, Emesa, were still in Moslem hands, and were never taken by the Christians, though their reduction must certainly have been possible at more than one crisis. The only great city which the Crusaders held in the interior, besides Jerusalem, was Edessa, and this they were soon to lose. The Latin Kingdom, with its subordinate principalities, counties, baronies, and fiefs, was more an armed occupation than a systematic conquest ; yet even as an occupation it was inefficient. At the time of its greatest extent, the "Frank" dominion extended along a zone over five hundred miles long from north to south, but rarely more, and often less, than fifty miles broad. In the north the County of Edessa (er-Ruha, Orfa) stretched from (and often over) the borders of Diyar-Bekr to a point not far north of Aleppo, and included such important fiefs as Saruj, Tell-Bashir (Turbessel), Samosata, and Ayn-Tab (Hatap). West and south of the County of Edessa lay the Principality of Antioch, which at one time included Tarsus and Adana in Cilicia, but

THE TAKING OF JERUSALEM.

(FROM A PAINTED WINDOW AT ST. DENYS, 12TH CENTURY.)

usually extended from the Pyramus along the sea-coast to a little north of Margat, and inland to near the Mohammedan cities, Aleppo and Hamah ; among its chief fiefs were Atharib (Cerep), Maarra, Apamea, with the port of Ladikiya (Laodicea). South again of Antioch was the County of Tripolis, a narrow strip between the Lebanon and the Mediterranean, includ-ing Margat (Markab), Tortosa, Crac des Chevaliers, Tripolis, and Jubeyl. Over all these states, as over-lord, stood the King of Jerusalem, whose own do-minions stretched from Beyrut past Sidon, Tyre, Acre, Cæsarea, Arsuf, Jaffa, to the Egyptian frontier fortress Ascalon, and were bounded generally on the east by the valley of the Jordan and the Dead Sea. The chief subdivisions were the County of Jaffa and Ascalon (including also the fortresses of Ibelin, Blanche Garde, and Mirabel, and the towns of Gaza, Lydda, and Ramla); the Lordship of Karak (Crac) and Shaubak (Mont Real), two outlying fort-resses beyond the Dead Sea, cutting the caravan route from Damascus to Egypt ; the Principality of Galilee, including Tiberias, Safed, Kaukab (Belvoir), and other strongholds; the Lordship of Sidon; and the minor fiefs of Toron, Beysan (Bethshan), Nablus, etc.*

A glance at the map will show that a large pro-portion of these Christian possessions were within a day's, or at most two days', march of a Mohamme-dan city or a garrisoned fort, from which frequent raids were to be expected in retaliation for the in-cursions of the Franks. The autobiography of one of Saladin's elder contemporaries, the Arab Osama,

---

* Archer and Kingsford, *Crusades*, ch. vii.

reveals a perpetual state of guerilla encounters, alternating with periods of comparative friendliness and tranquillity. The general tendency of the original settlers of the First Crusade was undoubtedly towards amicable relations with their Moslem neighbours. The great majority of the cultivators of the soil in the Christian territories were of course Mohammedans, and constant intercourse with them, and social and domestic relations of the most intimate nature, tended to diminish points of difference and emphasise common interests and common virtues. In the present day a European family can rarely live to the third generation in the East without becoming more or less orientalised. The early Crusaders, after thirty years' residence in Syria, had become very much assimilated in character and habits to the people whom they had partly conquered, among whom they lived, and whose daughters they did not disdain to marry; they were growing into Levantines; they were known as *Pullani* or creoles. The Mohammedans, on their side, were scarcely less tolerant; they could hardly approve of marriage with the " polytheists," as they called the Trinitarians; but they were quite ready to work for them and take their pay, and many a Moslem ruler found it convenient to form alliances with the Franks even against his Mohammedan neighbours.

We find this interesting approximation between the rival races clearly appreciated in the fascinating memoirs of the nonagenarian Osama, the Arab prince of Sheyzar. As an historical witness, Osama was fortunate in his epoch. He was born in 1095, three years before the capture of Antioch gave the Franks their *point d'appui* whence they advanced to the conquest of Jerusalem ; and he died in 1188, when the Holy City had just been retaken by Saladin. He witnessed nearly the complete tide, the flow and ebb, of Crusading effort. His long life of ninety-three years embraced the whole period of the Latin rule at Jerusalem, and only just missed the Crusade of Richard Cœur de Lion. His family, the Beny Munkidh, were the hereditary lords of the rocky fortress of Sheyzar, the ruins of which still overhang the Orontes. Strong as the castle was,—shielded by a bold bluff of the Ansariya mountains, approachable only by a horsepath, which crossed the river, then tunnelled through the rock, and was again protected by a deep dyke crossed by a plank bridge,—its situation in the immediate neighbourhood of Christian garrisons, half-way between the Crusading centres of Antioch and Tripoli, brought it into perilous contact with the forays that passed perpetually beneath its battlements.

Sheyzar was one of those little border states, between the Moslem and the Christian, which found their safest policy in tempering orthodoxy with diplomacy. No better post of speculation could have been chosen from which to observe the struggle that went on unceasingly throughout the twelfth century ; no witness more competent or more opportune could be found than the Arab chief who surveyed the contest from his conning-tower of Sheyzar. He knew all the great leaders in the war, and often took part in the fray. His first battle was fought under that truculent Turkman, Il-Ghazy, the man who did more than anyone, before the coming of Zengy, to spread dismay through the Christian ranks. Osama served under Zengy himself, and was actually present in the famous flight over the Tigris into Tekrit when the timely succour of Ayyub made the fortunes of the house of Saladin. He had seen Tancred more than once, when the prince led an assault against Sheyzar; and he remembered the beautiful horse which the Crusader received as a present from its castellan. King Baldwin du Bourg was a prisoner in the fortress for some months in 1124, and rewarded his host's kindness, *more Francorum*, by breaking all his engagements the moment he was released. Joscelin of Courtenay was another well-known figure in the armed expeditions which passed in perpetual procession over the Orontes; the autobiographer even saw the Emperor John Comnenus lay siege to his own eyry on the "Cock's Comb." Later on he visited King Fulk at Acre and explained to him through an interpreter, for Osama knew no *lingua Franca*, that he too, Arab though he was, might call himself "knight, after the fashion of my race and family; for what we admire in a knight is that he be lean and long." Nor was Osama's acquaintance limited to such high personages as he chanced to meet at Sheyzar or visited during brief excursions into Frank territory. He lived for long years at Damascus, at the court of Nur-ed-din, for whom he conducted a diplomatic correspondence with Egypt; he became for a time the guest of the Fatimid Caliph at Cairo, and farmed a fief near by at Kom Ashfin, where he

ROBERT OF NORMANDY UNHORSES A SARACEN.
(FROM A PAINTED WINDOW AT ST. DENYS, 12TH CENTURY.)

kept two hundred head of cattle, a thousand sheep, and reaped rich harvests of grain and fruit; and in his latter days he was intimate with Saladin, who delighted in his poetry and impromptu recitations.

Osama draws a firm line of distinction between the settled Franks, the families of the first Crusaders, who had grown accustomed to oriental life and become friendly with their Moslem neighbours, and the new arrivals, a set of bigoted pilgrims and needy adventurers, whose indiscreet zeal and lust of plunder embroiled the good understanding which had been established between the two creeds in Palestine. " Those Franks," he says, " who have come and settled amongst us and cultivated the society of Moslems are much superior to the others who have lately joined them. . . . The new-comers are invariably more inhuman than the older settlers, who have become familiar with the Mohammedans." Personal friendships were frequent between the settled Crusaders and the neighbouring Moslems, and it was not unusual for a Mohammedan to enjoy the hospitality of a Christian knight. Osama himself had acquaintances among the Templars, whom he called his " friends," and whom he preferred above all other Franks. When he visited Jerusalem, they gave him one of their oratories, close to the christianised mosque el-Aksa, wherein to say his Moslem prayers; he walked with them in the Sanctuary, and was taken to the Dome of the Rock and House of the Chain. Of the hospitality of the knights of St. John, too, he does not stint his praise. He was a witness of an ordeal by battle and ordeals by water, which did not in-

crease his respect for Christian jurisprudence, and
he cannot conceal his indignation at the frequent
breaches of sworn faith by the Crusaders, who seldom kept pact with the "infidel." Whilst generously
admiring their valour, he lays special stress upon their
defensive tactics, their cautious, orderly movements,
their precautions against ambushes and surprises,
and their self-control after victory in denying themselves the delights of a headlong pursuit. Like a
grave oriental, however, he cannot approve the idle
merriment, jovial roars of laughter, and mad pursuit
of pleasure, which he noticed among Franks of all
degrees. An eastern gentleman can never understand childish buffoonery or broad grins among men
of sense and position. Still less can he tolerate the
slightest public display of that gentle passion which,
like a true Moslem, he conceals behind the curtains
of his harim. He has no patience with the amazing
liberty allowed by Crusading husbands to their wives.

"They know not what honour means," he writes,
"nor jealousy neither. If they walk abroad with their
wives and meet another man, they let him hold the
wife's hand and take her aside to talk, whilst the husband stands aloof till the conversation be done! If the
lady prolongs it overmuch, her spouse walks off and
leaves her alone with her friend!"

So peaceful a scene of mutual toleration and goodwill between Christian and Moslem was not likely to
last long. The first breath of fanaticism would of
course blow all this fine cobweb to pieces. It came
from both sides. In proportion as the first Crusaders
became more tolerant and easy-going—not to say

careless and licentious—the later visitors found more reason for a display of zeal. To a political adventure, and a military annexation, succeeded an age of pious pilgrimage, attended by thinly veiled freebooting. As soon as the early Crusaders had made Palestine a safe field for devout tourists, the shrines were besieged by pilgrims whose narrower experience could not stomach the worldly toleration assumed by the earlier Christian settlers. Added to the fanaticism of honest bigots came the lawlessness of palmer-adventurers, freelances who disguised the lust of plunder under a pious cockle-shell. Both classes exasperated the Moslem population and incited the Crusading leaders to unprovoked forays. Describing the situation at the end of the first quarter of the twelfth century, a Mohammedan historian says:

"The Franks raided the country day by day; they worked unspeakable harm to the Moslems and brought ruin and desolation upon them. . . . Their forays pressed on into Diyar-Bekr, as far as Amid; they spared neither orthodox nor heretics; in Mesopotamia they despoiled the people of all the silver and valuables they possessed. As for Harran and Rakka, they oppressed them with contumely and shame, and gave them daily to drink of the cup of death. . . . All the roads to Damascus were cut, save that which passes Rahba and the desert, and merchants and travellers were forced to suffer the dangers and fatigues of a long journey across the wastes, in peril of life and property from the wandering Bedawis. The Franks even exacted black-mail from all the towns in their neighbourhood, and went so far as to send agents to Damascus to liberate Christian slaves. At Aleppo they forced the inhabitants to pay tribute up to the half of their revenue—even to the proceeds of the mill at the Garden Gate." *

On the other side, the Saracens, at least the Turkish Moslems, though for the moment divided and unable to offer any resolute opposition to the enemy, were by nature and training soldiers, and by race and teaching fanatics. The military system of the Seljuks bred up a nation of fighters; and their recent conversion to Islam, their ignorance and consequent subjection to the influence of fanatical *mullas*, imbued them with the convert's proverbial zeal. Every little court that assumed regal attributes on the decline of the central power became a nursery of warriors, each one of whom was a strenuous upholder of Islam. As with their Christian opponents, booty and Paradise no doubt combined to stimulate their enthusiasm for a religious war; but, whichever motive was uppermost, it was certain that only combination and a leader were needed to convert these straggling forces into a formidable army ready to die for the Faith. It was but necessary to preach the *Jihad*—the Holy War—and to show them a commander whose courage and military genius all must respect, and the Turkman chiefs and vassals would at once become a Church Militant with whom the Crusaders would have very seriously to reckon. The leader was found in Imad-ed-din Zengy.

* Ibn-el-Athir, *Atabegs*, 59 ff. We may make some allowance for oriental prejudice and exaggeration, but it must not be forgotten that the writer of the foregoing indictment lived soon after the events he describes, and that his father was an eye-witness of many of these scenes.

CRUSADERS PURSUING SELJUKS.

(FROM A PAINTED WINDOW AT ST. DENYS, 12TH CENTURY.)

CHAPTER III.

THE HARBINGER.

1127.

AMONG the numerous Seljuk officers, once slaves of Melik Shah, who were rewarded for their services with valuable appointments, Ak-Sunkur held a high place. As court chamberlain he was wholly in the confidence of his royal master, and enjoyed the special privilege of standing at his right hand at all public levees and councils of state. Later, as governor of the province of Aleppo, his rule was clement and enlightened*; his name became a proverb for loyalty and uprightness; and he died for his faithfulness to his old master's son (1094). He left a boy of ten, Zengy, surnamed Imad-ed-din or " Pillar of the Faith," round whom the retainers rallied. The greatest man then ruling in Mesopotamia was Kurbugha, lord of Mosil and many other cities, a vassal-in-chief of Melik Shah's son and successor. Kurbugha had not forgotten his old friend the " Gyrfalcon," and he summoned Zengy

---

* See above, p. 17.

and his mamluks to his court. "Bring the lad," he
wrote, "for he is the son of my comrade in arms,
and it behooves me to see to his nurture." So they
went to Mosil, were assigned becoming fiefs, and
followed their new lord on his campaigns. Once
near Amid, when the issue of a battle trembled in
the balance, Kurbugha embraced Zengy before the
army, and then consigned him to his own mamluks,
saying, "Behold the son of your old master; fight
for *him!*" They closed round the boy and set-to
with such fury that the day was won. This was
Zengy's first battle-field, and he was then about
fifteen.

Henceforward for many years he lived the life of
a privileged favourite at the court of Mosil under
successive leaders—a notable squire of the fighting
lords who held the borderland between the Crescent
and the Cross. He had grown tall and distinguished-
looking, of swarthy complexion and piercing eyes,
and his character was as upright as his carriage.
Up to his thirty-eighth year he continued to play a
secondary part in the wars and politics of Mesopotamia. Five great barons, one after the other,
held the government of Mosil with the defence of
the marches, and each of them treated him like a
son, endowed him with rich fiefs, and gave him high
command in their constant expeditions against the
Franks. On one of these occasions, at the siege of
Tiberias, Zengy distinguished himself by a conspicuous deed of valour. At the head of his men he
had repulsed a sortie of the garrison, and pursued
them to the gate of the city, which he dinted with

BATTLE BETWEEN CRUSADERS AND KURBUGHA.

(FROM A PAINTED WINDOW AT ST. DENYS, 12TH CENTURY.)

his lance. Then facing about, he found he was
alone; his troop had halted after the engagement,
and left him to follow the enemy singlehanded.
For some time he maintained his hazardous position,
and kept the Franks busy, in the hope that his men
would come up and join in an assault; but when
none appeared, he reluctantly beat a retreat, and
slowly returned to the lines unhurt. The fame of
his exploit was noised abroad and he was known
thereafter by the name of esh-Shamy, " the Syrian." *

In 1122 " the Syrian " was rewarded by the Seljuk
Sultan for his military services by the gift of his first
direct government, the fief of Wasit, then a large and
important city, together with the post of warden
of Basra.† He quickly justified the Sultan's choice.
The Arabs of " the Swamps " in Lower Mesopotamia, into which the Euphrates and Tigris in those
days poured their waters, were eager to recover their
lost supremacy in the fertile fields watered by the
Great River; but so long as Zengy commanded the
frontier, they were held in check. The Arab historian gives a graphic picture of the critical battle fought
on March 1st, 1123, between the Arabs and the Turks.
The former were led by the famous Emir of the Asad
tribe, Dubeys, son of Sadaka, who had settled at Hilla,
attacked Madaïn (Ctesiphon), and even marched upon
the " City of Peace," Baghdad itself, the seat of the

---

* Ibn-el-Athir, *Atābegs*, 34, 35.

† It was a settled principle of the Seljuk administration that no one
was eligible for a governorship until he was thirty-six; Zengy was
now thirty-seven, and had therefore gained his promotion almost at
the earliest possible date.

Abbasid Caliphate. The Caliph el-Mustarshid was
no laggard ; he put himself at the head of his Turkish guard, marshalled his troops, and clad in his black
robe and turban, with the cloak of the Prophet on
his shoulders and the sacred staff in his hand, he embarked in his galley. On landing on the other side
he was received by his great vassal, el-Bursuky, the
lord of Mosil, Zengy of Basra, the chief Kady, the
head of the noble Seyyids, the chief of the Ulema,
and other noted warriors and dignitaries, who, as
soon as they saw the well-known baldachin surmounting the Caliph's horse, fell on their knees and kissed
the ground before him. El-Mustarshid received them
in his tent, and one after the other the barons took
the oath of faithfulness. Then they marched upon
Hilla, the enemy's stronghold. Dubeys met them by
the canal called " Nile," which connected the Euphrates and Tigris, and both sides prepared for battle.

The Arabs numbered ten thousand horse and
twelve thousand foot ; the Caliph and his lords mustered but eight thousand horse, and their infantry
did not exceed five thousand. The Commander of
the Faithful stationed himself with his staff behind
the line of battle but in full view of the combatants.
In front of him stood his chaplains, each with an
open Koran before him ; all Baghdad was on its
knees that day, reciting the Holy Word and seeking
the protection of God ; and if it was read once, the
Book was read right through a thousand times in
that hour of stress. The right wing of the Caliph's
army was under the command of Zengy and another
emir, and received the brunt of the enemy's attack.

Antar led his Bedawy horsemen in two brilliant charges, and had almost put the Caliph's troops to flight, when Zengy, by an adroit movement, took the Arabs in flank, and, aided by el-Bursuky, drove the enemy into the canal. The rout was complete, the prisoners were slaughtered without mercy, their leader fled, and his women fell into the hands of the conquerors.

After the victory Zengy resolved to try his luck at court. He was tired of standing at the beck and call of temporary superiors. He called his henchmen and comrades together and addressed them: "Our position," he said, "is become unbearable. New governors are continually appointed, and we are to obey their whim and pleasure! They send us now to Irak, now to Mosil, to-day to Mesopotamia, to-morrow to Syria. What do ye advise me to do?" Then Zeyn-ed-din Aly, the friend whom Zengy trusted most of all, spoke up: "My lord, the Turkmans have a saying, 'If so be a man must needs set a stone on his head, let it be quarried withal out of a high mountain.' In like manner, if it be necessary that we serve somebody, let it be the Sultan himself." Zengy took this advice and went to Hamadhan, to the court of the Seljuk Mahmud. Here he remained in waiting, without gaining any reward beyond his father's privilege of standing in the post of honour next to the throne. This honour he enjoyed until his pockets were empty. "O Aly, my friend," he said to Zeyn-ed-din, "we have indeed put the stone on our heads, as you proposed, and, faith, it is heavy enough!"

At length one day the Sultan rode forth to play
polo, attended by his court. When it came to choos-
ing partners, he singled out Zengy and handed him
the *chogan* mall, saying "Come and play." After
the match he turned to the other courtiers and upbraided them for their boorish jealousy.

"Are ye not ashamed?" he asked. "Here is a well-
known man, whose father held an exalted place in the
state, and not one of you has so much as offered him a
gift, or bidden him to his table! By Allah, if I have
left him so long without providing for his charges or
allotting him a fief, it was only that I might see what ye
would do." Then to Zengy : "I give you to wife Kundughly's widow, and my people shall supply you with
gold for the wedding."

Kundughly had been the richest noble of the
court, and his widow was endowed like a king's
daughter. The day after his marriage the fortunate
Emir rode forth in great pomp, surrounded by his
own and his wife's retainers.

Zengy's visit to court had succeeded, and he returned in 1124 to the double fief of Basra and Wasit,
which he ruled with a firm yet generous hand. When
the Sultan and his spiritual suzerain came to blows,
Zengy defended Wasit against the Caliph's army,
and then, seizing every boat he could lay hands on,
embarked his troops and brought a timely reinforcement to the Sultan, who was then outside Baghdad,
and was equally amazed and relieved when he suddenly saw the device of his trusty baron displayed on
the approaching flotilla. In the result the Caliph

was forced to make peace; the Seljuk graciously consented to take up his undesired abode in the City of
Peace; and Zengy received the long coveted post of
warden of Baghdad, with the control and patronage
of the whole of Irak (Chaldæa). In the autumn of
1127 he was appointed to the government of Mosil
and Jezira (the "Island," Mesopotamia). Nor was he
merely a great feudatory and ruler of broad lands;
he was also given the important charge of bringing
up two of the Sultan's sons, and by virtue of this
office he attained the dignity of an *Atabeg* or Governor of Princes. The new position placed him in
the forefront of the struggle with the Latin power.
Henceforward we shall see him as the champion of
the Faith against the Franks—the Cid Campeador
of the East. His encomiast recites his achievements
in rhyming prose:

" He ravaged the Franks in the midst of their domain;
and wreaked revenge for the true believers' pain; till the
crescents of Islam waxed full, after their wane; and the
suns of faith, of late extinct, flashed forth again; and
the Moslems trod proudly, arrayed in victory's dress;
and drank of the ever-flowing wells of success; deprived the Trinitarians of keep and fortress; and dealt
back their lies and wickedness: so the worship of the
One was restored in the 'Island' and Syrian regions;
and there flocked to the cause of Islam defenders in
legions."

Before he could measure swords with the Crusaders,
however, he had to make good his position in his
new and important government. Hitherto he had

been but one of many peers—a great captain but no
king. But at Mosil, two hundred miles away up
the Tigris, he was practically independent, and permitted no interference in his government. His system
was that which had received the sanction of the ideal
emperor, Melik Shah, and which formed the model for
the administration of all the states that sprang up
from the ruins of the Seljuk empire. It depended
upon direct personal rule, carried out by an elaborate
network of inspectors, whose reports were checked
by an army of spies. Zengy had agents at the capitals of all the neighbouring princes and even at the
imperial court, and he knew exactly what the Sultan was doing from morning to night. Each day
brought couriers from various parts with despatches,
and he was always the first to hear of any news.
The widest hospitality was extended to visitors, but
it was combined with strict surveillance. No envoys
passed through his territory without due notice and
permission, and when they came they were furnished
with a trusty escort to check inconvenient question-
ing of the people and spying out of the land. His
subjects were not permitted to leave his dominions,
lest they should betray the weak points in his defences; if any escaped, he compelled their surrender. When a company of peasants migrated
from Mosil to Maridin, he called upon the Ortukid
Prince of that city to send them back. Timurtash
objected: "We treat our *fellahin* well," he wrote,
"and take but a tithe of their produce; had you
done the like, these peasants would not have quitted
you."

" Say to your master," replied Zengy to the messenger, " If thou didst take but one-hundredth of the produce it would be too much, seeing that thou livest in luxury and sloth on thy crag of Maridin ; whereas if I taxed my people up to two-thirds, it would be nothing for my services. For I have not only mine own enemies to fight but must wage the Holy War withal, and but for me thou couldst not drink even a cup of water in security at thy Maridin, for the Franks would have gotten possession of it. Wherefore, unless those peasants are sent back, verily I will bring out every clodhopper from Maridin and dump him down at Mosil."

The emigrants were hastily sent back. Another time Zengy made the Sultan deliver up a fugitive noble ; the unhappy man was cast into prison and heard of no more.

Evidently this was no lenient governor. The story is told how Zengy once surprised a boatman asleep at his post, when he ought to have been alert and awaiting him ; on being roused the man was so terrified to see his dreaded master standing before him that he dropped dead on the spot. His slaves complained, with too much reason, of his cruelty, and his servants went in such fear that they dared not ask him to repeat an order which they had not understood. It is told how he gave one of his waiting-men a rusk to hold, and the man did not dare to let it go. Nearly a year had passed when Zengy suddenly called for it; the man instantly produced it, carefully wrapped in a napkin. His obedience was rewarded by a rich appointment.

Zengy was a shrewd judge of men, and whenever

he found a capable servant or officer, that man was sure of steadfast trust and support. Moreover, severe as he was himself, he allowed no one else to tyrannise over his subjects ; " there can be only one tyrant at a time in the land," he said. Once, on a campaign, when he discovered that one of his favourite captains had turned a Jewish family out into the winter's cold, to make his quarters in their house, Zengy faced round on the man and gave him a single look,—and that emir went humbly forth from the city and pitched his tent in the mud and rain. Oppression and licence were never permitted among his officers, and no one in that age more rigorously punished assaults upon women. The wives of his soldiers, he held, were under his special protection, and no man insulted them with impunity during their husbands' absence at the war. He discouraged his followers from acquiring property. " So long as we hold the country," he said, " what boots your estate, when your military fief serves as well? If the country be lost to us, your estates go too. When a Sultan's followers own lands, they oppress and harass and despoil the folk." He never allowed his armies to trample on the people's crops,—they marched, says the chronicler, " as it were, between two ropes,"— and no soldier was permitted to take even a truss of straw from a peasant without paying for it. Acts of violence were rigorously punished by crucifixion. He was lenient in his taxation towards the poor, but rich cities like Aleppo were heavily mulcted for the cost of his campaigns.

After all he gave them a good return for their

ASTROLOGICAL CALCULATOR MADE BY MOHAMMED IBN KUTLUKH OF MOSIL, A. H. 639.

(IN THE BRITISH MUSEUM.)

money. The effects of his severe and resolute rule were seen in the security and prosperity of his dominions, and especially in the revival of his capital. The father of the historian Ibn-el-Athir relates:

" I saw what Mosil, the Mother of the ' Island,' was when our martyred * lord first came. The greater part of the city was in ruins, and waste land stretched from the Quarter of the Drummers as far as the Citadel and Palace. . . . The old mosque was deserted, and all the houses near the ramparts were abandoned to the distance of a stone's throw. . . . But as the Martyr's reign went on, the country enjoyed protection, the designs of the wicked were frustrated, and the powerful were restrained from tyranny. The tidings of improvement spread abroad, and the folk flocked into his territory and settled there. Verily ' Generosity breeds attachment.' Buildings multiplied at Mosil and the other towns, insomuch that the very cemeteries vanished under new suburbs."

Zengy built the great Government House opposite the Almeida,† doubled the height of the ramparts, deepened the fosse, and erected the gate called after him el-Bab el-Imady. Before his time Mosil was so poor in fruits that when a merchant sold grapes he cut off little bunches with scissors to make the weight exact ; but when Zengy restored its prosperity, fertile

---

* Zengy did not die in battle for the Faith, which is the highest title to the name of *Shehid* or 'martyr' ; but the term is also applied to those Moslems who fall, as he did, by assassination, and other causes.

† Almeida, Arabic *Meydan*, is a large square or open space used for horse-racing, polo matches, and other sports.

gardens grew up around it, pomegranates and pears, apples and grapes abounded, insomuch that last year's gathering was hardly exhausted before the new crop was ready to be plucked.*

---

* Ibn-el-Athir, *Atabegs*, 137–142.

A PARTY OF CRUSADERS RETURNING FROM A FORAGING EXPEDITION.
FROM A THIRTEENTH-CENTURY MS. OF WILLIAM OF TYRE.

CHAPTER IV.

THE FALL OF EDESSA.

1127–1144.

ZENGY'S historical importance rests not upon his benefactions to Mosil and its dependencies, but upon his championship of Islam against the Crusaders, at a time when the Mohammedan cause seemed desperate. The Turkman chiefs of Mesopotamia were disunited and as prone to fight each other as to "go on the Path of God," and they were in nowise disposed to follow the leadership of the new governor of Mosil. The whole country was parcelled out in military fiefs, corresponding to Zengy's own tenure, each with a number of vassals, and among the great feudatories were some of old standing and renown. The Ortukid princes had been settled at the castles of Keyfa and Maridin since the beginning of the century. The two sons of Ortuk, Sukman and Il-Ghazy, had been famous in their raids upon the Franks; and the latter had held the high office of warden of Baghdad. No leader so far had inspired half the terror in the Christian ranks that this truculent Turkman had aroused. From his mountain fastness he had raided northern Syria ; and when Aleppo put itself under his protection, he marched to the relief of the city at the head of three thousand horse and nine thousand foot, and storming the hill of Ifrin, where the Franks were strongly posted, he won a signal victory, in which Roger of Antioch was slain. Il-Ghazy died in 1122,—the very year of Zengy's first appointment,— but his son Timurtash succeeded to his eyry at Maridin and afterwards to Aleppo ; and though he was an easy-going prince, who preferred a quiet life, he was not likely to forget what was due to his father's son—at least, until he had received a lesson in deportment.

A more powerful and energetic leader of the Ortukids was his cousin David, who had succeeded to the castle of Keyfa in 1108, and became the most renowned chief in all Diyar-Bekr. When he sent one of his arrows round among the Turkmans, everybody girded his loins in delighted anticipation of the fray, and soon twenty thousand men mustered under his banners. Such a prince was not disposed to resign the first place to a new-comer, and Zengy soon found that he had to reckon with David before he could venture into wider fields. Diyar-Bekr must be subdued or disarmed, or he could never safely advance into Syria without fear of a flank attack. His first move was against the town of Jeziret-ibn-Omar, which had recently shaken off the yoke of Mosil ; he took his army across the Tigris, some swimming, some in boats, and, aided by treacherous inhabitants, entered the town just in time; for the next day there was a spate to the height of a man, and the river became impassable. From Jezira he marched against Nisibin, once a famous capital, from whose conquest Trajan derived his title of Parthicus. It was now one of the Ortukid cities, and Zengy won it by an unworthy artifice; he caught one of the enemy's carrier-pigeons, which commonly served as messengers in Mesopotamia and Syria, and substituted a false message, which procured the immediate surrender of Nisibin, quickly imitated by Sinjar.

Here a fresh danger awaited him. The cities commanding the upper course of the Euphrates, Edessa, Saruj, Bira, etc., formed outposts of the Christians, and, in the hands of Joscelin de Courtenay, their garrisons were a *corps d'élite*. They could not be left safely in the rear without precautions. Zengy met the difficulty by arranging an armistice with Joscelin, who was probably glad enough to postpone a struggle with so formidable an adversary; and the Atabeg was left free to advance into Syria. He was engaged in establishing order in his new territories when he received an appeal from Aleppo for deliverance from the exactions of the Franks. It was the very opportunity he was seeking. He straightway crossed the Euphrates (1128), passed through Manbij, and was welcomed with thanksgivings at Aleppo. The only Syrian lord who had been able to make any head against the Crusaders was Tughtigin, the Atabeg of Damascus; and he was just dead. In the very nick of time, Zengy, now "the Syrian" *par excellence*, came

4

to take his place and to champion the despairing
Moslems against the infidels.*

Master of Aleppo, Zengy stayed more than a year
in northern Syria, doing as much mischief as possible
to the Christians. Armed with the Sultan's letters-
patent as Governor of all the Western Provinces, he
laid siege to the strong castle of Atharib (the "Cerep"
of the Franks), a day's journey from Aleppo, to
which it had long been a standing menace. Its garrison was full of picked warriors, and from its position and the mettle of its defenders it was one
of the most formidable of the Latin strongholds.
For a long time Zengy's furious assaults were steadily repulsed, but he drew his lines closer and never
lost heart. The besieged were in sore straits, and
King Baldwin at Jerusalem held a council of war,
whether or not he should advance to their relief.
Some thought it a trifling matter and made sure
that the Saracens would beat a retreat, as they had
been used to do of late ; but one of the council, "a
devil to know," says the chronicler, saw something
more serious in Zengy's movements : "A blaze will
follow these sparks," said he, "and there is flame
under this smoke. Is not this the young lion who
left his spoor at Tiberias ?"

* A melancholy incident marred his arrival. Turning over the
treasury and wardrobe of the governors of Aleppo he chanced to
light upon a bloody tunic. It was the very coat in which his father
had been executed ; and the wife who stood by his side was a grand-
daughter of the Seljuk Tutush who had ordered the deed. In un-
controllable aversion Zengy put her aside, and in spite of her
entreaties and the remonstrances of the judge she was sternly
divorced.

Baldwin finally resolved to relieve the beleaguered city, and marched "with his horsemen and foot, his banners and crosses, his princes, knights, and counts," to meet the lion of Tiberias. Zengy's counsellors advised a retreat to Aleppo, but he would none of their counsel: "Let us put our trust in God, and meet them, tide well or ill." Instead of waiting for the relieving army, he went forth to the encounter, and a furious battle ensued. Zengy at the head of his men charged the enemy again and again, shouting the words of the Prophet, "Take a taste of Hell!" The Crusaders were utterly routed: "the swords of God were sheathed in the necks of his foes," and few indeed escaped to tell of the field of shambles. They turned to fly, but what could avail when "the bottle was hung on the peg, and the locust had ended its song"? No quarter was given; the "Martyr" plunged through a sea of blood, cleaving heads and laying bones bare, till the field was covered with mangled corpses and severed limbs. Only those escaped who hid under the heaps of slain, or "mounted the camel of night."

Deprived of its last hope, Atharib was taken by assault, its fortifications razed, and its garrison enslaved or put to the sword,—the piles of their bones could be seen for years. Thus was the terror of Cerep abated. The loss was not all on one side, however, and Zengy was anxious to get his wounded home and give his men rest. After making terms with the neighbouring fortress of Harim (Harenc), he returned to Mosil in 1130, the most famous leader in Islam. His deeds were bruited over the land,

and his name became a proverb for valour and
ferocity. *Sanguineus* the Christians wrote his name,
and he had signed it in blood on the field of Atharib.

Four years Zengy rested from the Holy War.
He had much to occupy him at Mosil, in maintain-
ing his supremacy over the neighbouring chiefs; and
the death of his sovereign the Sultan in 1131 brought
about another war for the Seljuk succession, in which
Zengy took his share. It was in this campaign
that he encountered the defeat from Karaja the Cupbearer which sent him and his army flying pell-
mell to the Tigris, where the ferry-boats of the
governor of Tekrit saved them from destruction.
The Caliph sought to profit by this reverse and to
pay off old scores against the Atabeg; but his siege
of Mosil in 1133 was literally circumvented by Zengy,
who completely surrounded the besiegers, and after
three months of futile attack his Holiness retired.
The eastern horizon being once more serene, the
Atabeg turned his eyes again to Syria. To wage
the *Jihad* with success, it was essential to have
possession of Damascus, the heart of Syria, yet
now little better than an outpost of the Franks.
Damascus must be his,—and then, massing the
armies of Syria and the " Island," he would drive the
" dogs of Christians " into the sea.

It was a dream destined never to be realised by
the dreamer, though it came to pass after his death.
His first attempt in 1135 was successfully repulsed.
Then the able statesman who governed Damascus
in the name of a series of nominal lords, Muin-ed-din
Anar (the Ainardus of the Latin chroniclers), took

the only possible measure to defeat Zengy's design : he made common cause with the Franks. The Crusaders themselves stood in no little dread of the furious champion of Islam, and were glad to aid Damascus in checking his advance. When Zengy again arrived in Syria in the summer of 1137 he found the Franks on the side of Anar, and his first act was to drive them, along with the King of Jerusalem, into the castle of Barin (Mont Ferrand). The Arab historians describe the fortress as " high as the crest of Orion, loftier than the mountain-peaks," the giddy summit of which was unattainable by the weary-winged birds; and the Franks held it impregnable. Nevertheless, after Zengy's mangonels * had played upon its walls, Mont Ferrand was forced to lower its flag. The Atabeg presented King Fulk—"*ab hoste satis humane tractatus*," as William of Tyre admits—with a robe of ceremony, and the exhausted and dispirited garrison was suffered to march out with the honours of war.

This unwonted clemency was the result of common prudence. Zengy had learned that strong reinforcements from Europe were landing in Syria, and hastily patching up a truce with Damascus he retreated to Mosil. In fact a formidable combination was gathering for his discomfiture. The Emperor John Comnenus brought an army into Syria,

---

* A mangonel or stone-sling was a machine for throwing stones worked by means of twisted ropes. The other chief siege-engine of the day, the catapult (balista), resembled a huge arbalest or crossbow.

and was joined not only by the Crusading states,
but by the Moslem lord of Damascus and its dependencies. John began by exchanging friendly embassies with Zengy, and we read of gifts of falcons
and hunting-leopards, and a treaty that guaranteed
the immunities of Aleppo. But such facts were
not worth their parchment in days when Christian
ecclesiastics laid down the rule that an oath to an
infidel was null and void. The Emperor next took
Bizaa and Kafar Tab, and then laid siege to Sheyzar,
Osama's family fortress on the Orontes, in April,
1138. Zengy was summoned to the rescue, and
pressed on with forced marches. Though not strong
enough to drive the enemy from their position on
the heights, his harassing skirmishes, the rumoured
advance of David of Keyfa, together with some
skilful diplomacy and the passing of hard cash,
changed the imperial mind, already disgusted at
the indifference and frivolity of the Latin princes ;
for on the twenty-fourth day of the siege "the
Dog of the Romans" departed, abandoning his
siege-train, including eighteen huge mangonels, which
Zengy instantly appropriated. "It was thus," quoth
Ibn-el-Athir, that "*God sufficed the faithful in the
fight.*" *

The Emperor's interposition had proved futile ;
but the understanding between Damascus and Jerusalem held good. In vain Zengy tried to conciliate
the rulers of the Syrian capital by marrying the
Lady Emerald (Zumurrud Khanum), the widowed

---

* *Koran*, xxxiii., 25.

mother of the reigning lord, and giving his own daughter to the emir himself. The young man was murdered soon after, and everything had to be begun over again. Nothing could tempt or intimidate Anar, the real ruler of the city, not even the savage execution of the garrison of Baalbekk— his personal fief—after it had surrendered in October, 1139, to Zengy's solemn pledge of safe-conduct on the Koran and the Triple Divorce. This treacherous butchery only strengthened the alliance with the Christians, which was now cemented by a formal treaty, whereby Anar agreed to pay the King of Jerusalem a monthly subsidy of 20,000 gold pieces and to give him Banias, if he would aid in taking it from Zengy and driving him out of the land. The town was duly taken by the strange allies, but Zengy saved them from the trouble of carrying out the last part of the agreement by himself withdrawing his army from Syria. Leaving Saladin's father as warden of Baalbekk in reward for long and tried services, he once more left Damascus unsubdued, and returned to Mosil.

The resistance of Damascus defeated Zengy's plans in Syria. He now developed an attack upon the Crusaders from a different quarter. Repulsed in the south, he would swoop upon them from the mountains of the north. His preparations were deliberate. He protected his rear and flank by overawing the Kurds, seizing Shahrzur and Ashib (which he rebuilt and named after himself el-Imadiya, Amadia, as it is called to this day), and allying himself by marriage with the Shah of Armenia. Then he gradually advanced towards the enemy. One after the other, the towns of Diyar-Bekr fell into his hands, until his army lay before the strong walls of Amid, to which he began to lay siege for no juster cause than the Arab adage, " The sword is a better title-deed than parchments." But Amid was not his objective; his eyes were elsewhere; and as the Eastern chronicler says, he " but coquetted with Amid to conceal his desire for Edessa."

So long as his old antagonist, Joscelin de Courtenay, had held the famous episcopal city, Callirrhoe of the sweet waters, Zengy had not dared to approach it. The restless Count had been a terror throughout Diyar-Bekr and Syria : a very " devil amongst unbelievers," the Mohammedan annalist called him ; and Edessa had been the strongest outpost of the Christian state. But Joscelin was dead, and a second and very different Joscelin sat in his seat. Valiant like his father, but only by fitful impulses, ordinarily sluggish and pleasure-seeking, Joscelin II. preferred the comfortable ease of his fief at Tell Bashir (Turbessel) to the rigours of the hill-country, and Zengy's ruse of a siege of Amid was quite enough to determine the Count to go away to his pleasant Syrian estate. His Latin followers were nothing loth to follow his example, and Edessa was left to the care of Chaldee and Armenian merchants, *imbelles viri*, unskilled in arms, who relied upon the protection of mercenaries whose pay was often a year or more in arrears. With such defenders the strongest walls were little worth.

Zengy's opportunity had come, and when the city

lay deserted by its lord and the picked Crusading
chivalry, he suddenly raised the siege of Amid and
advanced upon Edessa with a vast array. He first
summoned the garrison to surrender, being loth to
injure so queenly a city : but when they refused—
mindful, no doubt, of the fate of Baalbekk—he took
counsel with the Koran, and obtaining a favourable
augury, gave the order for the siege. He had
brought mangonels and skilled sappers, and covered
the approaches of the engineers with a devastating
bombardment and incessant assaults, till the besieged
realised the words of the Koran, " *The earth, all
spacious as it is, became too strait for them.*" * An
Arab poet sang of him :

> He rides in a billow of horsemen,
> > they roll o'er the earth like a flood ;
> His spears flash speech to the foeman—
> > incarnadined tongues of blood.
> Dark as the night is his beauty,
> > but his brow has a morning light ;
> Mercy he uses at pleasure,
> > but not in the stress of the fight :
> Heart to the Heart of his host,
> > and wings to its Wings, is his might.†

After repeated storming parties had been sent in
vain, the engineers at last brought their mines,
stuffed with burning faggots, up to the walls. Zengy
himself inspected the trenches, and then said, " Let
no man sup with me to-night unless he will ride with
me into Edessa in the morning." After a month's
siege, a breach of over one hundred ells was made,

---

* *Koran*, ix., 119.

† Ibn-el-Athir, *Atabegs*, 121.

and the Turkman troops poured into the devoted
city (23 December, 1144). They were mad with the
intoxication of victory, and burning to avenge the
thousand insults which the lords of Edessa had
forced down Moslem throats ; now was the time to
blot out in blood the raids and massacres, the sacking and burning, which had made the knights of
Baldwin and Joscelin a terror throughout the country side. In their first fury they spared nothing :
"they murder the widow and the strangers and put
the fatherless to death"; crosses were overturned,
monks and priests cut down, everything destroyed
and trampled under foot, save only the girls like
gazelles, the youths fit for slaves, and the treasures
of the merchants. It was ruthless, but did not the
Koran picture righteous punishments such as this?
"*Even such was the heavy hand of thy Lord God,
which He laid on the cities that had wrought wickedness : of a surety His grip is deadly, fearsome !*" *

Then Zengy himself entered the city, and was
amazed at its beauty and stateliness, and grieved that
it should suffer at his hands. He stopped the soldiery
in their destructive rage, and made them give up their
prisoners, the youths and girls like gazelles, and the
treasure and goods they had taken. He restored the
inhabitants—all that was left of them—to their homes,
that the city might recover its prosperity, and he
spared no pains to undo the mischief he had begun.

Edessa, in the words of the Arabic historian, was
"the conquest of conquests": the stoutest prop of
the Latin Kingdom was uprooted ; Saruj and the

---

* *Koran*, xi., 104.

other satellites of the great city immediately surrendered; and the valley of the Euphrates was finally
freed from the oppression of the infidel. *Truth is
come and Falsehood vanished away* * was proclaimed
through the length and breadth of the land; for Islam
had triumphed. The victory was the common talk
of the civilised world, and people delighted to relate
strange portents of the wonderful event. Far away,
a holy man, who afflicted his body with abstinence
and rigour, came forth one day from his cell with a
face transfigured with joy, and said to the people,
"One of the brethren has told me that Zengy has
taken Edessa this day." After a time, some of the
men who had fought in the siege chanced to come to
his retreat: "O master," said they, "we knew that
we should triumph, from the moment that we saw
thee standing on the ramparts and shouting the battle-cry, '*Allahu Akbar.*'" The saint denied that he
had been at Edessa, but they all swore with great
earnestness that they had recognised him on the wall.
Still more strange were the words of the pious Moslem
sage at Palermo, over whom King Roger of Sicily
was exulting in respect of some recent successes of
his troops over the Saracens: "Where was your
Prophet," he asked, "that he came not to the aid
of his Faithful?" The sage made answer, "He was
helping in the conquest of Edessa!" The courtiers
burst into laughter, but the king sternly checked
them: the words impressed him strangely. Soon
afterwards they were only too clearly explained. †

---

* *Koran*, xvii., 83.

† Ibn-el-Athir, *Atabegs*, 124, 125.

The great Atabeg did not long survive his crowning triumph. The next two years were spent, no
doubt, in organising his new dominions, for he never
returned to Mosil. In furtherance of his schemes of
Syrian empire, he was actively besieging Castle
Jaabar, hard by the Euphrates, in 1146, when one
night as he was sleeping, being heavy with wine,
some of his slaves stole into his tent and began drink-
ing what was left. The noise roused Zengy, who
roundly abused the fellows, and then fell asleep
again. It seems that the men dreaded the punishment that was certain to follow in the morning; but
the Atabeg was often so cruel a master that little was
needed to drive them to desperation, even if the governor of the besieged fortress had not offered them
blood-money. They plucked up heart and stabbed
him as he lay. The eunuch Yaruktash gave the fatal
blow, and then all three turned and fled into the castle. When the alarm was raised, the great Emir was
in the very article of death. One who was present
told how he had found his master still breathing:

"On seeing me he thought I had come to give him
the final stroke, and he raised a piteous finger, as though
praying for mercy. I stopped short, crying out, 'O my
master, who hath done this?' But he had no strength
to answer, and that instant he breathed his last." (14
September, 1146.) *

So died Imad-ed-din Zengy, "King of Emirs,"
"Pillar of the Faith," at the age of sixty-two, by the
sword which he had used without mercy—his great

---

* Ibn-el-Athir, *Atabegs*, 132.

ambition unsatisfied, his goal unattained. As he lay there stark, treacherously slain by men who had eaten at his table, none regarded him ; his sons and hench-men were all eager to claim their inheritance, or se-cure the favour of his successor ; the army, paralysed by the crime and the loss, disbanded in dismay ; and the man who had led them and fed them, and con-quered a kingdom with them, was left alone in his cold tent. It was reserved for strangers from Rakka to compose his limbs and bury him hard by on the field of Siffin, where so many of the Faithful had fallen five hundred years before. In calmer times, his sons built a dome over the grave, and admiring chroniclers called him hero and " Martyr." It even fell to a saint of those days to see him in a vision, his face all glorified with peace, and to ask him con-cerning his state : " How hath God treated thee ? " —" With forgiveness."—" For what cause ? "—" Be-cause of Edessa."

Meantime the Crusaders punned on the tragic end of " Sanguin " in their doggerel Latin :

> " *Quam bonus eventus ! fit sanguine sanguinolentus*
> *Vir homicida reus nomine Sanguineus.*"

But they rejoiced too soon. Zengy indeed was dead, but he had done a work that all the princes in Christ-endom could not undo, and he left in his son Nur-ed-din, and his follower Saladin, leaders who knew how to crown the task he had begun. Forty years after the great Atabeg's death, the Holy Land belonged to Saladin, and Jerusalem had fallen again into the keep-ing of the Moslems, who have held it to this day.

PART II.

EGYPT.

1138–1174.

CHAPTER V.

SALADIN'S YOUTH.

1138–1164.

WE left Ayyub in 1138 sadly departing from the castle of Tekrit, with his brother, on the very night of Saladin's birth. They betook themselves to Zengy at Mosil, and were not disappointed of their welcome. The great Ata-beg had not forgotten the ferry on the Tigris, and was never the man to turn away a good sword. The two brothers served in his armies in many wars, and when Baalbekk fell, in October, 1139, Ayyub became the governor of the conquered city. Baal-bekk, or Heliopolis, the old "city of the Sun," was celebrated not only for its antiquity and its temples, but for its lofty situation. It stood between Leb-anon and Antilibanus, overhanging the valley of the Litany, at a height of four thousand feet above the sea, and was said to be the coldest town in Syria. A legend tells how men asked the Cold, "Where shall we find thee?" and it answered, "My home is Baalbekk." Though far from being the

magnificent city that it was in the days when Anto-
ninus Pius built the great temple of which a part
still stands, Baalbekk in the time of Ayyub was yet
an important town, surrounded by fertile fields,
orchards, and gardens, and defended by a strong
wall, with a citadel, or acropolis, on the west.   It had
not yet suffered the vandal touch of the Mongols, or
the final upheaval of earthquake, which reduced it
to its present ruined state.   Its " presses overflowed
with grapes," sweet water ran through the town, and
mills and water-wheels all around bore witness to fertility.*   To be placed in command of so great and
prosperous a city was a convincing proof of Zengy's
confidence, especially when it happened to be the
southernmost outpost over against the hostile city
of Damascus, distant only thirty-five miles.

Here the governor's son Saladin spent some years
of his childhood ; and, according to the saying, they
ought to have been happy years, because they have
no history.   We know absolutely nothing of the
family of Ayyub between 1139 and 1146, the period
of their residence at Baalbekk.   No doubt Saladin
received the usual education of a Moslem boy ;
probably as the son of the commandant he had the
best teaching within reach.   Ayyub was particularly
devout, and even founded a convent for Sufy re-
cluses at Baalbekk.   His son was doubtless drilled
for years in the Koran, in Arabic grammar, and the
elements of rhetoric, poetry, and theology ; for, whatever the race of the Saracen rulers of those days,
their educational standard was Arabian ; and to in-

* El-Idrisy, writing in 1154.

stil the Koran and traditions, to teach a pure Arabic style and the niceties of Arabic syntax, formed the chief aim of the learned but limited men who were entrusted with the training of distinguished youth.

Whatever schooling Saladin had at Baalbekk must have been meagre compared with his later opportunities. He was not yet nine years old when his father's patron was murdered, and the death of the great Atabeg was of course the signal for the recovery of Baalbekk by its old Damascus owner. Ayyub made no effort to defend the town. He was ever a diplomatic, prudent sort of man, keenly alive to his own interests. He saw that the two sons of Zengy, who shared their father's dominions, were occupied in watching each other, and had no time to look after Baalbekk. Mosil was distant, and Aleppo timid. On the other hand, Damascus was near, and was resolved to get back her own. When her troops entered Baalbekk, Ayyub made terms from the citadel, and before he surrendered he had arranged to receive a handsome fief, including ten villages near Damascus, a good sum down, and a house in the capital. Here his statecraft and sagacity soon procured him a high position at the court of Abak, the grandson of Tughtigin, and in a few years he rose to be commander-in-chief of the Damascus army.

Ayyub held this exalted post when Zengy's son, the King of Aleppo, Nur-ed-din Mahmud, marched against Damascus in April, 1154. The name of Nur-ed-din (Noradin) is second only to Saladin among the great defenders of Islam. After the catastrophe at Jaabar, the Atabeg's kingdom had fallen into two

parts: his eldest son, Seyf-ed-din Ghazy, duly succeeded him at Mosil, whilst a younger, Nur-ed-din,
ruled the Syrian province. Hardly had he established himself upon the throne of Aleppo, when he
was called upon to defend Edessa. Immediately
after the death of Zengy, the Armenian inhabitants
invited their former Count, Joscelin de Courtenay, to
retake the city, and in November, 1146, he surprised
the Turkman guard in their sleep, and the town was
his. The citadel, however, held out till Nur-ed-din's
arrival, when Joscelin and his troops prudently retired, whilst the Armenians who sought to flee under
his protection were caught between the garrison and
the relieving army and cut to pieces. *Foris gladius
et intus pavor.*

"It was pitiful to see, and lamentable to tell,—the
helpless crowd, the peaceful populace, old men and
sick, matrons and tender maids, ancient grandams, and
little children even at the breast, in the jaws of the
gate, some trodden down by horsemen, some smothered
in the press, some slain by the merciless swords of the
enemy." *

Very few escaped with the outgoing army, which
Nur-ed-din pursued and harassed as far as the Euphrates.

Joscelin himself was captured later on, blinded,
and cast into prison at Aleppo, where he died
after nine years' misery. His failure was followed
by the complete extinction of the Frankish power
throughout the County of Edessa and along the

* William of Tyre, xvi., 16.

northern frontier. The disastrous Second Crusade, led by the Emperor Conrad and Louis VII., still further depressed the courage of the Christians. They came at the preaching of St. Bernard to wipe out the disgrace of Edessa; but they only disgraced themselves before Damascus, in 1148, where the vigilant Anar, no longer afraid of Zengy, and aided no doubt by Ayyub, held them at arm's length and eventually saw their forces evaporate.

" From the place of muster at Tiberias, the host, with the Holy Cross at its head, marched across Jordan ; first went the barons of the land under King Baldwin, next the French, and last the Germans. The mud wall that surrounded the famous gardens of Damascus offered no bar to the advance of such an army. But the thick orchards with their narrow foot-paths and their growth of fruit and herbage formed a far better protection to the city. Everywhere throughout the length and breadth of this vast stretch of green and trees the ambushed Saracens opposed the invaders' progress ; or, penned up in lofty buildings, which here and there rose up like stone islands out of a sea of green, shot down their arrows from above. At last, after long fighting, the woods were cleared, and the Christians, wearied out with heat and thirst, made for the river, only to find a fresh army drawn up against them. ' Why do we not advance ? ' cried Conrad from the rear, and, learning the cause, burst through the French battalions to the van. There, in true Teutonic fashion, he and his knights leaped off their war-horses, and, closing up behind their shield-wall, soon swept back the enemy within the city.

" ' The siege now began in earnest, and would have

been brought to a successful issue,' says William of Tyre, 'had it not been for the greed of the great princes, who commenced negotiations with the citizens.' At the advice of traitors, the camp was shifted to the south-west, where, so ran the rumour, the wall was too weak to withstand the feeblest onslaught. But here the Crusaders found a more deadly enemy than strong fortifications; for in their new position they were cut off from the river and deprived of the orchard fruits; and through lack of food and leadership despair fell upon the host, until men began to talk of retreat. There was jealousy, likewise, between the Syrian Franks and their Western allies, and out of this too fertile source of evil, Anar, the Vezir of Damascus, was not slow to reap profit for himself. He pointed out to the former the folly of helping their brethren to seize Damascus, the capture of which would be but the prelude to the seizing of Jerusalem also. His arguments, supported as they doubtless were by bribes, brought about the abandonment of the siege." *

By Easter, 1149, this valiant Crusade was on its way home.

In such a crisis no man who could bear a sword could have been idle in Damascus. Ayyub, though he probably did not attain the rank of commander-in-chief until after Anar's death in the August following the siege, must have played a prominent part in the defence. Saladin was of course too young to be more than an absorbed spectator. It is true that Western legend tells how Eleanor of France carried on her amours with the future " Soldan "; but as he was then but eleven years old, King Louis's jealousy

* Archer and Kingsford, *Crusades*, 217–219.

found a more probable accomplice for the divorce,
which afterwards took place, than a good little boy
at school.

Five years later, Ayyub was the chief agent in
changing the dynasty and admitting the son of
his old patron to the capital of Syria. It happened that whilst the elder brother had made
terms with Damascus and had there risen to high
power, the younger, Asad-ed-din Shirkuh, the
" Mountain-Lion," had taken service with Nur-ed-din,
and such was the valour he showed in every engagement, that his master not only gave him valuable
cities in fief—such as Emesa and Rahba,—but placed
him in command of the army which was destined for
the conquest of Damascus.

The great opportunity seemed at last to have come.
The Franks were discredited and dismayed after the
miserable collapse of the Second Crusade; Mesopotamia was quiet under the magnanimous rule of
Zengy's eldest son ; the indomitable Anar, who had
repeatedly withstood the great Atabeg himself, was
dead, and in his stead had risen Ayyub, whose
brother was Nur-ed-din's trusted marshal ; and already the Prince of Damascus had humbly paid homage to the King of Aleppo. If ever the hour had
struck for the realising of Zengy's dream of a Syrian
empire, centred at Damascus, it was now.

In April, 1154, Nur-ed-din's army appeared on
some pretext before the unconquered city. Shirkuh
opened negotiations with his politic brother within
the walls. In six days all was arranged ; Ayyub did
justice to his old devotion to the house of Zengy,—

and espoused the side of the strongest battalions.
Il devint traître pour n'être point ingrat. The people of Damascus, like sheep astray, now that Anar
was dead, abandoned their hereditary lord, and following Ayyub's advice opened their gates to the
powerfulest sovereign of the age. Nur-ed-din entered Damascus without a blow, and the brothers
were duly rewarded. Ayyub alone of all the court *
was granted the right to be seated in the presence of
the king, and was made governor of Damascus;
Shirkuh was established at Emesa, with the viceroy-
alty over the whole Damascene province. The ferry
on the Tigris had proved a sovereign talisman ; but
if they owed their first advance to a stroke of fortune, both brothers evidently possessed the talent
and courage to use their opportunities.

From 1154 to 1164, Saladin lived at Damascus, at
the Court of Nur-ed-din, with the consideration that
belonged to the son of the commandant. As to
what he did, what he studied, how he passed his
time, and with whom, the Arab chroniclers maintain
an exasperating silence. We are informed that he
showed himself a youth of " excellent qualities," that
he learned from Nur-ed-din how " to walk in the path
of righteousness, to act virtuously, and to be zealous
in fighting the infidels." As the favoured governor's
son, he naturally enjoyed a privileged position, but,
far from exhibiting any symptoms of future greatness, he was evidently a shining example of that
tranquil virtue which shuns "the last infirmity of
noble minds." This is all we are told of Saladin up

---

* Ibn-el-Athir, *Atabegs*, 314.

to the age of twenty-five. The Syrian nobles—and Saladin's rank was now high—spent their youth in study, and their manhood in war and hunting and the cultivation of letters. Stalking the lion was the king of sports, but coursing and hawking were practised with unflagging energy. We read of setters and falcons imported regularly from Constantinople, where they were bred with great care and science. But we are not told a word to favour the supposition that Saladin as a youth was a mighty hunter; all we know tends to the belief that he preferred a quiet seclusion, and like his sagacious father, rather than his impetuous uncle, governed his life on principles of prudence and placidity. When it came to a choice of ways, the one arduous but leading to honour and renown, the other to peaceful insignificance, Saladin, as we shall see, endeavoured to choose the latter; nor was it a case of a formal *noli episcopari*, but rather the protest of a retired nature against the rush and press of an ambitious career. He was one of those who have greatness thrust upon them; and though, when once fairly launched, he missed no opportunity of extending his power, it may well be doubted whether he would ever have started at all but for the urgency of his friends. An uneventful youth might have gently passed into a tranquil old age, and Saladin might have remained plain Salah-ed-din of Damascus with a name too obscure to be Europeanised.

Nor is it likely that he would have distinguished himself as a scholar or poet. To judge by later years, his literary tastes tended to the theological; he loved poetry indeed, but less than keen dialectic;

and to hear holy traditions traced and verified, canon
law formulated, passages in the Koran explained,
and sound orthodoxy vindicated, inspired him with
a strange delight. Like his father Ayyub, he was
above all things a devout Moslem ; and at Damascus he had ample opportunities for cultivating di-
vinity. Learning in those days meant theological
armory more than anything else, and wise men
came in throngs from the East and from the West,
from Samarkand and from Cordova, to teach and be
taught in the mosques and *medresas* of Damascus.
They must have brought with them the knowledge
of other lands and other customs and arts. Perhaps
Saladin sat and listened in the west corner of the
Great Omayyad Mosque, when Ibn-Aby-Usrun was
holding his lectures there.   He could have no better
master than one who was styled a " leader of his age
in talents and legal learning," and whom Nur-ed-din
not only brought with him to Damascus, but even
built colleges in most of the great cities of Syria for
him to lecture in, that his wonderful gifts might be
known of all.   He became a judge in Mesopotamia,
and it speaks well for Saladin's faithfulness to early
ties that, when the old man lost his sight, the
Damascus youth who had become the greatest of
Sultans refused to let him be deprived of his honourable office.

A negative proof of the retired life led by Saladin
in youth and early manhood is found in the fact
that Osama, who spent nearly the whole of the ten
years, 1154–1164, at Damascus in intimate relations
with the court (when it happened to be there), does

THE OMAYYAD MOSQUE AT DAMASCUS.

not once mention him, and when at last he met him
in 1174 it seems that a formal introduction had to
be made.*   Had Saladin been constantly at court,
Osama must have known him.   At the same time it
must be remembered that the Arab chief was between sixty and seventy at the period of his earlier
Damascus residence, and would hardly have paid
much attention to a mere youngster; and further,
that the old poet's impulsive Bohemian nature could
have had little in common with the staid young man
who preferred the society of divines.   Saladin possibly thought Osama a sad warning, and the wild
old Arab perhaps retorted with the opinion that the
governor's discreet son was no better than a prig.

The fact that Saladin, who was afterwards the
most renowned leader of his time, was apparently a
completely obscure individual up to the age of
twenty-five, is the more curious when it is remembered that his uncle Shirkuh, who afterwards brought
him into public life, was Nur-ed-din's right-hand man,
a conspicuously able and ambitious general, and was
even spoken of as almost his colleague in sovereignty.†   When in 1159 Nur-ed-din was apparently
dying of a malady which kept him stretched for
months on a bed of sickness at Aleppo, Shirkuh,
then unquestionably the premier noble of Syria, was
on the point of seizing the crown itself, and was only
deterred by the ever-prudent counsels of Ayyub,
who suggested that it might be wise to wait and see
whether their master was really going to die or not.

* Derenbourg, *Ousama*, 368.
† Ibn-el-Athir, *Atabegs*, 305.

In 1160 Shirkuh acted as leader of the Damascus caravan of pilgrims to Mekka, and displayed extraordinary pomp on the occasion; yet we do not hear of Saladin among his brilliant staff, nor did the latter, despite his religious instinct, ever perform that journey which to Moslems is the crowning act of grace. Shirkuh of course took a prominent part in the wars of Nur-ed-din, in the conquest of Harim (Harenc) from the Franks in 1162, and the ensuing capture of fifty Syrian fortresses, whereby the kingdom of Zengy's cautious son was extended to Marash on the border of the Seljuk Sultanate of Rum on the north, and southward to Banias at the foot of Mount Hermon, and to Bozra in the Hauran.

In all this Saladin had no share: if he had taken the smallest part in any warlike operation we may be sure his admiring biographers would have recorded it. It was not until Shirkuh made his memorable expeditions to Egypt that the future " Sultan of the Moslems " emerged from his voluntary retirement and stepped boldly into his uncle's place as the true successor of Zengy in the rôle of Champion of Islam.

CHAPTER VI.

THE CONQUEST OF EGYPT.

1164–1169.

FOR two centuries Egypt had suffered the rule of a dynasty of heretical Caliphs who boasted a descent from Fatima, the daughter of the Prophet Mohammed, and were hence known as the Fatimids. They professed the peculiar mystical philosophy of the Shiïtes, maintained the incarnation of the Divine Reason in the Imams sprung from Aly and Fatima, and believed in the coming of the Mahdy, the last inspired leader of the same elect descent. Notwithstanding the rigid orthodoxy of the vast majority of the Egyptians, who followed the teaching of the great Sunnite Imam esh-Shafiy,—whose tomb in the desert, outside the southern wall of Cairo, is still an object of profound reverence,—the Fatimid Caliphs imposed their authority with little difficulty upon a people accustomed to submission and pliable in matters of faith; and for several generations wielded a power which stood unrivalled among Mohammedan states.

Their navies disputed the command of the Mediterranean with those of the Caliphs of Cordova; they
successfully occupied Sicily, and raided Sardinia and
Corsica; their ships frequented the Red Sea and the
Indian Ocean, and even coasted West Africa through
the Straits of Gibraltar; their caravans traded with
Asia and Europe, and penetrated the heart of Africa
even to Lake Chad; their armies held Syria and
Arabia as well as Egypt, and excited perpetual
alarm in their decayed rivals, the orthodox Abbasid
Caliphs of Baghdad. Their wealth, the fruit of the
great Indian trade, which passed through their cus-
toms-houses to the merchants of Venice and Pisa,
was fabulous, if we may credit the amazing inventory of jewels and treasure recited by the Arab historians; the luxury and prodigality of their court were
the wonder of foreign envoys; the walls and gates
and mosques of Cairo bear witness to their splendid
conception of what was due to the royal city, yet
what remains of their architecture is but a vestige of
the noble works upon which they are known to have
lavished all the resources of decorative art.

Egypt has proved herself the Capua of more than
one conquering race. The Fatimid Caliphs, abandoning the simplicity of their early days, when they
ruled as missionaries among the simple hardy Ber-
bers of Kayrawan, revelled in the wealth and luxury
of their beautiful palaces at Cairo, and were content
after a while to devote themselves to the unique pursuit of pleasure, and to leave the obnoxious labour
of government to their servants. Their vezirs gradually usurped all sovereign powers, and even assumed

the title of King, whilst the Fatimid pontiff, buried
in the cushions of his harim, retained only the mysterious spiritual authority with which the "true
Imam" was invested in the eyes of all devout followers of the sect of Aly.   The Caliph of Cairo, on
his jewelled throne, became as much a puppet as his
rival of Baghdad.   Cabals and factions were the
natural consequences of bureaucratic rule, and the
Fatimid kingdom, divided against itself, with a population imperfectly reconciled to the Shiïte sect,
might easily have fallen a prey to any determined
invader.   The long immunity of Egypt was due
chiefly to the weakness of her neighbours.   The Seljuks had indeed deprived her of Syria, but the Seljuk
empire had split into fragments before an invasion of
Egypt had been attempted.   The only power that
menaced the Fatimid government in the first half of
the twelfth century was the Kingdom of Jerusalem.
The Franks were not only in possession of the
Syrian coast and many inland fortresses, but were
ambitious fighting men, bent upon plunder.   Fortunately for Egypt, the Crusaders fought at least as
much for gold as for glory, and there is no doubt
that the later Fatimids procured their indulgence
by a prudent application of subsidies, if not a settled
annual tribute.*

The arrival of Nur-ed-din upon the scene of Syrian
politics, especially after his conquest of Damascus,
introduced a highly disturbing influence.   The King
of Syria and the King of Jerusalem were now rival
powers : neither could allow the other to increase his

---

* *Annuam tributi pensionem*, William of Tyre calls it (xix., 5).

strength by the annexation of Egypt, and thus to acquire a vantage-ground from the south. Each coveted the delta of the Nile, and each watched his rival with jealous vigilance. The Egyptian vezirs, the real governors of the country, fully alive to the possibilities of the situation, set themselves to co-quet with both parties, and to play off one against the other. In the end they carried the game too far, and gave Saladin an opportunity which he did not neglect.

The cause of Nur-ed-din's first interference in arms in the affairs of Egypt was an appeal from a deposed vezir. In a time of frequent assassinations and changes of ministers, Shawar, the Arab governor of Upper Egypt, made his way to the vezirate in Janu-ary, 1163, only to be deposed in seven months' time and driven out of the country by Dirgham, the War-den of the Gate and commander of the Barkiya bat-talion. Shawar fled to Nur-ed-din at Damascus and implored succour. It was not the first time that an Egyptian vezir had proposed terms of alliance to the Syrian King, but Shawar's proposals were the prodi-gal pledges of desperation. He offered to pay the whole cost of an invasion, and afterwards to give Nur-ed-din a third of the Egyptian revenue in annual tribute. The King of Syria was not indifferent to the importance of obtaining a hold upon Egypt : he knew that it was the master-key of the political situ-ation, and would form a prolific source of revenue. Yet he hesitated to accept Shawar's overtures. Dis-trust of the man himself, and apprehension of the risks to which an expedition would be exposed when

CRUSADERS AND EGYPTIANS BEFORE ASCALON.
(FROM A PAINTED WINDOW AT ST. DENYS, 12TH CENTURY.)

marching through the desert on the Crusaders' flank, made him pause.

Events, however, moved too fast for his prudence. Dirgham quarrelled with Amalric over the yearly subsidy, and the new King of Jerusalem with prompt decision invaded Egypt in September, 1163, to exact the usual tribute. Dirgham, after a severe defeat near Bilbeys, ingeniously avoided total discomfiture by breaking down the dams and causeways and flooding the country with the imprisoned waters of the Nile, then at its height. Amalric had already retired to Palestine, but half satisfied with some sort of composition, when Dirgham, hearing of Shawar's negotiations at Damascus, perceived his error in not conciliating the Latin King, and hastened to proffer an eternal alliance, to be cemented by increased tribute. This step must have been known to Nur-ed-din: fortified by an auspicious consultation of the Koran, he immediately cast his former scruples to the winds; and before Amalric could intervene, Shawar was on the march to Egypt (April, 1164), supported by a strong force of Turkmans from Damascus, led by Asad-ed-din Shirkuh, with Saladin on his staff. The Egyptians were defeated at Bilbeys, but rallied again under the walls of Cairo.

For several days indecisive conflicts took place, Shawar holding Fustat, and the other the castle of Cairo. Then, to raise funds, Dirgham possessed himself of the *wakf*, the "money of the orphans," and at once the people began to fall away from him. Worse still, he was deserted by the Caliph and the army. Driven to bay, for the last time he sounded the " as-

6

sembly." In vain "the drums beat and the trumpets
blared, *ma-sha-llah !* on the battlements " : no man
answered.   In vain the desperate Emir, surrounded
by his bodyguard of five hundred horse, all that remained to him of a powerful army, stood suppliant
before the Caliph's palace for a whole day, even until
the evening call to prayer, and implored him by the
memory of his forefathers to stand forth at the window and bless his cause.   No answer came ; "the
guard itself gradually dispersed, till only thirty troopers were left.   Suddenly a warning cry reached him :
' Look to thyself and save thy life ! '—and lo ! Shawar's trumpets and drums were heard, entering from
the Gate of the Bridge."

Then at last the deserted leader rode through the
Zuweyla gate out into the streets beyond, calling on
the people, who had once adored him and battened
on his favour, to rise and do battle in his cause ; they
only hooted and cursed, as is the manner of the multitude towards fallen favourites.   Still he rode on,
till his horse, maddened by the tumult, threw its
rider, beside the sacred chapel of " our Lady Nefisa."
Instantly the fickle folk hacked off his head, and bore
it in triumph through the streets ; his body they left
to be worried by the curs.   Such was the tragic end
of a brave and gallant gentleman, poet, and paladin ;
courteous and comely in face and bearing, cultivated
in mind and accomplished in every manly sport ;
" one who could write like Ibn-Mukla, and composed
poems with double rhymes " ; " the best horseman of
his age," and as stout an archer as ever drew bow in
Egypt.

NICHE FROM THE CHAPEL OF SITTA NEFISA, ARAB MUSEUM, CAIRO.

Shawar, restored to power, in May, 1164,* was
eager to see the backs of the allies who had effected
his reinstatement. He cautiously excluded Shirkuh
from the fortified city of Cairo, and kept him in the
suburbs. Then safe, as he thought, within his own
strong walls, he defied his ally, broke all his promises, and refused to pay the indemnity. Shirkuh
was not the man to forego his rights or condone
broken faith; he sent Saladin to occupy Bilbeys and
the eastern province. This hostile movement compelled Shawar in turn to appeal to Amalric. Now
the King of Jerusalem plainly foresaw the ruin of
the Christian cause in Palestine, penned in "between the devil and the deep sea," if Nur-ed-din
should once gain a firm footing in Egypt, and he
willingly sent the same army with which he had
intended to support Dirgham against the very man
whom he was now to protect. The tables were thus
turned: the Franks were now the allies of their
former enemy, and the saviour of the Egyptian
vezir had become his foe.

On the arrival of the Crusaders the Syrian army
entrenched itself at Bilbeys, where it resisted all the
assaults of Amalric for three months. A fortunate
diversion at last came to its relief. Nur-ed-din was
waging a successful campaign in Palestine. After a
reverse at the hands of Gilbert de Lacy and Robert
Mansel, he had taken Harim (Harenc) and was laying siege to Banias (Cæsarea Philippi) then commanded by Walter Chesney; and Amalric was sorely

---

* In his chronology of the first expedition to Egypt, Baha-ed-din
is a year too early (1163). I follow Ibn-el-Athir in his *Kamil.*

wanted at home to protect his own kingdom, always dangerously exposed upon its eastern marches.
Nor was Shirkuh less anxious to extricate himself
from a situation where, attacked all day and every
day, penned in behind weak earthworks, and running
short of food, his position was neither safe nor agree-
able. An armistice was accordingly arranged, and the
two parties came to terms. On the 27th of October,
the Syrians marched out of their camp and filed off
between the lines of the allied Crusaders and Egyptians, Shirkuh himself, battle-axe in hand, bringing
up the rear. A Frankish officer, surprised at this
warlike attitude, asked the truculent old warrior
whether he was afraid that the Christians would attack him in spite of their pledge. " Let them try!"
said Shirkuh, and passed on. In accordance with the
agreement, the army returned to Damascus, where
they found that Nur-ed-din's victories had been
crowned by the surrender of Banias in mid October,
and the capture of Bohemond Prince of Antioch,
Raymond Count of Tripoli, with Hugh of Lusignan,
and other noted knights, who were led in chains to
Aleppo.*

The expedition to Egypt had ended without glory,
but it had accomplished its object; it had spied out
the land, and Shirkuh was able to report favourably
on the possibility and advantages of annexation.
Egypt was a country, he said, "without *men*, and
with a precarious and contemptible government."
Its wealth and defencelessness invited aggression.

---

* William of Tyre, xix., 9.

The ambitious general was devoured by desire for a viceregal throne at Cairo, and from this time forth he persistently urged Nur-ed-din to authorise the conquest of Egypt. The bolder spirits at court supported his importunity, and the Caliph of Baghdad accorded his blessing and encouragement to a project which involved the deposition of his heretical rival. Nur-ed-din, ever cautious, resisted these influences for a while, but at last gave way,—possibly because rumours had reached him of a closer union between Shawar and the Franks, which soon proved to be well founded.

It was, in fact, a race for the Nile. Shirkuh started first, at the beginning of 1167, with two thousand picked horsemen, and, taking the desert route by Gazelle Valley (Wady-el-Ghizlan) to avoid a collision with the Franks, but encountering on the way a violent and disastrous sandstorm, reached the Nile at Atfih, some forty miles south of Cairo, where he might cross to the west bank without fear of molestation. He had hardly carried his army over, however, when Amalric appeared on the east side, having hurried from Palestine as soon as he heard of the enemy's movements. The two armies followed the opposite banks down to Cairo, where Amalric pitched his camp close to Fustat, whilst Shirkuh took up a position exactly facing him at Giza. There each waited for the other to begin operations. Meanwhile Shawar had recovered from his surprise at the sudden irruption of the Franks, whom at first he had not recognised with certainty as foes or friends, and began to testify his gratitude

for their protection in a substantial form. Amalric
took the opportunity of the vezir's amicable dispo-
sitions to place their alliance on a more formal basis.
Convinced of the unstable character of the Minister,
he resolved to have a treaty ratified by the Caliph in
person. The conditions were that Egypt should pay
the King two hundred thousand gold pieces * then
and there, and a further like sum at a later date, in
return for his aid in expelling the enemy. On this
agreement Amalric gave his hand to the Caliph's
representatives, and claimed a like ratification from
the Caliph himself.

The introduction of Christian ambassadors to the
sacred presence, where few even of the most exalted
Moslems were admitted, was unprecedented; but
Amalric was in a position to dictate his own terms.
Permission was granted, and Hugh of Cæsarea with
Geoffrey Fulcher the Templar were selected for the
unique embassy. The vezir himself conducted them
with every detail of oriental ceremony and display to
the Great Palace of the Fatimids. They were led by
mysterious corridors and through guarded doors,
where stalwart Sudanis saluted with naked swords.
They reached a spacious court, open to the sky, and
surrounded by arcades resting on marble pillars; the
panelled ceilings were carved and inlaid in gold and
colours; the pavement was rich mosaic. The unaccustomed eyes of the rude knights opened wide with
wonder at the taste and refinement that met them at

---

* In Arabic, *dinars*. The dinar was a gold coin weighing a few
grains more than the present half-sovereign, and containing a larger
proportion of gold (.97).

every step;—here they saw marble fountains, birds
of many notes and wondrous plumage, strangers to
the western world; there, in a further hall, more exquisite even than the first, "a variety of animals
such as the ingenious hand of the painter might
depict, or the license of the poet invent, or the
mind of the sleeper conjure up in the visions of
the night,—such, indeed, as the regions of the
East and the South bring forth, but the West
sees never, and scarcely hears of." At last, after
many turns and windings, they reached the throne
room, where the multitude of the pages and their
sumptuous dress proclaimed the splendour of their
lord. Thrice did the vezir, ungirding his sword,
prostrate himself to the ground, as though in humble supplication to his god; then, with a sudden
rapid sweep, the heavy curtains broidered with
gold and pearls were drawn aside, and on a golden
throne, robed in more than regal state, the Caliph
sat revealed.

The vezir humbly presented the foreign knights,
and set forth in lowly words the urgent danger from
without and the great friendship of the King of Jerusalem. The Caliph, a swarthy youth emerging from
boyhood,—*fuscus, procerus corpore, facie venusta,*—
replied with suave dignity: He was willing, he said,
to confirm in the amplest way the engagements made
with his beloved ally. But when asked to give his
hand in pledge of faithfulness, he hesitated, and a
thrill of indignation at the strangers' presumption
ran through the listening court. After a pause, however, the Caliph offered his hand—gloved as it was—

to Sir Hugh.   The blunt knight spoke him straight :
" My lord, troth has no covering : in the good faith
of princes, all is naked and open."   Then at last,
very unwillingly, as though derogating from his
dignity, the Caliph, forcing a smile, drew off the
glove and put his hand in Hugh's, swearing word
by word to keep the covenant truly and in all good
faith.*

The treaty thus ratified, Amalric attempted to
throw a bridge of boats across the Nile; but the
presence of the enemy on the other side defeated
the plan, and he resorted to another.   Finding an
island where the river forked into its two main
streams, he conveyed his army over to it by night,
and thence to the other side, in ships.   Shirkuh discovered the movement too late to oppose, and finding the enemy landed he retreated to Upper Egypt.
The King pursuing came up with him at " the two
Gates " (el-Baban), ten miles south of Minya.   Here
was a plain, on the border where the cultivated land
touched the desert, and numerous sandy hills gave
cover to the combatants.   Shirkuh's captains at first
advised him not to risk a battle ; but one of them
stood forth and said stoutly, " Those who fear death
or slavery are not fit to serve kings : let them turn
ploughmen, or stay at home with their wives."   Saladin and others applauded ; and Shirkuh, always
ready for hard knocks, gladly gave battle (18th April,
1167).   He put the baggage in the centre, covered

---

* William of Tyre, *Historia rerum in partibus transmarinis gestarum*, lib. xix., cap. 19, 20.   The embassy is not recorded by the
Arabic chroniclers.

by Saladin's troop, which was to bear the first brunt of the attack. Saladin's orders were to fall back when pressed and draw the enemy in pursuit, and then to press them in turn, as the fight might allow. Shir-kuh himself took command of the right wing, com-posed of a body of picked horsemen, which was to cut up the enemy's rear, consisting of the less war-like Egyptians. It fell out as he expected. The Franks were drawn away by Saladin; the Egyptians were cut up and routed; and when the Crusaders, returning from the pursuit, found their allies fled, they also hastily retreated, abandoning their baggage and leaving Hugh of Cæsarea among the prisoners.* The victors, however, were not strong enough to fol-low up the success, march on to Cairo, and run Sha-war and Amalric to earth. Taking the lesser risk, Shirkuh went north by a desert route and entered Alexandria without opposition. Here he installed Saladin as governor, with one half of his army, while with the other he again turned southwards to levy contributions in Upper Egypt.

The joint forces of the Franks and Egyptians now invested Alexandria, whilst the Christian fleet held the coast. The defence of the city was Saladin's first independent command, and he quitted himself

---

* Ibn-el-Athir, *Kamil*, 548; according to his *Atabegs* it was a month earlier. The numbers engaged are variously estimated. The Arab historians give Shirkuh only 2000 horsemen. William of Tyre, on the other hand, puts the Saracen force at 9000 men mailed (*loricis galeisque*), 3000 archers, and at least 10,000 Arabs armed with spears. The Latins, he says, had only 374 knights, an uncer-tain number of light infantry (Turcopoles), and a body of Egyptians who were more a burden than a help (xix., 25).

well. He had but a thousand followers of his own, in the midst of a mongrel and partly foreign populace, who, as malcontents, were not sorry to take part against a feeble government, or to defend their city against the savage and bloodthirsty Franks ; yet, as merchants and tradesmen, could not conceal their terror of the siege-machines and infernal engines which the " infidels " brought against their walls. Provisions, moreover, ran short ; and short rations make a humble stomach. At last they rose in a tumult and openly talked of surrender : " Why suffer we these things for a stranger and a cause which is not ours?" Saladin meanwhile had sent to his uncle for help, and Shirkuh was hurrying down from Kos laden with treasure. The news put fresh heart into the people, already spurred on by Saladin's spirited exhortations and the promise of reinforcement, or frightened into a desperate courage by his tales of the monstrous barbarities inflicted by the Franks upon the vanquished. They held out for seventy-five days, in spite of hunger and incessant assaults, till it became known that Shirkuh was at the Abyssinians' Lake, laying siege to Cairo. On this, Amalric gave up all thoughts of Alexandria, and a peace was arranged (4 August, 1167), by which both parties * agreed to leave Egypt to the Egyptians. Alexandria was surrendered to Shawar ; prisoners were exchanged ; and Shirkuh led the exhausted remnant of his two thousand troopers back to Damascus. Before leaving, Saladin was honourably

---

* It is fair to state that the Franks did not fully admit this pledge for their part of the treaty of peace.

entertained in Amalric's camp for several days but rather, one suspects, as a hostage than as a guest. The experience, nevertheless, may have been valuable. He must have seen something of knightly order and discipline, and may here have formed a friendship with Humphrey of Toron, who was on terms of brotherliness (*fraterno fœdere junctus erat* *) with at least one Saracen emir. It is even probable that this was the occasion when Saladin received Christian Knighthood at Humphrey's hands.†

The Christians claimed the campaign as a triumph, and the evacuation of Alexandria as a surrender ; but if the Arab chroniclers are right in saying that Amalric paid Shirkuh fifty thousand pieces of gold to go away, the advantage would appear to have been on the side of the Moslems. On the other hand, the Franks, in violation (apparently) of their agreement, not only left a Resident or Prefect at Cairo, but insisted on furnishing the guards of the city gates from their own soldiers ; they also increased the annual subsidy to be paid by Shawar to the King of Jerusalem to one hundred thousand gold pieces. The apparent inconsistency of these arrangements at Alexandria and Cairo may be explained by the supposition that the Christians, alarmed by the news of Nur-ed-din's successes in Palestine, were eager to get home at all costs, and therefore abandoned their chances against Shirkuh, however propitious ; yet did not leave Egypt without clinching their hold upon the shifty vezir at Cairo.

---

* William of Tyre, xvii., c. 17.

† *Itinerarium Regis Ricardi*, i., c. 3. See below, Chap. XXIII.

Not content with this hold, the more impetuous
among Amalric's counsellors presently began to urge
the complete conquest of Egypt, and their advice was
strongly supported by the garrison they had left at
Cairo and Fustat, who had naturally the best means
of discovering the weakness of the defences. The
King of Jerusalem withstood these counsels in vain.
He had doubtless discovered by this time that the
only safe policy was to conquer Damascus first, and
make the Kingdom safe on the east, with the great
Syrian desert for its frontier, before attempting to
annex Egypt—since invasion meant exposing his
rear to the assaults of Nur-ed-din. Moreover, Egypt,
he said, was their milch cow ; and he pointed out
the bad policy of turning a friend into an enemy
and throwing Shawar into the arms of Nur-ed-din—
with whom he was already supposed to be intriguing,—but he argued to no purpose. His captains
were bent upon invasion and confident of success,
and at last he allowed himself to be persuaded. In
open violation of his word, as understood by the
Saracens, and at least without the shadow of an excuse, he once more marched into Egypt ; but now
he entered as an enemy where before he had been
bidden as an ally. Arrived at Bilbeys on the 3d of
November, 1168, he added to perfidy the crime of
wholesale massacre,—he spared neither age nor sex,
says the Latin chronicler, in the devoted town.

This barbarous act at once ranged the Egyptians on
the side of Nur-ed-din, and inspired them to heroic exertions. They took advantage of the Christians' fool-
ish loitering, to marshal their forces and strengthen

their defences. The old city of Fustat, for three hundred years the metropolis of Egypt, and still a densely populated suburb of Cairo, was by Shawar's orders set on fire, that it might not give shelter to the Franks (12 November, 1168). Twenty thousand naphtha barrels and ten thousand torches were lighted. The fire lasted fifty-four days, and its traces may still be found in the wilderness of sandheaps stretching over miles of buried rubbish on the south side of Cairo. The people fled "as from their very graves," the father abandoned his children, the brother his twin; and all rushed to Cairo for dear life. The hire of a camel for the mile or two of transit cost thirty pieces of gold.* The capital itself was in a tumult of preparation for the attack. Amalric did not keep it long in suspense, but he was forced to abandon the usual camping ground (the Birket-el-Habash) on account of the suffocating smoke from Fustat. The assault, however, was postponed by the negotiations which Shawar adroitly contrived, to buy off his greedy assailants. There was more pretence than honesty in his diplomacy, for he was sending at the same moment couriers to Damascus to implore the aid of Nur-ed-din. The young Caliph of Egypt wrote himself, and even enclosed some of his wives' hair as a supreme act of supplication which no gentleman could resist.†

This time the King of Syria did not hesitate; he was nettled at the poor results of the two previous

---

* *Kamil*, 555 ; el-Makrizy, *Khitat*, i., 286 ; Wüstenfeld, *Geschichte der Fatimiden Chalifen*, 338–339.

† Ibn-el-Athir, *Kamil*, 556.

expeditions, and indignant with the Franks for what
he held to be a flagrant breach of faith. He might
even have gone in person, but that he was preoccupied with the unsettled state of Mesopotamia. He
lost no time, however, in despatching a force of two
thousand picked troopers from his own guard, with
six thousand paid Turkmans of approved valour,
under the command of Shirkuh, supported by a
large staff of emulous emirs. The only one to hold
back was, strange to say, Saladin himself. He had
been his uncle's right hand in the former campaigns,
but he still loved his old retirement and the discourse
of pious men ; and when Shirkuh, in the presence of
Nur-ed-din, said " Now, Yusuf, make ready for the
march," Saladin answered " By Allah, if the sovereignty of Egypt were offered me, I would not go :
what I endured at Alexandria I shall never forget."
Then Shirkuh said to Nur-ed-din, " Needs must he
come with me," and Nur-ed-din turned to the young
man and repeated the words, " *La budd min mesirik
maa ammik,*" " Needs must that you go with your
uncle." In vain Saladin pleaded his aversion to the
campaign and his lack of means ; Nur-ed-din would
not listen, but supplied him with horses and arms
and bade him make ready : " So I went," said Saladin, recounting the scene in later years, " I went like
one driven to my death." Thus were accomplished
the words of the Koran * : "*Perchance ye hate a thing
although it is better for you, and perchance ye love a
thing although it is worse for you: but God knoweth and
ye know not.*" Nur-ed-din himself superintended the

* *Koran,* ii., 113 ; *Kamil,* 563.

marshalling of the army at the Spring Head, a day's march from Damascus, and gave every man a present of twenty gold pieces, whilst he committed to Shirkuh two hundred thousand dinars for his military chest.

On the 17th of December, 1168, the third expedition began its march to Egypt, once more to rescue Shawar, in name, but in fact with far larger designs. Amalric, always needy and greedy, was still waiting before Cairo for more of the vezir's promised gold, when Shirkuh suddenly effected his junction with the Egyptians (8 January, 1169), evading the Frank army which had gone out to intercept his advance. Deceived by Shawar and outgeneralled by Shirkuh, the discomfited king retired to Palestine, without offering battle, having gained, as the proverb has it, nothing better than the "boots of Honeyn." The Syrians entered Cairo in triumph, and were welcomed as deliverers. The grateful Caliph gave audience to Shirkuh and invested him with a robe of honour, clothed in which he returned to display himself to the army. Shawar, inwardly devoured by jealousy and alarm, rode out daily to the Syrian camp, in great state, with all his banners, drums and trumpets, and overwhelmed the general with protestations of devotion; but meanwhile he took no steps to perform his engagements to Nur-ed-din, but was actually meditating a treacherous arrest of Shirkuh and his officers at a friendly banquet. The Syrian leaders soon determined that he was not to be trusted, and Saladin and Jurdik resolved to get rid of him. As the vezir was riding out to visit the general, who chanced to be paying his respects to

the venerated tomb of the Imam esh-Shafiy, Saladin
and his men dragged him from his horse and made
him prisoner. Whatever doubts Shirkuh may have
entertained as to the fate of Shawar were set at rest
by a peremptory order from the Caliph himself, who,
like a slave emancipated from a rigorous master, demanded the head of the vezir. It was sent, and
thus ended the brief and checkered career of a remarkable and politic minister ; an Arab chief, moreover, of ancient lineage, with all the Bedawy's daring
and the ancestral love of poetry—insomuch that he
once filled Omara's mouth with gold in delight at an
ode—and, it must be added, with the Arab's full
share of falsehood and deceit.

The Caliph el-Adid, who was much impressed by
the gallant bearing of his deliverers, immediately appointed Shirkuh to the vacant office, clad him in the
robes of vezir, invested him with plenary powers, and
gave him the titles of " Victorious King " and " Commander-in-chief " (18th Jan., 1169). The people were
as pleased as the pontiff ; they had liked the jolly
soldier as he rode over the country a year and a half
ago, even though he was levying taxes ; and the
Cairenes appreciated the liberal manner in which he
had disbursed from his heavy military chest, and had
refreshed them with the looting of Shawar's palace,
where they left not so much as a cushion for his lav-
ish successor to sit on ! The Arab poet saw more
clearly when he remarked that the claws of "the
Lion " * were now fastened in his prey. The " Lion

* Asad-ed-din, " Lion of the Faith," was the Arabic surname of
Shirkuh, which is itself Persian for " Mountain-Lion."

MOSQUE OF IMAM ESH-SHAFI'Y, CAIRO.

of the Faith," however, lived scarcely more than two months to enjoy his quarry, but died suddenly on the 23rd of March, 1169—the result of over-eating; for he was a mighty trencherman and addicted to heavy feeding. In person, Shirkuh was short and stout, choleric of face, and fierce by nature; nor had Allah endowed him with a superfluity of intelligence. Yet he was a bold and capable soldier, emulous of glory, patient under hardships, liberal beyond his means, and beloved of his men; and he had the grace to die at the right moment. The way was now open for Saladin.*

---

* William of Tyre's portrait of Shirkuh is worth quoting: it was evidently drawn by one who knew him. He describes him as "virum industrium, et in armis strenuum, liberalem supra vires patrimonii sui, gloriae cupidum, et in re militari admodum exercitatum, militibus carum, efficiente munificentia, et acceptum. . . . Erat autem homo jam senior, pusillus statura, pinguis multum et corpulentior . . . in altero oculorum habens albuginem; laboris patientissimus, sed et sitim et famem aequanimiter tolerans, supra id quod aetas illa soleat sustinere."—*Hist.*, xix., 5.

7

GOLD COIN OF NUG-ED-DIN ISSUED BY SALADIN AT CAIRO IN 1173.

CHAPTER VII.

VEZIR OF EGYPT.

1169–1171.

"I MEANT Amr; but God meant Kharija," is the Arab version of *l'homme propose et Dieu dispose.* Saladin had been dragged to Egypt against his will, foreseeing nothing but misery; and now the very step he had tried to avoid was to lead him to the pinnacle of fame. The Prophet indeed said truly, "*God will make men wonder when they see folk hauled to Paradise in chains.*" In such happy bonds was Saladin led to the throne. The Fatimid Caliph chose him from among all the Syrian captains to be the successor of his uncle, and on the 26th of March, 1169, three days after Shirkuh's death, he was invested * with the mantle of vezir and decorated with the title *el-Melik en-Nasir,* "The King Strong to aid." His comrades in arms, many of whom were older and more experienced than him-self, were not easily reconciled to the promotion of

---

* The actual diploma of appointment is preserved at Berlin, and runs to ninety-eight folios.

the young man of thirty over their heads. They
thought him a well-behaved and intelligent subal-
tern, too quiet and unambitious for high command;
—it was indeed this opinion of Saladin's docility that
had procured him an office where a tractable tool was
wanted:—but to raise him above the war-worn captains of Nur-ed-din's campaigns was more than they
could stomach.   It needed all Saladin's tact and diplomacy, supported by the specious arguments of
el-Hakkary the lawyer, and a liberal opening of treasury coffers, to induce the jealous warriors to submit;
and several of them returned to Syria rather than
serve under their junior.

On his side, Saladin began to order his life more
rigorously.   Devout as he had always shewn himself, he became even more strict and austere.   He
put aside the thought of pleasure and the love of
ease, adopted a Spartan rule, and set it as an example to his troops.   He devoted all his energies
henceforth to one great object—to found a Moslem
empire strong enough to drive the infidels out of the
land.   " When God gave me the land of Egypt,"
said he, " I was sure that He meant Palestine for me
also."   It may well be that natural selfish ambition
quickened his zeal; but the result was the same:
thenceforward his career was one long championship of Islam.   He had vowed himself to the Holy
War.

The new vezir's position was curiously anomalous.
He was at once the prime-minister of an heretical
(Shiïte) Caliph, and the lieutenant of an orthodox
(Sunnite) King.   With admirable inconsistency, the

two names were duly prayed for every Friday at the
mosque.   The anomaly would have to be abolished,
but only by degrees : violent changes might be fatal
so long as the people of Egypt retained the affection
for the (Shïïte) doctrines which two centuries of
Fatimid rule had instilled, and which was fostered
by the very nature of the tenets.   Saladin's relations with Nur-ed-din were also delicate.   The King
of Syria congratulated him, indeed, on his appointment, and confirmed him in his command of the
Syrian army in Egypt, but was clearly resolved to keep
him in his place.   His despatches from Damascus
were addressed merely " To the Emir Salah-ed-din,
Commander-in-chief, and the other Emirs," to show
him that he was but *primus inter pares*, liable to be
recalled or degraded at his sovereign's pleasure.   To
gradually strengthen his own position without awak-
ening the distrust of the people of Egypt or the
jealousy of Nur-ed-din, was the prudent policy which
Saladin must necessarily pursue.

His first step was to surround himself by his family.   Like another Joseph, also vezir of Egypt, but
under a Pharaoh instead of a Caliph, he sent for his
father and brethren from Syria, and made them
share his splendour.   He even offered to surrender
his high office to his father, * but Ayyub refused
the honour.   " My son," said he, " God had not
chosen thee for this great position hadst thou not
been fitted for it ; it is not well to play with one's
luck."   Ayyub, however, took upon himself the

---

* Ayyub arrived in Egypt in the middle of April, 1170, a year later
than his sons (Ibn-Khallikan, i., 245).

duties of treasurer, and his other sons loyally supported their brother in his difficult situation. They
had their reward, for Saladin gave them the fiefs of
obnoxious Egyptians, whom he banished to places
where they could do no hurt. His plan was to
weaken the Caliph's party, and he did not care how
much he was hated by the Egyptian courtiers and
officers, so long as he gained the confidence of the
people. This he set himself seriously to win, and
his Arab biographer says that the folk came from all
parts of Egypt to see him, and seldom went away
empty-handed : there was ever a petitioner at his
ear, and none appealed to him in vain.

He needed all his popularity among the people;
for the palace, with its numerous troops and dependents, was openly hostile. The Caliph had discovered that he was mistaken in Saladin's character,
—that he had adopted not a slave but a master;
and intrigues were soon a-foot to destroy the new
vezir. Nejah, the chief black eunuch and *major
domo*, headed a conspiracy among the upholders of
the Fatimid dynasty. They planned an understanding with the Franks, who were to invade Egypt and
entice Saladin from Cairo, when the conspirators
would take him in rear, and thus attacked on both
sides he and his Turkmans would perish. An accident revealed the plot to Saladin, and he had the
chief eunuch watched, until at length he succeeded
in catching him at his country house, outside the
protection of the palace, and the unlucky Black was
quickly beheaded (July, 1169). This summary execution of their countryman and leader aroused the

fury of the Caliph's troops, then (as in modern
Egypt) composed largely of Sudanis; and fifty
thousand, it is stated, of these Blacks rose up to
avenge him.   A bloody struggle ensued in the wide
quadrangle that divided the palaces (Beyn el-Kasreyn), and many houses and streets were set on
fire; but at last the Blacks were overcome, their
quarter, el-Mansuriya, was burnt, and they were
compelled to beg for mercy.   They were sent over
the Nile, to Giza, and thence away to Upper Egypt,
where rebellion smouldered for several years.   In
the winter of 1171–2, Saladin's eldest brother, Turan
Shah, reduced them to temporary submission, but in
the following winter he had to fight them again,
and even pursued them into Nubia, where he took
the city of Ibrim (Primis), near Korosko, pillaged the
church of the monophysite Christians, tortured the
bishop, and slew seven hundred of the pigs which
were found there in great abundance, to the proper
disgust of all pious Moslems.   In 1174 there was a
formidable rising of the Blacks at Aswan, led by
Kenz-ed-daula; and it needed some hard fighting
before he was defeated and killed in September by
Seyf-ed-din (el-Adil), another of Saladin's brothers.
Yet another insurrection, at Koptos, had to be suppressed by the same general in 1176.   After this we
read no more of risings among the Blacks, but, as the
Arab historian piously concludes, "God made an end
of their villainy."   It is evident that the struggle
was obstinate, and that Upper Egypt was for six
years in a state of intermittent rebellion; and there
can be little doubt that the Blacks who repeatedly

revolted were stirred up by the fugitive Sudany
slaves and other partisans of the Fatimids.*

Hardly had Saladin expelled the mutinous Blacks
from Cairo, when a still more urgent danger arose.
The Crusaders were not slow to grasp the significance
of the political change in Egypt.   The possession of
the Nile by Nur-ed-din's general placed the Kingdom
of Jerusalem as it were in a cleft stick, squeezed on
both sides by armies controlled by the same power.
The harbours of Damietta and Alexandria gave the
Moslems the command of a fleet, and enabled them
to cut off the communications of the Crusaders with
Europe, stop the annual pilgrim ships, and seize their
supplies.   Every effort must be made to break this
fatal chain, which threatened the very existence of
the Latin power in Palestine.   Accordingly the most
formidable attack that Saladin ever had to meet in
Egypt was organised, probably in connexion with
conspirators in Cairo.   Amalric joined hands with
the Eastern Emperor, and a Greek fleet of 220 sail
co-operated with a strong land force of Crusaders in
besieging Damietta.   Fortunately for the defenders,
contrary winds delayed the fleet on its way from the
Golden Horn, and Saladin availed himself of this
respite to strengthen the garrison and prepare for
the attack.   At the same time he sent messengers to
Nur-ed-din to report the state of affairs, and espe-

---

* See the ingenious memoir of M. Paul Casanova on *Les derniers
Fatimides* in the *Mémoires de la mission archéologique française au
Caire*, tome vi., fasc. 3 ; and Ibn-el-Athir, *Kamil*, 566–8 ; Baha-
ed-din, 56 ; Abu-Salih, *Churches and Monasteries of Egypt*, ed.
Evetts, f. 96. ; Mrs. Butcher, *Church of Egypt*, ii., 104.

cially to point out the risk of leaving a hostile faction behind him at Cairo whilst he went himself to
the assistance of Damietta. In response, the King
of Syria poured troops into Egypt, battalion on battalion, and began to distract the attention of the
enemy by a demonstration against Palestine.

The siege of Damietta was begun in November,
1169. Amalric took up a position between the sea
and the town, and awaited the arrival of the Greek
fleet. In three days it appeared, but an iron chain
guarded by an impregnable tower prevented its entering the harbour, and it was unable to render the
aid that had been expected. *Nocuit differre paratis :*
the chances of success were weakened by delay ; and
when at last, led in person by their gallant king, the
Franks attacked with all their elaborate machinery
of mangonels and fighting towers,* the garrison was
more than equal to repelling them, and sallying forth
burnt their siege engines and even set fire to part of
the fleet. Saladin meanwhile had brought up his
troops, with ample stores and munitions of war, and
a million gold pieces in his chest, and perpetually
harassed the besiegers. The garrison was easily kept

---

* " The movable towers [*castra* or *castella*], or ' belfreys ' [*berefridi*],
were brought in pieces, which were framed together. They were
then pushed across the ditch of the fortress, which was filled up with
hurdles and fascines to facilitate their passage. The towers protected
the ' besieging engines' with which the walls were battered, and the
mining operations " (Sir C. W. Wilson, R.E., note to Baha-ed-din).
They were the *machinae, par excellence*, of medieval warfare. They
ran on wheels, and were often protected from fire by a covering of
raw hides. Mr. Archer states (*Crusade Rich. I.*, 88) that Amalric's
machina at Damietta was seven stories high.

supplied, since the arm of the Nile was open and protected by the troops from Cairo ; but the Franks ran short of bread ; a diet of fruit disordered their unaccustomed stomachs, and disease and famine thinned their ranks. The Greeks on the ships were starving, and the Latins ashore could spare them nothing.

The very elements seemed to conspire with the improvidence of the commanders to complete their discomfiture. Heavy rains swelled the Nile, flooded the plain, and saturated the camp. The storm upset their tents and siege-scaffolds, and the garrison took advantage of their plight to pelt them with stones slung by powerful catapults. Murmurs arose in the ranks ; the wretched soldiers, half starved and half drowned, begged to go home ; and after fifty days of fruitless efforts, Amalric was forced to give up the siege. Peace was made, and the generous and businesslike Alexandrians opened their markets to the famished invaders, who, when they had well eaten, set out in great dejection on their return to Palestine (19 December). To crown the disaster, a tempest wrecked nearly the whole fleet, and the dead bodies of the Greeks were cast up on the coast which they had come to conquer. As the proverb says, " The ostrich set out to find itself horns, and came back without ears." * Henceforward, instead of going forth to attack, the Latin Kingdom was on its defence.

Encouraged by the failure of the Franks at Damietta, Saladin took the field in the following year—

---

* *Kamil*, 568–70.

a year memorable for the earthquake which devast-
ated Syria and laid low many of its ancient cities,—
and began the series of attacks which continued until his treaty with Richard of England, twenty-two
years later.   His first raid was against Gaza, the
frontier city of the Latin Kingdom.   On his way he
laid siege to the small castle of Darum, the southern
outpost of Christianity, which had been recently
fortified by Amalric, and was held by the Knights
Templars.   Their commander, Ansel de Pass, made
a vigorous defence, and gave time for Amalric to
come up with 250 knights of both the military orders, and 2000 foot-soldiers, who speedily dislodged
the Saracens from their positions.   Saladin did not
wait for a pitched battle : at dead of night he slipped
away, and almost before they were awake the inhabitants of Gaza found their town taken.   The citadel,
however, a strong fortress built by Baldwin II., held
out, and its warden, Milo de Planci, sternly refused
to admit the fugitive citizens, who were thus forced
to stand outside the gates and fight to the death.
Saladin had no mind for a long siege, and after
plundering the town left the castle alone, and returned to Egypt with the spoils.   On his way he
passed close to Amalric, who got his men under
arms, but was relieved to see him depart without
offering battle.   The year's successes ended in December, 1170, with the taking of Eyla at the head of
the gulf of Akaba,—the same Elath whence Solomon's fleet sailed to Ophir,—the key of the Red Sea
route for pilgrims to Mekka.   In order to rescue
this important post from the Crusaders, Saladin had

ships built in sections at Cairo, carried the parts on camels to the Red Sea, where he put them together, and took the fort after a combined attack by sea and land.

These successes against the "infidels" brought Saladin much renown among the Egyptians, who were ready enough to forget their jealousies and religious differences when a campaign was on foot and booty within sight. As their champion against the common enemy, Sunnites and Shiïtes, Egyptians and Turkmans, eagerly followed the banners of the young leader, against whom they had no less willingly plotted when no Holy War was at stake. Saladin's valour and generalship convinced the army of his right to command, and the mass of the people, so far as they understood at all, recognised in him a powerful protector. His authority was now so firmly established that he could venture upon a momentous step. The anomalous situation of a Sunnite vezir holding office under a Fatimid Caliph was peculiarly distasteful to a man of Saladin's orthodox views. For some time the King of Syria and the Abbasid Caliph of Baghdad had pressed him to do away with this political and theological inconsistency by introducing the name of the true instead of the false Caliph in the public Friday prayer (*khutba*)—the recognised form of allegiance. Hitherto Saladin, despite his religious tenets, had combatted this proposal on the ground that the change might cause a revolution in Egypt. Another reason, which he did not mention, was that his popularity among the heterodox Egyptians might prove a valuable support in the very probable event of a rupture with Nur-ed-din.

In 1171, however, his position had become much stronger, and he could afford to run some risk. The Fatimid Caliph was no longer personally a factor in politics. Since the assassination of his black chamberlain, he and his palace had been placed under the vigilant control of the white eunuch Karakush, Saladin's right-hand man, whose name, curiously enough, instead of being associated with acts of fidelity and severity, has become in the Turkish empire the designation of the ridiculous puppet, Punch. The seclusion and impotence of the Caliph had lowered the influence of Shïïte doctrine in Cairo, and Saladin had provided sound religious instruction according to the Sunnite rules by founding colleges * and establishing approved teachers of orthodoxy in the capital and the chief provincial towns.

The ground was thus prepared, and advantage was taken of the illness of the helpless captive who still called himself Imam, or God-directed leader, to carry out the long-determined change in the Caliphate. On the first Friday in the sacred month Moharram, the first month of the year of the Flight 567 (the 10th of September, 1171), a bold divine from Mosil, anticipating the regular preacher in the chief mosque, recited the bidding-prayer for the preservation and prosperity of the orthodox Caliph of Baghdad:

" O God, assist him and assist his armies ; O Thou Lord of the Faith and of the world present and the world to

---

* The Nasiriya or Sherifya and the Kamhiya colleges near the mosque of Amr in Fustat, were founded by Saladin in 1170.

come, O Lord of the beings of the whole world. O God, assist the forces of the Moslems and the armies of the worshippers of Thee Only. O God, frustrate the infidels and polytheists, Thine enemies, enemies of the Faith."

This ecclesiastical revolution took place without a sign of opposition,—"there was not so much as the butting of two goats," says the chronicler ; nothing worse than surprise was shown by the crowded congregation. The Caliph at Baghdad was overjoyed, illuminated his capital, and sent Nur-ed-din and Saladin robes of honour and the famous black flags borne by the Abbasid legions. To Nur-ed-din he sent, besides, two swords; one for the dominion of Syria, the other for Egypt, and hailed him Sultan. Meanwhile the person most affected lay dying in his great palace at Cairo. El-Adid, the last of the Fatimid Caliphs, never heard of his supersession in the public prayers ; Saladin had forbidden his servants to tell him, saying, "if he recover, he will learn the truth soon enough, but if not, let him die in peace." He died three days later, not quite twenty-one years old. On his deathbed he had asked to see Saladin, but the vezir suspected a plot, and excused himself. Afterwards, when he found the wish was sincere, he repented his neglect, and spoke highly of the young Caliph's many virtues, his gentle character, his good qualities, and friendly advances.

Thus ended in feebleness and neglect the Fatimid dynasty, which had been the greatest Mohammedan power on the shores of the Mediterranean for nearly three centuries. The family indeed survived for two generations, but they could do nothing against the assured authority of Saladin. El-Ádid left eleven sons, four sisters, four wives, and other relations, to the number altogether of one hundred and fifty-two; but Karakush, the *major domo*, shut them up under strict guard, the men in one place, the women in another, according them the luxuries and respect to which they were accustomed. The great palace of the Fatimids owned a new master.

EAGLE ON THE WALL OF SALADIN'S CITADEL AT CAIRO.

GOLD COIN OF SALADIN STRUCK AT ALEXANDRIA IN 1183.

CHAPTER VIII.

SALADIN AT CAIRO.

1171–1173.

VISITORS to modern Cairo see very little of Saladin's capital. Besides the three ancient gates, three ruined mosques, and part of the old walls, nothing remains of the city he traversed when he first rode out from the Fatimid palace at the head of his guard. The most conspicuous feature of the present Cairo, the Citadel, with its slender Turkish minarets and commanding battlements, did not exist : only a rounded spur of Mount Mukattam suggested the place where a fortress should be built. Most of the wide expanse, now covered by the European houses of the Ismaïliya quarter, between the Ezbekiya and the river, was under water ; for in Saladin's day the Nile ran much further east and almost washed the city wall at the part where the river-suburb of el-Maks then stood. Bulak and its island were not as yet risen above the surface of the water, and there was no Abbasiya suburb on the north. Houses and streets indeed

stretched then, as now, beyond the old Zuweyla
Gate, towards the south, as far as the chapel of " our
lady Nefisa," and there were many buildings or ruins
of former habitations beyond this, where we now see
only hill after hill of rubbish-heaps smothered in
sand—the melancholy memorials of what was once
the stately city, bowered in gardens, of old Fustat,
and still older Babylon.

These suburbs and ruins were not then part of
Cairo. The real Cairo, the city of the Fatimid Caliphs, was never more than an immense royal castle,
called " The Victorious," *el-Kahira*, the *Cahere* of
William of Tyre, which Italians corrupted into our
modern Cairo. It was also known as " the city " *el-
Medina*, and it was founded, in 969, expressly for the
residence of the Caliph and his vast harim and slave-
household, with quarters round his palace for the
separate brigades of his army, the vezir and officers
of state, and the departments of government. The
spacious enclosure of the castle, guarded by massive
walls and imposing Norman-like gates, was forbidden
ground to all but high functionaries of state. Even
ambassadors of foreign powers were required to dismount outside, and were led to the Caliph's presence
by both their hands in the manner of the old Byzantine and the medieval Ottoman courts.

The chief buildings were the " Great East Palace "
the Caliph's personal residence, where he kept his
women, children, slaves, eunuchs and servants, estimated at from eighteen to thirty thousand in number,
and the " Lesser West Palace," or pleasure-house,
which opened on the spacious garden of Kafur, where

BAB ZUWEYLA, CAIRO.

A FATIMID GATE OF THE 11TH CENTURY.

a *meydan* or hippodrome provided exercise for the court. The two were separated by the square called "Betwixt the Palaces" (*Beyn el-Kasreyn*) where as many as ten thousand troops could parade; the name is still preserved in part of the Suk-en-Nah-hasin or Coppersmiths' Market. An underground passage connected the two palaces, by which the Caliph could pass without violating that mysterious seclusion which was part of his sacred character. Hard by were the mausoleum where lay the bones of his Fatimid ancestors, brought from far Kayrawan; and the mosque (el-Azhar) where the Caliph was wont to lead the Friday prayers as Prince and Pre-centor of the Faithful; and near this, the Arab his-torian remarks, as if it were a common architectural feature, was "the well into which the Caliph used to throw the slain." The people believed that some-thing more valuable than corpses of murdered ca-liphs, slaves, or disgraced favourites, was hidden in its gloomy depths; but when they searched for gold and precious stones, they were supernaturally re-pelled; and since no man can safely contend with "the Jinn," the well was filled up, lest worse should happen.

Of the size and splendour of the Great Palace the Arabic historians speak with bated breath. We read of four thousand chambers;—of the Golden Gate which opened to the Golden Hall, a gorgeous pavilion where the Caliph, seated on his golden throne, surrounded by his chamberlains and gentle-men in waiting (generally Greeks or Sudanis), sur-veyed from behind a screen of golden filigree the

8

festivals of Islam ;—of the Emerald Hall with its
beautiful pillars of marble ;—the Great Divan, where
he sat in state on Mondays and Thursdays, at
a window beneath a cupola,—the same window,
perhaps, under which Dirgham stood suppliant in
his downfall ;—and the *sakifa* or Porch, where the
Caliph listened every evening, while the oppressed
and wronged came below and cried aloud the *credo*
of the Shiïtes, till he heard their griefs and gave orders for their redress. The historians say little of
the splendour within the palace, but some idea may
be formed of its treasures by the marvels observed
by Hugh of Caesarea,* and from the statement that
among the amazing wealth of jewels and precious
stones which Saladin discovered on the death of el-
Adid were an emerald four fingers long, and a ruby
known as "the Mountain," the weight of which, in
our terms, was over 2400 carats (" I have seen and
weighed it myself," says Ibn-el-Athir). The wealth
of the Fatimids in jewels and works of the goldsmith's
art had long been proverbial. In the inventory of
the treasures of one of these Caliphs we read of
quantities of emeralds and pearls, cut crystal vases,
chased and enamelled gold plate ; coffers inlaid with
designs in gold ; furniture and ornaments of san-
dalwood, ebony, and ivory, adorned with precious
stones ; cups and pitchers of fine porcelain filled
with camphor and musk ; metal mirrors framed in
silver and gold with borders of emeralds and carnel-
ian ; tables of sardonyx ; countless vessels of bronze
inlaid with silver and gold ; tapestry, silk, and bro-

---

* See above, p. 86.

AIRO IN THE DAYS OF SALADIN - 1170

Bâb-el-Bahr Ard-et-Tabbâla
KAL'AT-EL-MAKS

N.

River Nile

Bâb-esh-Shariya

Bahâ-ed-din (Karakûsh) Quarter
Bâb-el-Futûh
MOSQUE OF EL-HÂKIM
Bâb-en-Nasr
Berjuwân Quarter

Bâb-el-Kantara
PEARL PAL.
Inner Greek Quarter
VEZIR'S PALACE

CAIRO
Kâfûr's Garden
E. PALACE
Akmar Mos.

Bâb-el-Faraj
Emirs' Quarter (Founded 969)
Deilem Quarter
W. PALACE
Barkiya Quarter

Bâb-es-Sa'âda
Jaudariya Quarter
AZHAR MOSQUE

Mahmûdiya Quarter
Turks' Quarter
Bâb-el-Barkiya

El-Lûk
Zuweyla Quarter
Greeks' Quarter
Bâb-el-Mahrûk

Canal (El-Khalij)
Bâb Zuweyla
MOSQUE OF TALÂ'I

Saladin's Wall

El-Mansûriya (Quarter of the Blacks)
Bâb-el-Vezir

Elephant's Lake (Birket-el-Pil)

Ruins of El-Katâi' (Founded 870, destroyed 905)
SALADIN'S CITADEL (1176-1207)

Kal'at-el-Kebsh
MOSQUE OF IBN-TÛLÛN

Ruins of El-'Askar (Founded 751)

CHAPEL OF S. NEFISA

Ruins of El-Fustât (Founded 641, burnt 1168)

MOSQUE OF 'AMR

CEMETERY (El-Kerâfa)

Er-Rôda I.

Abyssinians' Lake (Birket-el-Habash)

Nilometer

CASTLE OF BABYLON (Kasr esh-Shema')

TOMB OF IMÂM-ESH-SHÂFI'Y

Mukattam Hills

Scale of 1 Mile
0   ½   1

...ted Lines show additions to the Fortifications made by Saladin.

cade, heavy with gold embroidery, and adorned with the portraits of kings.

Of all the treasures that he found, Saladin kept nothing for himself. Some he distributed among his followers, or presented to Nur-ed-din ; the glorious library of 120,000 * manuscript volumes he gave to his learned chancellor the Kady el-Fadil; the rest of the treasure was sold for the public purse. Nor did it suit his simple and austere mode of life to take up his residence in the stately palace of the late Caliph. Silken divans and " Pavilions of Pearls " were nothing to him. He remained in the " House of the Vezir," and gave up the Great Palace to the captains of his army, allotting the western pleasure-house to his brother el-Adil. No longer a royal residence, the beautiful mansions of the Fatimids gradually fell into decay. " O censurer of my love for the sons of Fatima," cried Omara the poet of the Yemen, " join in my tears over the desolate halls of the twin Palaces ! " One of the doorkeepers remarked that he had seen no wood brought in, and no rubbish thrown out, for a long time ; and when the woodwork is used for fuel and the refuse is left to accumulate, the end of a building is not far off. So it happens that not a vestige remains of these once splendid palaces, which were the wonder and envy of princes.

Outside the " city " or castle of Cairo there was a large population to the south-west, and when Sala-

---

* Some say 2,600,000 volumes, including 1220 copies of one book, the famous history of Tabary. The numbers and statistics of Oriental writers are seldom to be trusted.

din rode forth to visit the holy tomb of the Imam
esh-Shafiy in the desert, he passed by the sites of
three earlier capitals. Going out of the Zuweyla
gate, he would first traverse the comparatively recent quarters which had sprung up since the building
of the royal and official " city " ; he would pass by
the ruins of the Mansuriya, out of which he had
smoked the rebel Blacks like a nest of hornets.
Further on, the " Lake of the Elephant," long since
dried up, would be on his right, whilst on the left
the craggy spurs of the Mukattam range prompted
the building of the citadel which he afterwards
began. All the way his road lay through the
crowded suburbs of the populace, whose houses
covered the site where once had stood the famous
city of " the Wards " (el-Katai), where Ibn-Tulun
three centuries before had kept his kingly state.
El-Katai was, like the " city " of Cairo, essentially
an official capital, and was inhabited chiefly by the
king and his court, his soldiers, and his purveyors,
each class in a separate " ward." It was the third
capital built since the Arabs conquered Egypt, and
of all its magnificence nothing remains but the
ruined mosque of Ibn-Tulun, of which the grandeur
and admirable designs reveal something of what has
been lost. Beyond, still to the south-west, once
stood el-Askar, " the Camp," another official centre,
where the governors dwelt who were sent from
Baghdad to rule Egypt in the days when the Abbasid Caliph held undivided sway from the borders
of India to the Atlantic Ocean. Furthest south of
all, between the Abyssinians' Lake and the Nile, lay

MOSQUE OF IBN-TULUN, CAIRO.

what remained of the oldest capital of Mohammedan Egypt, at once the official centre and the metropolis of commerce, called el-Fustat, " the Tent," in memory of the pavilion of the Arab conqueror. In spite of the devastations of the great fire of 1168, the inhabitants had begun to return to their ruined homes and were trying to re-people the desolate streets. But Fustat never recovered its lost prosperity, when its bazars were renowned for wealth and commerce, and its houses reared their six stories aloft, and gardens of fruit and flowers stretched all around. Now nothing remains but the old Mosque of Amr, so often repaired and altered that its founder would not know it, and the Roman fortress of Babylon, the " Castle of the Beacon " of the Arabs, now a hive of Coptic churches served by Coptic drones, but once the guardian of a busy Christian city, the ancient and populous " Babylon of Egypt." The scanty suburb of " Old Cairo," or Masr * el-Atika, is not a relic of Fustat, for it stands on ground which was covered by the Nile in the days when Fustat was a city.

The history of the capital of Egypt under its Mohammedan rulers had thus been a series of transplantings from the south to the north-east. First *el-Fustat*, "the Tent," was founded by Amr the

---

* The capital of Egypt was called by the Arabs by the same name as Egypt itself—*Misr*, and this name was commonly used for Fustat, which remained the commercial metropolis long after the building of Cairo. Misr is now pronounced *Masr*, and it is possible that it was so pronounced as early as the time of Saladin, for we find in William of Tyre, who certainly knew Arabic, the spelling *Macer*.

conqueror in 641 ; then *el-Askar*, " the Camp," was
built, as a government centre, on the site of the
camp of the Abbasid general in 750 ; thirdly, *el-Katai*,
"the Wards," was laid out, still further to the north-
east, in 869, by Ahmad ibn Tulun, as the capital of
his dynasty ; and lastly, in 969, Johar, the general
of the Fatimid Caliph of Kayrawan, after annexing
Egypt, founded el-Kahira " the Victorious," as a
fortified residence for his master. Saladin carried
on the tradition of building, in which every great
eastern ruler took pride ; but, instead of pushing the
capital still further to the north-east, he sought to
unite the sites of all the four capitals, and to build a
Citadel—the famous " Castle of the Mountain "—
on the westernmost spur of Mount Mukattam, to be
the centre of government and to form a military
stronghold capable of overawing the whole city and
resisting assaults from outside. His plan was to
connect this fortress by a bastioned wall with the old
fortifications of the Fatimid " city," and to extend
it so as to enclose the site of Fustat and Katai, and
thus to sweep round to the river ; but the plan was
not completed, and even the Citadel was not finished
till long after his death. Saladin's enlargement of the
area of the city was accompanied by the demolition
of whole suburbs between the old " city " and the
shrine of Nefisa. These were replaced by pleasure
gardens, and it is recorded that the tall Zuweyla
gate could be seen from the door of Ibn-Tulun's
mosque. Jehan Thenaud, who accompanied an embassy from Louis XII. to Cairo at a later period,
found these gardens still a striking feature of the city :

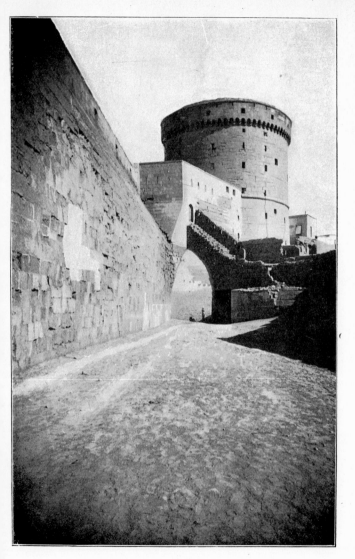

A TOWER IN THE CITADEL OF CAIRO.

" moult somptueulx et grans jardins plains de tous
fruictiers : comme cytrons, lymons, citrulles, oranges,
aubercotz, cassiers et pommes de musez ou d'Adam
pour ce que l'on dict estre le fruict duquel Adam oul
trepassa le commandement de Dieu. Lesquelz jardins
tous les soirs et matins sont arrousez de l'eau du Nil
que tirent beufz et chevaulx." *

Traces of some of these pleasure grounds may even
now be seen from the battlements of the Citadel.

It has been supposed that Saladin designed the
Citadel of Cairo to protect himself against a possible
insurrection of the partisans of the late dynasty.   A
sufficient explanation, however, is found in his early
associations : every Syrian city had its citadel or
fortress, and experience had shown many a time that
the town might be taken whilst the citadel remained
impregnable, a refuge for the people and a means of
recuperation.   Therefore Cairo must have a citadel
too.   It might soon be needed as a tower of defence
against his liege-lord Nur-ed-din himself.   Saladin
had propitiated the King of Syria with presents from
the treasures of the Fatimid palace ; prayers were
offered for him as sovereign lord every Friday in the
mosques, above all in the great mosque of el-Hakim,
which now supplanted the Azhar as the chief mosque
of the city ; and his name appeared on the coins struck
by Saladin at Cairo.   But in spite of this nominal subjection and the absence of all symbols of personal
sovereignty, Saladin was virtually his own master ;
and supported as he was by a strong army com-

---

* *Le voyage et itinaire de oultre mer faict par Frère Jehan Thenaud*,
cited in Schefer's *Nassiri Khosrau*, 133.

manded by his brothers and nephews, he was in fact
King of Egypt. Nur-ed-din was well aware of this,
but his difficulties with the Franks, with the Seljuk
Sultan of Rum, and with various contentious rulers
in Mesopotamia, left him no leisure to clip the wings
of his vassal in Egypt. He could not even count
upon Saladin's coöperation in the Holy War ; for,
whether rightly or wrongly it is difficult to decide,
Saladin was convinced that if once his suzerain had
the chance of seizing his person, there would be an
end of his power; and nothing could induce him to
venture within Nur-ed-din's reach. Not only this,
but he seems to have carried this dread so far that
he preferred to have the Franks on his borders as an
obstacle to Nur-ed-din's advance.

An instance occurred immediately after the death
of the Egyptian Caliph. Amalric was absent at Constantinople, concerting further measures against the
Saracens with his wife's uncle, the Emperor Manuel
Comnenus ; and Saladin, probably acting on orders
from Damascus, seized the opportunity for an attack
upon Mont Real (esh-Shaubak), an irritating little
fortress built by Baldwin I. in 1115. Its glittering
white battlements crowned a hill clothed with olives,
and its gardens of apricots below formed a delicious
oasis in the desert south of the Dead Sea. But it
stood like a sentinel on the frontier between Syria
and Egypt, and commanded the caravan road between the two countries to the perpetual annoyance
of their commerce. To hold it or destroy it was for
many years an object dear to Saladin, but it constantly eluded his grasp. On this first attempt he

set out on the 21st of September, 1171, and established his leaguer round the white walls with little
opposition. Indeed after a brief defence the garrison
asked for an armistice of ten days, to arrange terms
of capitulation, or more probably to gain time for
rescue. During this interval Nur-ed-din himself left
Damascus to join his Egyptian viceroy; whereupon
Saladin broke up his camp and retreated to Cairo.
Writing to his liege-lord he pleaded a convenient
rumour of a conspiracy in favour of the late dynasty
as an excuse for his sudden retreat. It was true, but
insufficient; his brothers were fully competent to
deal with the rising of the Blacks in Upper Egypt.
Nur-ed-din was not deceived, and resolved to invade
Egypt and make an end of such contumacy.

Rumours of the coming attack soon reached Cairo,
and an anxious council was held by the family of
Ayyub and the leading captains of the army, to
whom Saladin communicated the news. There was
a dead silence. Then a fiery young nephew, Taki-
ed-din Omar, spoke up: "If Nur-ed-din comes,"
said he, "we will fight him and drive him out of the
land." But Ayyub, prudent and sagacious as ever,
sternly rebuked the hot-headed youngster, and turning to Saladin said:

"I am thy father, and here is Shihab-ed-din thy mother's
brother: bethink thee, is there one in this assembly who
loves thee and desires thy welfare as we do?" "No,
by Allah!" exclaimed Saladin. "Know then," said
Ayyub, "that if I and thine uncle were to meet Nur-ed-
din, nothing could stop our dismounting and kissing the
ground at his feet. Even should he bid us cut off thy

head with the sword, we should do it. From this, judge
what others would do. All whom thou seest here, and
all the troops, must needs do homage to Nur-ed-din,
should he come. This land is his, and if he would de-
pose thee, we must instantly obey. This therefore is
my counsel : write to him, and say : ' News has reached
me that you intend to lead an expedition to this country ;
but what need is there for this ?   Let my lord but send
hither a courier on a dromedary, to lead me to you by a
turban about my neck ; no one here will offer to resist.' "

Then he dismissed the meeting : " Retire and leave
us. We are Nur-ed-din's mamluks and slaves, and
he may do with us as he chooses."

All this was said for effect, for Ayyub knew that
some of the jealous emirs would be sure to write and
report the whole proceedings to Damascus. When
he was alone with his son, he took him to task for
letting the officers see his secret ambition, and reiterated his conviction that not a man of the army
would dare to take up arms against the King of Syria, and that the only prudent course was conciliation. He repeated the message he proposed before,
and then added : " When he reads this he will give up
his project. Meanwhile time is on our side, and
every moment God is doing something." Then the
old warrior broke out : " By Allah ! if Nur-ed-din attempted to take but a sugar-cane of ours, myself
should fight him to the death ! " Saladin followed
his father's counsel, and, as Ayyub had foreseen, the
King thought it wise to accept the message of submission,—without risking the experiment of the
dromedary.

The reality of Saladin's obedience was soon put to the test. In May or June, 1173, he set out, by Nur-ed-din's instructions, to lay siege to Karak. This celebrated fortress, north of Mont Real, and close to the southern extremity of the Dead Sea, was also on the caravan route, the very key of Syria, and a perpetual thorn in the side of the Saracens. It stood, and still stands, on the site of Kir Moab, which, in the days of Mesha, repelled the attack of Jehoshaphat, King of Judah ; and it nobly sustained its tradition. "The Crow's Castle," as the Arabs called it, was rebuilt on Roman foundations by Payen, King Fulk's cupbearer, on a lofty hill of the range of Mount Seir, nearly three thousand feet above the sea, and overlooking a fertile valley, warmed by hot springs, where fruits grew in abun-dance. The position and the strength of the fortifi-cations, the towers of which, carved with lions, may still be seen, made the fortress almost unassailable : a deep moat divided it from the town below, which was also fortified, and whence access was obtained to the castle only by two steep and narrow tunnels cut in the living rock. A sheer precipice defended the east side. In its general construction it was a typical Crusading fortress ; and, well supplied with water and provisions, it resisted siege after siege.

Saladin was not destined to take it yet. Scarcely had he begun to skirmish with the enemy's outposts, when the news came that Nur-ed-din, as arranged beforehand, was approaching with his Syrian army. Up to this, Saladin had seemingly braced himself up to meet his suzerain, but at the last moment his heart failed him. He feared a snare, and hastily beat a retreat to Egypt.* His excuse was valid enough —the illness of his father, whom he had left in command at Cairo, and whose death might entail a revolution. Nur-ed-din took the desertion in good part, saying, "The holding of Egypt is our paramount object." As it was, Saladin returned too late to see his father alive. Ayyub had been thrown from his horse outside the Gate of Victory, whilst taking his daily ride to exercise his troops, and died on the 9th of August, before his son's arrival. The loss of his politic sagacity could not easily be replaced.

Saladin was well aware that, in spite of smooth words, Nur-ed-din still cherished feelings the reverse of friendly towards him, and he cast about for a safe refuge in the event of the threatened invasion. He continued to strengthen the fortifications of Cairo, to increase his army, and to accumulate stores and arms; but he was far from confident in his ability to resist an attack from Syria, and he turned his mind to preparing a place of retreat in case he were forced to abandon Egypt. He had already conquered the provinces on the African coast, Barka and Tripoli, as far as Kabis (Gabes), in an expedition commanded by a second Karakush (not the builder of the citadel of Cairo) in 1172–3; but this strip of territory was too open to invasion by sea and land to offer a

---

* There is evident confusion in the accounts of the Arabic historians of the two similar expeditions to Mont Real and Karak in 1171 and 1173, and some of the incidents may have been transposed. It is probable that Saladin never really intended to meet Nur-ed-din on either occasion.

THE GATE OF VICTORY (BAB EN-NASR), CAIRO.

secure asylum, and the expedition was undertaken chiefly in order to keep his numerous troops occupied, and to supply them with fresh booty and prize-money. The same objects, and the removal of intriguing officers to a safer distance, as well as the castigation of the still rebellious Blacks, no doubt prompted in some measure the expedition which he sent into the Sudan about the beginning of 1173; but in this he had a deeper design. If Egypt proved untenable, then the Sudan, or perhaps southern Arabia, might serve as a place of retreat, whither Nur-ed-din would not be likely to follow. The Sudan, however, proved anything but a desirable sanctuary. Saladin's elder brother, Turan Shah, a brave and dashing soldier, but rash, and unstable as water, successfully accomplished his immediate object, reduced the Blacks to submission, and occupied Ibrim, as has been related. But to live permanently in a country which produced nothing but maize, and where the only occupation was fighting and enslaving an irreconcilable population under a blazing sun, was not at all to his mind, so he returned to Cairo with a caravan of slaves, and reported that the Sudan would not answer Saladin's purpose.

There remained the resource of Arabia. Omara, a poet and historian of the Yemen, then living at Cairo, exhausted the refinements of language in extolling the beauty and fertility of his native land, renowned in antiquity as Arabia Felix. It was afterwards believed that his enthusiasm was partly dictated by a wish to remove so fierce and warlike a leader as Turan Shah to a distance before a con-

spiracy that was hatching came to the birth. The
poet's representations, however, which were true
enough, were taken in good faith, and Turan Shah
organised a well-found expedition, which left Egypt
on the 5th of February, 1174, for Mekka, on its march
to the Yemen. There he was joined by a powerful
Arab chief, and the two made short work of the resistance of the Yemenites. Zebid, Jened, Aden,
Sana, and the other strongholds fell one after the
other, in May to August, and Turan Shah established
his seat of government at Taïzz and ruled Arabia
Felix until his return to his brother early in 1176.
The province remained under the authority of the
Ayyubid dynasty for fifty-five years, but was never
put to its intended use as a refuge from the vengeance of Nur-ed-din.

Meanwhile insurrection and intrigue had troubled
the serenity of Egypt. The plot was ripening of
which Omara was believed to be the instigator. A
number of Egyptians and Sudanis, and even some of
the Turkman officers and troops, joined in the conspiracy; the Kings of Sicily and Jerusalem were engaged to assist by promises of gold and territory;
and preparations were a-foot for a combined attack
by sea and land, in which Saladin was to be enmeshed.
Fortunately the whole plan was betrayed to the intended victim by a divine to whom the conspirators had unwisely confided their secret. Saladin
waited until his information was fully confirmed, and
then swooped down upon the plotters, seized the
leaders, including the too political poet, and had
them all crucified on the 6th of April, 1174. The

revolting Egyptians and black slaves were exiled
to Upper Egypt.

The sea attack, which was to have supported the
Cairo conspiracy, did not take place till the late summer. The Franks of Palestine did not move when
they heard that the plot had failed ; but the King of
Sicily, less well-informed, despatched a large fleet, estimated at 282 vessels,* which arrived off Alexandria
on the 28th of July. The inhabitants of the scanty
garrison were completely taken by surprise, but they
tried to resist the landing, which was nevertheless
effected near the pharos. The catapults and mangonels which the Sicilians had brought were soon playing upon the curtain of the city walls, and the
defenders were obliged to fight desperately all the
first day till night fell, to resist the storming parties.
The next day the Christians advanced their machines
close up to the walls, but reinforcements had joined
the garrison from the neighbouring villages, and
again the attack was beaten off. On the third day,
there was a vigorous sortie : the machines were burnt,
the enemy lost severely, and the garrison returned
flushed with triumph. Scarcely were they within
the gates, when an express arrived from Saladin, to
whom they had sent for support. The courier had
ridden from Cairo that same day with relays of horses,
and, reaching Alexandria between three and four in
the afternoon, loudly proclaimed the approach of
Saladin's army. The tidings put fresh heart into

---

* Ibn-el-Athir's account of the siege of Alexandria is here followed.
Baha-ed-din puts the ships at 600, and the troops at 30,000, and
dates the beginning of the siege 7th September.

the defenders, and they rushed out again in the
gathering darkness, fell upon the camp of the Sicilians, and drove them, some to the ships, some into
the sea. The news that Saladin was on the march
finished the fiasco : the Sicilians slipped their moor-
ings and fled, as suddenly as they had come.

The danger from the Franks was over, but it had
been very grave. Nevertheless the Sicilian invasion,
the conspiracy at Cairo, and the insurrection up the
Nile, weighed nothing in the balance against the important news which had been brought from Syria.
The greatest of dangers was past, the greatest of
rivals was no longer formidable ; for on the 15th of
May the Sultan of Syria lay dead.

SIEGE OF A SARACEN FORT.
FROM A 13TH CENTURY MS.

PART III.

EMPIRE.

1174–1186.

SILVER COIN OF SALADIN STRUCK AT DAMASCUS IN 1177.

CHAPTER IX.

THE CONQUEST OF SYRIA.

1174–1176.

THE news of the death of Nur-ed-din fell like a thunderbolt among the Saracens. It was wholly unforeseen. On the 6th of May, 1174, he was out riding with one of his courtiers, discoursing in his philosophic way upon the uncertainty of human life : on the 15th he was carried off, in his fifty-sixth year, by a contemptible quinsy. No sovereign since Melik Shah had been so revered. To his subjects he was a model of all virtue, the embodiment of Moslem piety, "a second Omar ibn Abd-el-Aziz," as religious, just, and clement a king as ever ruled. Even the Crusaders bore witness to his chivalrous character, and William of Tyre admits that, in spite of his race and creed, " Noradinus was a just prince, wise, and religious," though a great oppressor of Christians. Justice was the quality he valued next to—indeed as a part of—godliness. He would himself appear in the kady's court to answer the process of a subject, and he in-

sisted on no favour being shown to his rank. He
remitted all customs' dues and tithes throughout
his dominions, and lived simply and frugally on his
private means, without touching the public revenue.
When his wife complained of her poverty, and dis-
dained his offer of three shops at Emesa, belonging
to his estate, and worth about twenty gold pieces a-
year, he rebuked her : " I have nothing more, for all
the rest I hold only in trust for the people." In
pursuance of that trust he built citadels for their defence, and founded many colleges, convents, hospitals, and caravanserais, for their spiritual and bodily
welfare. No man delighted more in the conversation of the learned and devout. None was more
diligent in the observance of the minutest rules of his
religion. There was a holy calm in the grave but
gentle eyes, which relieved the massive brow and
ennobled the swarthy, almost beardless, face. He
possessed the dignity and serenity of the true Eastern gentleman ; in his presence there was silence and
stillness—

> " Tum, pietate gravem ac meritis si forte virum quem
> Conspexere, silent, arrectisque auribus adstant :
> Ille regit dictis animos, et pectora mulcet."

Nur-ed-din's greatness consists rather in his just
and able administration than in his victorious campaigns. Yet he was a bold and fearless warrior, a
splendid horseman, ready to expose himself in the
front of every battle ; and he organised his feudal
levies very carefully, made the soldiers' fiefs hereditary, and kept a strict register of the men and arms
that each of his vassals was bound to furnish at his

demand.* But his power of conquest was restricted
at the very outset by the division of his father
Zengy's dominions, and the jealousy of his elder
brother of Mosil. He had to build up a kingdom,
and secure it from attack both on east and west, before he could attempt larger schemes; and to this
Jerusalem owed its temporary safety. His early
wars with the Crusaders had been little more than
forays; and after he had taken Damascus (1154) and
reduced the rest of inland Syria, his attention was
chiefly occupied with Egypt; as a rule he only
skirmished with the Franks, and kept them at arm's
length. He had indeed taken Harenc and Banias,
and in the north he had made his power felt as far
as Marash. At the time of his death, however, he
was preparing for greater efforts. He had overrun
Mesopotamia on his brother's death in 1170, and
though he left the brother's son in nominal authority
at Mosil, all Jezira and Diyar-Bekr were really under
the sway of Damascus. Relieved from any menace
from this quarter, and strengthened by the widened
area for recruiting his army, he was gathering forces
to reduce Saladin to more becoming humility when
the hand of death arrested his plans. Whether he
would have succeeded, and whether after deposing
Saladin he would have led a united Egyptian and
Syrian army against the Franks and expelled them
from the Holy Land, are merely speculative questions; but the Christians, we may believe, had less
to fear from the cautious policy of Nur-ed-din than
from the zeal of his great successor.

---

* Ibn-el-Athir, *Atabegs*, 308.

Upon Nur-ed-din's death, Saladin became the most powerful ruler between Baghdad and Carthage. Es-Salih Ismaïl, the heir of the late King, was a child of eleven years, a luckless shuttlecock between rival guardians. The dominions of the descendants of Zengy in Mesopotamia were cut up among jealous factions. The knell of the Latin Kingdom tolled in July, when the Franks lost Amalric, and Raymond of Tripolis became regent over Baldwin, the afflicted heir, a boy of thirteen, and a leper. Two children with cliques of envious counsellors formed no very formidable obstacles to the progress of a determined ruler, backed by a powerful and seasoned army. Mere personal ambition would have led most men in Saladin's position to take advantage of the weakness of his neighbours, but to ascribe any such conscious motive to him would be to misread his character. Unless he could persuade himself that the general interests of the Saracens, and especially of the Moslem faith, required his intervention, he would hesitate to aggrandise his power at the expense of one whose sister was his own wife and whose father had once been his lord and benefactor. The state of Syria left him no alternative, unless he were content to look on whilst the kingdom laboriously built up by Zengy and his son fell piecemeal to rival emirs, or even to the " infidels." Disunion and anarchy prevailed ; the young King's cousin of Mosil threw off his allegiance and even annexed Edessa and other dependencies of Syria : the emir who had charge of Aleppo was at enmity with those who surrounded the boy sovereign at Damascus; many of the great vassals made themselves independent; Islam in Syria had no leader, and if the Franks had not been in a similar case they might have done what they pleased with the fragments of Zengy's realm.

In these straits, Saladin, as the chief among the officers of the late King, naturally came forward with advice and proffers of assistance, which might almost be interpreted as commands, despite the respectful terms in which they were couched. He sent an ambassador to the young King with assurance of his loyalty, and ordered the name of "es-Salih, son of Nur-ed-din," to be recited in the prayer and engraved upon the money of Egypt.* He wrote to the lords of Damascus to upbraid them with their jealousies:

"If Nur-ed-din," he said, "had thought any one of you capable of taking my place or of being trusted as he trusted me, he would have appointed him to the government of Egypt, the most important of all his possessions. If death had not prevented him, he would have bequeathed to none but me the guardianship and bringing up of his son. I perceive that to my hurt you have arrogated to yourselves the care of my Master, the son of my Master. Assuredly I will come to do him homage and repay the benefits of his father by service which shall be remembered for ever; and I shall deal with each of you according to his work, [especially] the abandoning of the defence of the King's dominions." †

---

* There are copper coins in the British Museum bearing the joint names of es-Salih and Saladin (see my *Catalogue*, vol. ix., *Additions*, p. 308), but these were probably issued, after the occupation of Damascus, from the mint of that city.

† *Kamil*, 607, 608.

Not only had the council of Damascus sat tamely
still whilst the Mesopotamia prince was filching
cities; they even purchased with gold the goodwill
of the Franks, to Saladin's fierce contempt. They
were indeed equally afraid of their neighbours on
either hand, Seyf-ed-din of Mosil and Saladin of
Cairo, and to protect themselves from both they
had made terms with the "infidels," as their predecessor Anar had done in the days of Zengy.

But when in August the child-King was removed
to Aleppo, a more imminent danger threatened them.
The vigorous captain of Nur-ed-din's veterans, who
ruled Aleppo and now assumed the guardianship of
the King, was prepared to trample on all rivals, and
would certainly begin at Damascus. In this emergency they appealed to the King of Mosil to come
to their aid; and when he refused, they invited
Saladin. He waited for no second bidding, but, taking only seven hundred picked horsemen, rode
straight across the desert for Damascus, trusting to
his luck to bring him safe through the Frank borders.
He came out of the waste untouched, and, entering
the ancient city amid general acclamations, rested at
his father's old house, until the citadel also opened
its gates to him, on the 27th of November.* Then
he installed himself in the castle and received the
homage and salutations of the citizens, winning
general applause by a liberal distribution from es-

---

* Different dates are assigned by Ibn-el-Athir and Baha-ed-din for
the entry into Damascus. Ibn-el-Athir's " end of Rabi I," *i. e.*, end
of October, may be a miscopying of Baha-ed-din's more precise
"30th of Rabi II," *i. e.*, 27th of November.

Salih's royal treasury. All this he did as the agent of the youthful King, whose "mamluk" he still professed himself to be, and whose sovereignty was formally attested by prayers and coinage.

Leaving his brother Tughtigin, surnamed the "Sword of Islam," as governor of Damascus, Saladin instantly pressed forward to reduce other cities which belonged to Nur-ed-din's kingdom, but were now practically independent. It was the depth of winter, and the cold and snow were severe on the highlands; but his business brooked no delay. Traversing the beautiful Bikaa, the wooded valley of the Litany river, on the 9th of December he victoriously entered the opulent city of Emesa, where Aurelian once made sacrifice to the gods for his victory over Zeno-bia; and then, masking its castle, which was too strong to be taken by assault, descended the fertile valley of the Orontes to the land of lush fields and water-wheels, to Hamah,—the same Epiphania where the heroic queen of Palmyra lost her throne and liberty. The city opened its gates, and the citadel presently surrendered, on Saladin's oath that he came as the viceroy and servant of es-Salih. Then he passed on to Aleppo, to the famous "Grey Castle" towering on its round hill above the plain, "a very bride for beauty," which held within its strong walls his nominal sovereign. The Governor and Vezir Gumushtigin had no mind to abdicate his authority to so dangerous a visitor, and prudently shut the gates in his face. Saladin opened a siege on the 30th of December, on the plea that he had come to rescue his liege-lord from evil counsellors; but es-Salih, as

much afraid of his deliverer as he was distrustful of
his governor, came out of the palace, and riding
amongst the people threw himself on their mercy.
The child made so moving an appeal to the crowd,
entreating them, with the tears running down his
cheeks, not to deliver him up to this fierce invader
who had stolen his heritage, that their hearts were
touched ; they redoubled their efforts, and their vigorous and repeated sorties made the invader pause.

The energy of the defence, joined to a new and
disquieting danger, decided Saladin to abandon the
siege.   Gumushtigin, the vezir, resolved to leave no
stone unturned to escape falling into the hands of
the Egyptians, sought help from the Sheykh Sinan,
the so-called "Old Man of the Mountain," Grandmaster of the Assassins of Syria. This redoubtable
secret society, partly religious, still more political,
had spread abroad from its cradle at the castle of
Alamut in the mountains on the south of the Cas-
pian Sea. Its corps of *fidawis*, or emissaries, trained
to murder as a fine art, had used their daggers to
some purpose in the wars which had tormented
Syria, and the Society had been rewarded by the
gradual acquisition of nine forts among the Ansariya
Mountains, forming an almost impregnable chain of
fortresses from Valenie (taken in 1125), on the coast,
to Masyaf inland. These "Assassins"—*Hashshashin*
or smokers of hashish (their name among the vulgar),
more properly Ismaïlis, or Batinis, "Esoterics"—
had taken firm root in Syria at the time of Saladin's
invasion, and were the terror of the country. Nur-
ed-din had vainly attempted to subdue them, and

had gained nothing by his endeavour except the unpleasant discovery of a warning pinned to his pillow by a poisoned dagger. In Egypt they had supported the lost cause of the Fatimids, from whose sect they were derived, and they probably had a share in instigating Omara's conspiracy. The Master was therefore willing enough to assist the vezir of Aleppo by sending his fanatics to murder Saladin in his camp. They gained admission without difficulty, but were detected just in time. One of the wretches was cut down by Tughril, the lord chamberlain, at the very tent of Saladin, and the rest made a desperate defence before they were overpowered and slain.

This narrow escape may well have deterred him from incurring further risks. He was threatened from other quarters, moreover : the King of Mosil was raising troops to defend his cousin of Aleppo ; and the Franks had already cut the road to Saladin's base at Damascus. Raymond, Count of Tripolis, had been for many years a captive of Nur-ed-din at Aleppo, and after his release on ransom (which was not paid) had become regent of the Latin Kingdom during the minority of Baldwin IV. The vezir of Aleppo, hard pressed by Saladin, appealed to the Count for assistance, and Raymond saw advantages, political and pecuniary, in helping the beleaguered city against the new aggressor. He therefore made a diversion, marching upon Emesa, which was still masked and blockaded by part of Saladin's army. The governor seems to have had some negotiations with Raymond, involving, as usual, solid cash.

Cheered by this golden hope, the Christians opened the attack on the 1st of February, 1175, and had the satisfaction of succeeding in their main object—of raising the siege of Aleppo; for Saladin was heard of next day. He had already reached Hamah, and was taking up a strong position near the great stone bridge over the Orontes, where lies the village of Arethusa (er-Rastan). The Franks immediately deserted the famous city, which once gave birth to Julia Domna and taught the child Elagabalus those Syrian rites which he afterwards brought as Emperor to Rome. Saladin entered Emesa, and reduced the citadel, after a stubborn resistance, in the middle of March. At the end of the month he occupied Baalbekk. He was now master of all Nur-ed-din's Syrian kingdom, except the districts immediately depending on Aleppo.

These successes finally roused Seyf-ed-din Ghazy II., the Atabeg of Mosil, who, as head of the descendants of his grandfather Zengy, regarded Syria and Mesopotamia in the light of a family estate. As a member of the family he had felt no scruple in taking advantage of his cousin's youth and annexing his Mesopotamian possessions; but it was another matter when an upstart, who had no drop of Zengy's blood, ventured to usurp the family prerogatives. Seyf-ed-din accordingly mustered a large army and despatched it to Aleppo, where its arrival was anxiously expected. The combined forces marched against the common enemy, and found him near Hamah. Though he had recently been reinforced by the arrival of a contingent from Egypt, Saladin was evidently outnumbered; for he made overtures for an accommodation, even offering to abandon all his conquests north of the province of Damascus. The enemy, however, would listen to no terms, and roughly told him to retire to Egypt. Driven to an issue at arms, he took up a position by the gorge of the Orontes, on the hills called the Horns of Hamah, where a superior position made up for disparity in numbers. On the 13th of April, 1175, the troops of Mosil and Aleppo marched to the attack, confident in their strength; but taken at a disadvantage and caught in a ravine between the tried veterans of Damascus and Cairo, they were cut to pieces, and the battle ended in a shameful rout.   Saladin pursued the fugitives to the gates of Aleppo, and es-Salih's advisers were compelled to agree to a truce, whereby each side retained the territory it then possessed. By this agreement Saladin remained the undisputed master, not only of the provinces of Damascus, Emesa, and Hamah, but even of the towns of Kafar Tab, Barin, and Maarra, not far from Aleppo itself.

Now, for the first time, Saladin asserted his independence, proclaimed himself King, and suppressed the name of es-Salih in the prayer and coinage.* This year he was prayed for in all the mosques of Syria and Egypt as sovereign lord, and he issued at the Cairo mint gold coins in his own name: " el-Melik en-Nasir Yusuf ibn Ayyub, ala ghaya," " *The*

---

* There are gold coins of this date (A.H. 570), struck at Cairo and Alexandria, in the Khedivial Collection and that of Artin Pasha at Çairo,

*King Strong to Aid,** *Joseph son of Job ; exalted
be the Standard !* " So far as his words prove, he
had done his best to convince the young King at
Aleppo that he was ready to serve him loyally,
though he had made it clear enough that he would
allow no rivals near the throne. Es-Salih naturally
perceived that such nominal service meant real mas-
tery, and would have nothing to do with him. Posi-
tively repulsed in every overture of conciliation,
Saladin felt himself absolved from further fealty, and
in the circumstances there was no reason why he
should not take to himself the dignity of King.† His
assumption of royal prerogatives received the gracious sanction of the Caliph of Baghdad, who sent
him the customary diploma and robes of investiture
as King of Egypt and Syria ; they reached him at
Hamah, where he was organising his new possessions, in May, 1175.

Administrative duties and the mustering of troops
occupied the rest of the year, and nothing of any
moment happened until the following spring. But
the contest between the houses of Zengy and Ayyub

---

  * It is difficult to render the exact meaning of Arabic titles. *En-
Nasir* is *one who aids* another to victory, especially who aids in the
triumph of Islam, a champion of the faith. It connotes the idea of
success, and hence is often rendered " Victorious." A coin with this
inscription, struck at Cairo in 570 of the Hijra, *i. e.*, 1175 A.D., is
preserved in the Khedivial Library at Cairo. I think Sir Charles
Wilson suggested the appropriate rendering " Strong to aid."

  † Saladin has often been charged with disloyalty, but with little
reason. The nominal King was in the hands of Saladin's rivals, and
never gave him the opportunity to be loyal. Had Saladin left Syria
alone, it would have fallen, not to the boy King, but to other ambitious emirs.

was not ended by Saladin's victory at the Horns of Hamah. Both sides were actively gathering strength for a fresh struggle. Seyf-ed-din was levying troops among the minor states of Diyar-Bekr and Jezira, with which, in the spring of 1176, he was able to cross the Euphrates at Bira. His army numbered 6000 men, and was further reinforced when he picked up es-Salih's contingent at Aleppo. Saladin, who left Cairo with only 700 horsemen, had by this time brought up his forces from Egypt to join the troops of Damascus.

As he crossed the Orontes on the 11th of April, 1176, to meet the approaching storm, the sun was eclipsed, the earth was in darkness, and the stars shone clear in the midday sky.* Despite this omen, he continued his march, but he had not advanced far beyond Hamah when the sinister import of the eclipse was revealed, for he narrowly escaped a serious disaster. Seyf-ed-din came up unexpectedly whilst Saladin's men were dispersed at the Turkman's Wells (Jibab et-Turkman) watering their horses. Had he attacked at once, the result must have been a victory; but he hesitated, and when he took the field next morning, Thursday 22nd April, he found Saladin ready for him near the Little Caravanserai on the "Mound of the Sultan," fifteen miles from Aleppo. A bloody hand to hand fight ensued. The lord of Irbil over-threw Saladin's left wing, and was driving it be-

---

* Imad-ed-din makes this eclipse occur on Saladin's return from Hamah to Damascus in May, 1175; but no total eclipse of the sun occurred in 1175, whilst there was a total eclipse visible in northern Syria on April 11, 1176. *Cp.* Oppolzer's *Canon der Finsternisse.*

fore him, when the King himself charged at the head
of his guard and turned the fortune of the day.
A sudden panic seized upon the enemy, and every
man ran for his life.   Most of the Atabeg's officers
were killed or taken prisoners, and Seyf-ed-din with
difficulty made his escape from the field.   The camp
and horses, baggage, tents, and stores, all fell into
the conqueror's hands.

Saladin showed himself worthy of victory.   He
treated his prisoners generously, set them free, and
sent many of them away with gifts.   The wounded,
especially, owed their lives to his care, and many were
eager to enter his service.   As for the rich booty of
the enemy's camp, he gave it all to the army, and
kept not a thing for himself.   In this he displayed
alike the instincts of a generous nature and the fore-
sight of a statesman.   He bound both his own troops
and the enemy's to him with ties of gratitude and
personal devotion.   The prisoners he had freed, some
of whom were men of rank and influence, went back
to their homes by the Great River full of his praises,
extolling his clemency and greatheartedness, and
prepared to be his willing subjects.   His own men,
flushed with triumph and enriched with spoil, were
ready to follow him anywhere.

After a few days' halt before Aleppo, which still
closed its gates, he led them on whilst their blood
was hot.   A day's march brought them to Buzaa,
which they took ; next day they stormed Manbij ;
then they turned west to the strong fortress of
Azaz, which cost them thirty-eight days' siege and
heavy losses, and nearly sacrificed Saladin's life.   The

leaguer began on the 15th of May,* and on the 22nd
Saladin was resting in the tent of one of his captains,
when a fanatic rushed in upon him and struck at his
head with a knife. The cap of mail which the King
wore under his *tarbush* saved him for the moment,
and he gripped the assassin's hands; but, seated as he
was, he could not prevent his going on stabbing at
his throat. The dagger slashed the collar of his
gambeson,† but the rings of the armour kept it out of
his neck. All this was the work of an instant, and
in another, Bazkush had grasped the knife and held
it, though it sawed his fingers, until at last the des-
perado was killed, with the knife still clenched in his
hand. Another cut-throat followed, and fell dead;
and yet a third; but the guard was now on the alert.
Saladin mounted and rode to head-quarters in
panic fear, scarcely realising that he was alive. The
sudden assault of the secret assassin had terrors
which he never felt on the battle-field, and this second attempt by the agents of the "Sheykh of the
Mountain" unnerved him. It was found that the
three desperados had contrived to be enrolled in
the bodyguard itself: Saladin hastened to change it,
and searched the ranks for suspicious faces; but the
emissaries of Sinan had the art to assume every disguise and elude all precautions, and there could be

---

* Baha-ed-din says the siege lasted from May 15 to June 24; Ibn-
el-Athir, May 14 to June 21. Neither period exactly agrees with
the 38 days stated by the latter to be the length of the siege; but a
compromise between the two meets the difficulty.

† Persian *kazaghand*, a thick quilted tunic, always worn by Saladin
on horseback.

no real sense of security until their master was either crushed or propitiated.

Convinced that Gumushtigin was at the bottom of this dastardly attempt, Saladin redoubled his assaults against Azaz, and at last on the 21st of June the fortress capitulated. Then he hurried to Aleppo, to punish the plotter, and on the 25th began his third siege of the Grey Castle. His attacks were resisted as before, but sooner than risk being starved out, the garrison consented to treat. A general agreement was arranged (29 July) between the young King of Aleppo, the neighbouring Ortukid princes of Keyfa and Maridin (who had throughout supported him), and Saladin, by which he was finally recognised as sovereign over all the dominions he had conquered, and the four signatories bound themselves solemnly by an oath of mutual alliance.

When the treaty was concluded, there came to Saladin a young girl, the little sister of es-Salih. He received her with honour, and asked her " What is thy wish?" "The Castle of Azaz," she said. So he restored the castle to its old owners, loaded the princess with presents, and escorted her back to the gate of Aleppo at the head of his staff. The great Constable Humphrey of Toron had cause to be proud of his Knight.

CHAPTER X.

TRUCES AND TREATIES.

1176–1181.

FOR six years there was peace between Saladin and the house of Zengy. Es-Salih remained at Aleppo in undisturbed enjoyment of what was left to him of his father's kingdom. The Atabeg of Mosil did not invite a repetition of the disasters at the Horns of Hamah and the Sultan's Mound. There was also a nominal truce with the King of Jerusalem, which Saladin had concluded in the summer of 1175, with the assistance of handsome presents and the mediation of Humphrey of Toron, with whom he probably maintained the friendly relation which dated from the time of his own knighthood. His object was to secure himself in the rear whilst he was occupied in the north. Treaties with the soldiers of the Cross, however, were worse than useless, so long as the doctrine prevailed in Christendom that no faith need be kept with the "infidel"; and scarcely had they concluded the pact of amity, when they began to ravage the beautiful

valley of the Litany, burned the standing corn, set
fire to the villages, and returned in triumph, laden
with booty, and driving great flocks of stolen sheep
and cattle.

The raids of the Franks, however, cannot have
been very serious, or involved any loss of territory,
for Saladin seems to have paid no attention to them.
There was another power, independent both of the
Franks and the Zengids, with which he was forced
to deal. It was impossible to carry his life at the
disposal of the Sheykh of the Assassins. Saladin
accordingly determined to enter their country and
destroy them root and branch. As soon as he had
concluded his treaty of peace at Aleppo, and dismissed his Egyptian troops to recruit their strength
at home, he marched with the rest of his army into
the rocky passes of the Summak range, or Ansariya
mountains, where the fanatics had their forts. He
went into this gloomy region in August, and in
August he came out; but the Old Man still ruled on
his Mountain, and the Assassins were unconquered.
What happened is variously related. It is agreed that
Saladin laid waste much of the country and that he
set siege to Masyaf, the chief among the nine castles
of the society—a veritable eagle's nest, perched
on a scarcely accessible peak, and commanding a
desolate ravine. It is equally certain that his siege
artillery and storming parties made no impression
on the rocky fortress. The divergence arises when
the cause of his abrupt retreat is explained. The
Moslem historians naturally put the best colour on
it, and assert that Sinan obtained peace through the

mediation of Saladin's uncle; but even by these apologists the humility of the Master's overture is considerably weakened by his accompanying threat of a wholesale murder of the Ayyubid family in the event of refusal. The story told by Sinan's pane-gyrist * is more probable, when divested of its super-natural absurdities. This story is as follows.

When Saladin laid siege to Masyaf, Sinan was ab-sent, and the King's summons to surrender reached him at a village near Kadamus. He told the mes-senger that he must have a personal interview with Saladin; and then, since access to Masyaf was blocked by the leaguer, he retired with only two companions to the top of a neighbouring mountain, whence he looked down upon the siege and awaited the event. Saladin, believing that he had the arch-enemy in his power, sent a body of troops to surround him; but hostile soldiers and peaceful messengers were alike held back by a mysterious force which numbed their limbs. Such was the miraculous power of the holy Master, in whom his followers were taught to recog-nise a veritable incarnation of the Divine Reason. The awed reports of his baffled and perplexed en-voys worked upon Saladin's fears. He remembered the two former attempts upon his life, and began to doubt whether anything human could save him from the supernatural agencies of this devil or saint. He had chalk and cinders strewed around his tent, to detect secret footsteps; his guards were supplied with linklights, and the night watches were fre-

* Abu-Firas, published by S. Guyard: "Un Grand-Maître des As-sassins," in the *Journal Asiatique*, 1877.

quently relieved. But unearthly terrors surrounded him, and his sleep was troubled. One night the watchers on the battlements of Masyaf perceived a spark like a glow-worm slowly gliding down the hill where the Master sat. It vanished among the tents of the Saracens. Presently Saladin awoke from his uneasy dreams to see a figure gliding out at the tent door. Looking round he noticed that the lamps had been displaced, and beside his bed lay some hot scones of the shape peculiar to the Assassins, with a leaf of paper on the top, pinned by a poisoned dagger. There were verses on the paper:

" By the Majesty of the Kingdom ! what you possess will escape you, in spite of all, but victory remains to us :
   We acquaint you that *we hold you*, and that we reserve you till your reckoning be paid."

Saladin gave a great and terrible cry, and the guard and the officers rushed in. He showed them the scones, the dagger, the verses. The dread Master had been actually at his pillow : it was nothing short of a miracle. No one had heard a step or seen a living soul : there were footprints on the cinders— but they all pointed *outwards*. Then Saladin said : " I have *seen* him—and that is very different from hearing of him. Go to this man and ask him for a safe-conduct, and pray him not to punish me for my past errors." A messenger went to seek Sinan on the mountain ; but the Master made an- swer that there could be no warranty for the King's life so long as he continued the siege. Saladin therefore departed, in such haste that he even left his artillery behind him ; and at the Bridge of Ibn-

Munkidh he received a safe-conduct from the Master of the Assassins.

This is the narrative of a partisan and a visionary, but it may well be based upon fact. Sinan may actually have groped or bribed his way to Saladin's tent, and thus convinced him in person that no precautions could avail him against the knives of the secret society. The dread of assassination, joined to the impracticable character of the district and the strength of its fastnesses, may reasonably have induced the King to abandon his design of uprooting the abhorred sect; and if he could not wholly destroy them, the only prudent alternative was to make them his friends. As a political measure, moreover, the binding of the Master by ties of mutual toleration was a master-stroke. It cut away from the still disaffected Shïïtes in Egypt their hope of Sinan's sinister support, and deprived the Crusaders of a secret weapon.

After leaving the mountains, Saladin returned to Damascus (25 August), dismissed his Syrians to their homes, left his brother, Turan Shah, the conqueror of the Yemen, in command in Syria, and taking with him only his personal followers, went to Cairo (22 September). He had been absent two years, and there was much to organise and superintend. He now was able to devote his energies to the fortification and reconstruction of the city which he had already designed. The walls were repaired, and their extensions were laid out, and the building of the Citadel was begun. The Moorish traveller, Ibn-Jubeyr, in 1183 saw Christian

captives sawing stones and quarrying out the moat
or fosse beneath the massive walls of the castle.*
It was reserved, however, for a nephew thirty years
later to complete the fortifications which his famous
uncle had planned, and at the present day, so often
has the Citadel been remodelled by Mamluk Sultans, and finally by Mohammed Ali, that it is difficult to identify with precision any large part of the
original defences.†

The founder's inscription, however, may still be
read over the old "Gate of the Steps," Bab el-Mu-
darraj, a dark mysterious portal in the west face of
the original enceinte. It records how "the building
of this splendid Citadel,—hard by Cairo the Guarded,
on the terrace which adds use to beauty, and space
to strength, for those who seek the shelter of his
power,—was commanded by our Master the King
Strong to Aid, Honour of the World and the Faith
(el-Melik en-Nasir Salah ed-dunya wa-d-din), Father
of the Conquering, Yusuf son of Ayyub, Restorer of
the Empire of the Caliph; with the direction of his
brother and heir the Just King (el-Adil) Seyf-ed-din
Abu-Bekr Mohammed, friend of the Commander of
the Faithful; and under the management of the
Emir of his Kingdom and Support of his Empire
Karakush son of Abdallah, the slave of el-Melik en-
Nasir, in the year 579 (or 1183–4 A.D.)." ‡ The

---

* Ibn-Jubeyr, *Travels*, ed. W. Wright, 49.

† The subject has been elaborately treated by M. P. Casanova in
the *Mém. de la mission archéol. au Caire*, vi. See also Lane's
Cairo Fifty Years Ago, ch. iv.

‡ See Berchem in the *Mémoires de la miss. archéol. au Caire*, xix. 80 *ff.*

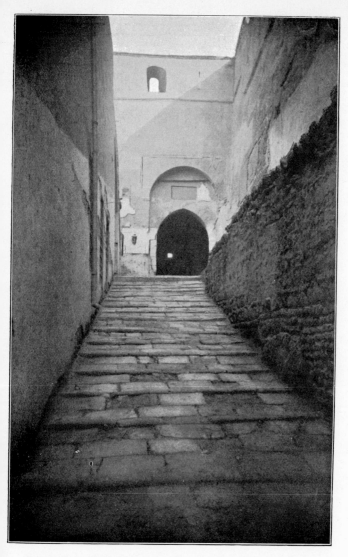

THE GATE OF STEPS, IN THE CITADEL OF CAIRO, WITH SALADIN'S
INSCRIPTION OVER THE ARCH.

famous " Well of the Winding Stairs," 280 feet deep,
still called the Bir Yusuf, " Joseph's Well," was
certainly excavated in the solid rock by Karakush
under Saladin's orders*; but the other buildings
lately existing in the Citadel and called after his
name really belonged to later times. The people of
Egypt were accustomed to name public works after
the famous Sultan. His memory, but not his act, is
preserved in the long aqueduct of Cairo, and even in
the great canal of Upper Egypt, still known as the
" River of Joseph," Bahr Yusuf, though it dates
from the time of the Pharaohs. The chief public
work, however, that he carried out, beyond Cairo
itself, was the great bridge or dyke of Giza, which
was built, like the Citadel, with stones from the
pyramids, in 1183-4, and carried on forty arches
along the border of the desert, seven miles from
Cairo, and was intended to form an outwork of
defence against an invasion of the Moors, which
never happened.†

Saladin remained at Cairo, occupied with these
improvements, building colleges like the Medresa of
the Swordmakers, and ordering the internal administration of his principal province, for a whole year,
till November, 1177, when he set out upon a raid
into Palestine. The Franks had lately forayed the
Damascus country, and the pretence of a truce was
no longer worth preserving. The Christians had now
sent a large portion of their forces north to besiege
Harim, a fortress belonging to the King of Aleppo,

---

* El-Makrizy, *Khitat*, ii., 204.

† Ibn Jubeyr, 49; el-Makrizy, ii., 151.

and the south of Palestine was comparatively bare of defenders. The occasion was propitious, and Saladin marched gaily to Ascalon, " the Bride of Syria." William of Tyre says that he heard, on careful inquiry, that the Saracens numbered 26,000 fighting men, of whom 8000 were *Toassin** or élite, including the bodyguard of a thousand Mamluks in yellow tunics—Saladin's colour—and 18,000 were *Caragholam* (black slaves) of inferior rank—doubtless the old Egyptian heavy-armed infantry from the Sudan. Meeting with no opposition, they began to raid the country in perfect confidence, sacked and burned Ramla and Lydda, and dispersed over the land, even up to the gates of Jerusalem, in a joyous orgy of plunder and devastation.

So secure were they in their strength that they treated the enemy with contempt, and allowed King Baldwin to get into Ascalon, and the Templars of Gaza to join him, without taking any precautions against a sudden attack. It is true the King of Jerusalem had only 375 knights to his back; but Saladin must have known by this time that 375 knights were not to be despised, especially when led by such warriors as Balian, Reginald of Sidon, Odo the Master of the Temple, and Joscelin the Seneschal, and encouraged by the presence of " the True Cross," borne by the Bishop of Bethlehem. How it happened is not clear, but this much is certain, that on the 25th of November, 1177, in the absence of the

* Perhaps *Taushiin*, " Peacocky," for *taush* is used of " goodly men." *Toassin* can hardly be from *Tawashi*, " eunuch," though many of this class commanded in Saladin's armies.

INSCRIPTION OF SALADIN AND KARAKUSH OVER THE GATE OF STEPS, RECORDING THE FOUNDATION OF THE CITADEL OF CAIRO, DATED 1183.

greater part of his army, Saladin's men were surprised at Tell Jezer, near Ramla,* and before they
could form up, the knights were hacking them down.
At first the Sultan retired fighting, and tried to get
his men into order of battle ; but his bodyguard was
cut to pieces around him, and he was himself all but
taken prisoner. Seeing that the day was lost, he
turned at last, and mounting a swift camel rode for
his life. A remnant of his troops escaped with him,
and throwing away armour and weapons, and leaving
the wounded to their fate, fled under cover of night
pell-mell to Egypt, where they arrived after great
privations. Of the rest of the army that had marched
so gleefully to the despoiling of the Holy Land, few
survived. Famine, cold, and heavy rains completed
what the sword began. Never had Saladin's arms
known such disaster.

Far from giving way to discouragement, however,
the great captain, who had for once thrown away an
army, hastened to collect another. Writing to his
brother Turan Shah at Damascus, Saladin admits the
desperate character of the battle, but is equal to
quoting poetry on the subject—" I thought of thee,"
he wrote (and Ibn-el-Athir saw the very letter)—

" I thought of thee, amid the thrusting of their spears,
   While the straight browned blades quenched their thirst in our
      blood "—

and adds " again and again we were on the verge of
destruction ; nor would God have delivered us save

---

* *Mons Gisardus*, according to the report of Roger de Molines
(Röhricht, *Regesta Regn. Hieros.*, 564).

for some [future] duty." In three months he was
ready to meet the Franks again, and the spring of
1178 found him encamped under the walls of Emesa.
Some skirmishes took place between his generals
(who were also his kinsmen) and the Franks. The
troops of Hamah won a victory over the enemy, and
brought the spoils, together with many heads and
prisoners, to Saladin, who ordered the captives to be
beheaded. They were " infidels," and they had been
plundering and laying waste the lands of the Faithful. The rest of the year was spent in Syria, without
any considerable action on either side. Saladin
wintered at Damascus, and in the spring prepared to
undo the latest manœuvre of Baldwin.

The King of Jerusalem had followed up his triumph at Ramla by pushing forward towards the
Saracens' country and setting an outpost on the road
to Damascus. There was a passage over the Jordan
called " Jacob's Ford," because here Jacob wrestled
with the angel*; it was also known as the "Ford of
Sorrows"; and here the King restored a fort which
not only defended the passage of the river, but commanded the approach to the plain of Banias, the
granary of Damascus, where rice and cotton fields
and groves of lemon trees lay thick at the foot of the
"Mount of Snow." Hitherto this fertile plain had

---

*"Cil lius qui est apielés li Gués Jacob, c'est là u Jacob luita à
l'angle, et là u il ot brisie le cuisse, quant il repairait d'Aran, là u il
estoit fuis pour Esaü, son frere." Ernoul, ed. Mas Latrie, 52. Ernoul adds that the King rebuilt the castle despite the treaty with the
Saracens, and against his own judgment, but was overpersuaded by
the Templars. Chesney says the ford is 80 ft. wide and 4 deep.

been divided in the friendliest manner between the
Franks and Moslems, and a mighty oak tree marked
the boundary between the two nations, whose flocks
grazed side by side. Saladin had vainly offered first
60,000 and finally 100,000 gold pieces to induce the
King to abandon a project which was peculiarly
offensive to the Saracens. He now resolved to raze
the fortress to the ground. His nephew Ferrukh
Shah had already won a success over the Franks by
an ambuscade in April, 1179: he had caught King
Baldwin with a scanty following in a rocky gorge
near Belfort, and it was only the courage of the
valiant Constable Humphrey of Toron that rescued
his young sovereign from capture, at the cost of his
own life. The loss of this gallant knight was a heavy
blow to the Franks. "No words can describe Hun-
fary," says the Arab historian; "his name was a
proverb for bravery and skill in war. He was indeed
a plague let loose by God for the chastening of the
Moslems."*

Following up this advantage, Saladin, who had
now removed his headquarters to Banias, pushed
forward, and in June again encountered the King of
Jerusalem. For Baldwin, hearing that the Saracens
were pillaging in the direction of Sidon, went forthwith to the rescue, burning to wipe out his late disgrace. Marching north by way of Safed and Toron,
he ascended a height of the mountains to the village
of Mesafa ("the station"), whence he commanded a
wide view, and beheld the camp of Saladin, as it
were at his feet, spread out on the "Meadow of

---

* Ibn-el-Athir, *Kamil*, 635.

Springs " (Marj Oyun, Mergion).   Hurrying down to
the attack, his troops fell into disorder, the infantry
dropped behind, and the army went into battle piecemeal.   At first they had it all their own way and put
part of the enemy to flight; but Odo at the head of
his Templars rashly pursued the fugitives too far,
and severed still further the already scattered forces
of the Christians.   Saladin, taking advantage of this,
rallied his flying troops, and calling upon them for a
great effort, made one of his furious charges.   The
enemy, who had thought the day won, were taken
by surprise; and burdened by the spoils of the slain,
had no time to form up.   Many were killed or made
prisoners, and the rest, escaping over the Litany
river, sought refuge in the neighbouring stronghold
of Belfort; some did not stop till they reached
Sidon.   The victory was specially notable for the
high rank of the prisoners.   The Masters of the Hospital and the Temple, Raymond of Tripolis, Balian
of Ibelin, Baldwin of Ramla, and Hugh of Tiberias,
were among the seventy knights whom the Secretary
Imad-ed-din counted as they stood in Saladin's tent.*
Baldwin obtained his liberty on paying a ransom of
150,000 Tyrian gold pieces and setting free a thousand Saracen prisoners; but when Saladin offered to
exchange Odo for an emir who had been taken by
the Franks, the Master—" a haughty, arrogant man,
with the breath of fury in his nostrils, who feared not
God nor respected man " †—whose frantic fighting
had been the wonder and the ruin of the day, replied

---

* Quoted by Abu-Shama (Goergens, *Arabische Quellenbeiträge*, 10).
† William of Tyre, xxi., 29.

proudly: "A Templar can give for his ransom nought but his belt and dagger." * Odo died in captivity: "he went from his prison to Hell," says Abu-Shama.

The road was now clear to King Baldwin's Folly, the Castle of Sorrows at Jacob's Ford. On the 25th of August Saladin marched thither, and as soon as his pioneers had collected enough vine-poles to make screens for the sappers, he began the attack. At the first assault a man in the crowd, in a tattered shirt, sprang on to the outwork and began to engage the enemy on the curtain; others followed, and the outwork was won. The Franks, however, still defended the walls resolutely, in confident expectation of being relieved. The next morning the Saracens mined the wall, and made the mine deep and filled it with burning wood, and waited for the wall to fall. But they waited two days, the fire burning all the time, and still the wall stood firm, for it was nine cubits thick, not ordinary cubits neither, but carpenters' cubits half as long again; and the mine was but a third through it. Saladin saw that it was useless, and called for water: "Every man who brings me a skin of water, shall have a gold dinar." Water was brought with such enthusiasm that the works were fairly flooded. Then the sappers returned and deepened the mine and pierced the wall, and put fire in again, and at last it fell on Thursday, the 30th of August, 1179. The Saracens

---

* "Non esse consuetudinem militum suae religionis, ut aliqua pro eis daretur redemptio praeter cingulum et cultellum." (Robert de Monte, in *Mon. German.*, ad 1180.)

poured in through the breach and took the castle by
storm, and made prisoners of the defenders to the
number of seven hundred, and set free the Moslem
captives ; but of the Franks, Saladin killed many
and threw them down the castle well, and sent the
rest to be imprisoned at Damascus. He remained
on the spot till the Castle of Sorrows was razed level
with the ground, and not a vestige of it remained.
As Aly of Damascus, the clockmaker, sang :

" How can we leave in the Patriarch's house those who break faith
    after they have sworn it ?
 I admonish you sincerely—sincerity is part of religion—quit Ja-
    cob's House, for *Joseph* is come." *

When the King of Jerusalem at last arrived to
raise the siege of his favourite castle, he found only
heaps of stone blackened with fire. The Crusaders
tried no more conclusions with Saladin that year.
Their King's disease was increasing, and there was
anxiety about the succession ; a truce would be welcome. There was rest during the winter, indeed,
which Saladin devoted to equipping a powerful navy
to assist in the next expedition. His fleet of seventy
vessels had done considerable execution in the autumn of 1179; harried the coast, and brought back
a thousand Christian prisoners.† This encouraged
him to try combined action by sea and land. In the
spring of 1180 he was once more in the parts about
Safed, waiting for his fleet to arrive off the coast, be-

---

* Ibn-el-Athir, *Kamil*, 636–9 ; Imad-ed-din in Abu-Shama, 16, 17.
† Ibn-Aby-Tay in Goergens, 16.

fore opening a vigorous campaign. Baldwin wisely chose the prudent course, and sent messengers to propose peace. Saladin was not sorry to agree, for droughts and bad harvests were seriously hampering his commissariat. In the summer he consented to a truce for two years by sea and land, for natives and new-comers alike, and it was confirmed by solemn oaths. For the Franks it was an humiliating concession : never before had they set seal to a treaty drawn up on equal terms which reserved no advantage for themselves. It was no wonder that their pride rebelled. The Count of Tripolis, no friend to the King, loudly denounced the compact; but a rapid raid of the Saracens upon his territory in May, and the appearance of Saladin's fleet off Tortosa, brought Raymond to reason. The Holy War ceased for a while.

There were other parties to the peace which now reigned over the Hither East, and the immediate cause of this widespread pacification was—a singing girl. Nur-ed-din, Prince of Keyfa, had been given to wife a great lady, the daughter of Kilij Arslan, the Seljuk Sultan of Konia. Unhappily he did not treat her well, but bestowed his affections upon a singing girl of no family at all. The neglected wife appealed to her father, and Kilij Arslan declared war. By the treaty of Aleppo, Saladin had agreed to stand by his allies, among whom was the Prince of Keyfa. Moreover he had himself a quarrel with the Sultan of Konia concerning the fortress of Raaban on the northern marches, and blood had been spilt. He was therefore in no humour to hear of a punitive expedition against his ally. " Tell your master, in God's name," he said to the Seljuk's envoy, " by my faith in two days I will march with my men into his capital and seize all his dominions." So in his wrath he had come as far north as Raaban, where he was again met by the ambassador, this time with peaceful arguments. Saladin, seeing the situation, put pressure upon his amorous ally, and the quarrel was compounded by the summary dismissal of the singing girl. This happy result was followed by an expedition into Cilician or Lesser Armenia, as far as Mopsuestia (el-Massisa), to compel its king Rhupen to keep faith with the Turkmans who pastured in his territory and under his protection. After the destruction of the castle of el-Menakir, Rhupen submitted.

Saladin's power had now made itself felt as far as Asia Minor; he was admittedly the chief of Saracen rulers from the Euphrates to the Nile, and was invited by other princes to act as arbiter in their disputes. This high position he used for a noble purpose, whatever motive urged him. He brought about a general peace, a *Truga Dei*, among all the peoples whom he could influence,

"nexuque pio longinqua revinxit."

On the 2nd of October, 1180, he presided over a memorable Congress, on the banks of the Senja, near Sumeysat, at which the princes of Mesopotamia—Mosil, Jezira, Irbil, Keyfa, and Maridin,— the Sultan of Konia, and the King of Armenia set their seals to a solemn pact, whereby they bound

themselves on oath to keep peace one with another
for the space of two years. For this time war was
to be unknown within their borders, and a holy truce,
a *Magna Pax Saracenica*, was to reign throughout
the land.

" Hae tibi erunt artes, pacisque imponere morem. . . . "

It was a great conception : but how it was observed
will be seen.

COPPER COIN OF SEYF-ED-DIN, ATABEG OF MOSIL, STRUCK IN
MESOPOTAMIA (JEZIRA) IN 1179-80

SILVER COIN OF SALADIN STRUCK AT ALEPPO IN 1186.

CHAPTER XI.

THE CONQUEST OF MESOPOTAMIA.

1181–1183.

THE Great Truce was made, and Saladin was free to return to Egypt. He left his nephew Ferrukh Shah in charge of Syria, and reached Cairo at the beginning of 1181. The year that was past had brought changes to many thrones. Louis le Jeune of France had died and Philip Augustus had succeeded; Pope Lucius had followed Alexander, and Alexius II. sat in the seat of the Emperor Manuel Comnenus. In Asia there had been a succession in the Caliphate; el-Mustady was dead, and en-Nasir, the most energetic of the later Abbasids, was pontiff at Baghdad. Seyf-ed-din, the Atabeg of Mosil, was gathered to his fathers, and Izz-ed-din his brother reigned in his stead. The close of 1181 witnessed an event of still greater importance to Saladin. On the 4th of December Nur-ed-din's heir, es-Salih Ismaïl, ended his gentle inoffensive life at Aleppo in a mortal attack of the colic—not without the usual suspicion of poison. When he knew his death was at hand, he sent for his chief officers and made them swear the oath of fealty to his cousin of Mosil—the only prince of the house of Zengy powerful enough to cross swords with its great supplanter. The dying youth could not forgive Saladin his trespass against the sovereign rights of the dynasty.

The Atabeg of Mosil hastened to take possession of Aleppo, where he was joyfully welcomed by his cousin's retainers. Other cities of Syria were disposed to revert to their old allegiance, and Hamah openly avowed its sympathy. The Atabeg nevertheless remained true to the treaty which he had sworn, and refused all inducements to invade Saladin's dominions. His later conduct suggests that fear had its share in this moderation, for he never ventured to meet his rival in the open field. Even the possession of Aleppo was too great a strain upon his energy ; and harassed by the apprehension that he could not defend at once both his Syrian and Mesopotamian capitals, he yielded to the urgency of his brother, Imad-ed-din, the ruler of Sinjar, and consented to exchange cities with him. Imad-ed-din entered Aleppo on the 19th of May, 1182.

To these transactions Saladin offered no opposition. He was bound by his treaty to respect his ally of Mosil, and he never broke a treaty in his life. At the same time he was closely watching events on his northern frontier. He had of course determined, long before, that the death of es-Salih should be the signal for his own advance to Aleppo. Its possession

by so ambitious and unscrupulous a ruler as Imad-
ed-din was an unforeseen obstacle to his plans.   But
nothing could be done so long as the peace was in
force ; and it would not expire till the 9th of September, 1182.   It is true the other parties to the
treaty would have justified him in tearing it up.
The Franks had again broken their faith.   Reginald
of Châtillon, released from his weary captivity at
Aleppo, and thirsting for revenge, had now become
master of the Dead Sea fortresses, by virtue of his
marriage with Stephania, the widow of the third
Humphrey of Toron and heiress of Karak.   He
used his position unscrupulously, and had lately
captured a peaceful caravan of merchants in time of
truce ; in return, Saladin had detained a pilgrim ship
that had run ashore at Damietta.*   When he prepared to re-enter Syria to protect his subjects, he
learnt, further, that the Zengid princes had so far
forgotten their honour and their religion as to make
a formal treaty with the Christians and even with
the Master of the Assassins for joint opposition to the
common enemy †—himself.   Even this did not tempt
him to depart from his word.   He advanced into
Syria, to be on his guard ; but he took no measures
against his deceitful allies until the treaty lapsed.

* William of Tyre admits the report (*dicebatur*) of Reginald's outrage, but charges Saladin with breach of faith in seizing the ship, as
a hostage against further infractions of the treaty. It is clear, however, from the Latin account itself, that Saladin held the ship and
captives as a set-off against previous breaches of the treaty by the
Franks.   Ernoul, 96, 97, distinctly records the breach of faith.

† Baha-ed-din, 68 ; Imad-ed-din and Kady el-Fadil, in Abu-Shama
(Goergens, 28, 35, 37).

On the 11th of May, 1182, Saladin left Cairo. The chief officers and grandees of his court assembled at the Lake to bid him farewell. One after the other they advanced to his stirrup and took their leave of the sovereign whom they had learnt, during fourteen years of glory abroad and equity at home, to honour and admire. Odes were recited, rhapsodies declaimed. Suddenly a discordant voice jangled the harmony of gracious words. " Enjoy," it cried, in the lines of the old Arab poet,

> " Enjoy the perfume of the ox-eyes of Nejd :
> After to-night, there will be no more ox-eyes."

The discordant note jarred upon Saladin, sensitive like all Easterns to the presage of ill-omen, and he rode away from Egypt with a weight at his heart. The prophetic verse did not err. There were no more ox-eyes for him in Egypt : he never saw Cairo again.

Knowing that the Christians were massed upon the frontier to intercept him, Saladin took the desert route across the peninsula of Sinai to Eyla at the head of the Gulf of Akaba, and thence marched north over the barren flinty plain beside Mount Seir (the Shera range), reconnoitring in search of the enemy. Meeting with no opposition, he ravaged the country about Mont Real, whilst Baldwin's army watched him from their entrenchments near Karak, without moving a finger, either to fight him or cut him off from the wells. Profiting by their lethargy, he marched unmolested through Moab to Damascus in the middle of June. He found

that his active nephew Ferrukh Shah had seized the
opportunity of Baldwin's absence in the south to
cross the Jordan, lay Galilee waste, sack Deburiya
among the oaks and myrtles of the wooded western slopes of Mount Tabor, and even to secure
possession of a rocky fortress (Habis Jeldek), to
which the Franks attached great importance. The
raiders lifted twenty thousand head of cattle and a
thousand captives.

Following up this advantage in July, Saladin despatched Ferrukh Shah again into Palestine. He
went by way of Ras-el-Ayn, and crossed the Jordan
towards Beysan (Bethsan), once Scythopolis, the third
city of Palestine, but then a small town situated in
the rich champaign beneath the naked peaks of
Mount Gilboa. The Franks meanwhile broke up
their camp at the Springs of Saffuriya, and hurried
south to protect Belvoir, a new castle near Beysan,
where they had large stores of ordnance. Following the Jordan down stream, they camped beneath
the hill of " the Star," whereon stood the ramparts
of Belvoir. Saladin was himself near Tiberias, but
he sent his two most capable generals, Taki-ed-din
and Ferrukh Shah, at the head of a large body of
horse-archers, to attack the position. The Saracens,
according to their enemies, had 20,000 men in battle
array, to their own 700 knights with their followers;
but William of Tyre would have us believe that,
thanks to the valour of the brothers Balian and
Baldwin of Ramla, and other gallant warriors, the
Christians had much the best of the skirmish, in
spite of the defection of " many whose names for

very shame we will not write." The Moslems, on the other hand, whilst admitting heavy losses, claimed the victory. Both sides retired after the battle, the Franks to Forbelet (Afrabela) and Saladin to Damascus.

The Saracens do not seem to have been disheartened; for in August Saladin led his troops in person across the Bikaa. His object was to seize Beyrut, which he hoped to surprise and storm with the assistance of his Egyptian fleet, with which his brother el-Adil was harrying the coast of Palestine. The ships bombarded Beyrut; whilst Saladin coming down from the hills, whence his scouts had signalled the fleet, directed a general attack on the land side. The arrows fell so thick that the inhabitants "dared not lift a finger," but the town was well fortified and garrisoned, and made a sturdy resistance. The Saracens, expecting to storm, had brought no mangonels for a regular siege. Moreover, King Baldwin was hastily equipping ships at Acre and Tyre for the relief of the port, and the Christian army was approaching. The surprise had failed, and Saladin, having more important affairs to attend to in the north, abandoned a leaguer which promised little success.

His change of plan is explained by the fact that he had received an invitation from Kukbury, the Emir of Harran, to enter and occupy Jezira. Any reason was good enough for Saladin, who was counting the hours till he could pay off his reckoning with the house of Zengy. At last the truce had come to an end; there were allies actually impatient to welcome him at the Great River; and the moment he could advance with honour he collected a siege-train and set out. After a feint attack on Aleppo, before which he lay but three days (19–21 September) he crossed the Euphrates at Bira. His partisans hastened to meet him. First Kukbury, whose fear of Mosil had led him to invite invasion; then Nur-ed-din of Keyfa, brought their war-bands to his colours. One after the other the cities of " the Island " fell before them. Edessa, Saruj, Rakka, Karkisiya, Nisibin, one and all bowed down, as subjects in a royal progress. In the midst of this triumph, the news came that the Franks were again foraying about Damascus. " Let them," said Saladin : " whilst they knock down villages, we are taking cities; when we come back we shall have all the more strength to fight them."

So he pushed on to Mosil, the capital of his only Moslem rival. Once more strong walls proved a match for his sappers. Karak first, then Beyrut, and now Mosil, resisted all assaults. The double ramparts were closely packed with zealous defenders, and there was not a weak joint in the armour. The place was crammed with stores, provisions, ammunition, and engines of war, providently prepared for this very emergency. Nevertheless Izz-ed-din would gladly have spared his city the rigours of a siege if an honourable arrangement could be come to; but Saladin's one persistent demand was the cession of Aleppo, which Izz-ed-din had not the will, nor perhaps the power, to force his brother to abandon. The neighbouring rulers of Armenia and

Persia vainly endeavoured to mediate; Saladin had but one answer: "Aleppo—or Mosil."

The investment was therefore begun on the 10th of November, 1182. Saladin himself took the position over against the Kinda gate; his brother Bury "Crown of Kings" (Taj-el-muluk) commanded the attack on the Imadiya gate; whilst Nur-ed-din, of Keyfa, took charge of the gate of the Bridge. All their efforts, however, made no impression on the solid masonry, and after a month of fruitless endeavour, Saladin drew off his army and marched three days to Sinjar, thinking to break the spirit of the Mosilis by reducing the surrounding country on which they depended for supplies. Sinjar made a spirited defence, and for fifteen days Saladin lay before the walls under which Constantine once fought his great battle with Sapor; but on the 30th of December the ancient city was stormed and sacked by the irritated soldiery, who broke all discipline in greed of plunder. Saladin only succeeded in protecting the governor and his officers, and sent them to Mosil with every mark of honour. After establishing a garrison at Sinjar, he prepared to meet a coalition which had been formed by the Atabeg of Mosil and the Shah of Armenia, aided by the retainers of the Prince of Maridin and troops from Aleppo. By the end of February, 1183, a large army had assembled on the plain of Harzem, below Maridin ; but, on hearing of Saladin's approach, they hastily sent messengers to treat for peace. He said they should have their answer on the plain of Harzem. The menace was sufficient. Each of the allies fled incontinently

to his own city, and when Saladin reached the rendez-
vous, there was no enemy. "They advanced like men,"
says the Chancellor; " like women they vanished."

The Atabeg had once more retreated behind the
walls of Mosil; but Saladin did not pursue him.
He abandoned all attempts upon that city for the
present, and when he had completed the organisation of his Mesopotamian conquests in his usual
system of military fiefs, he marched north, and after
eight days' siege, on the 6th of May, 1183, took the
city of Amid, in spite of the double enceinte of its
massive walls of black basalt, its iron gates, and the
natural moat formed by the crescent bend of the
Tigris. The place was full of precious spoil, of
weapons and engines of war, stores and treasure.
The famous library of "a million volumes" was
made over to the learned Chancellor, the Kady el-
Fadil, who took away a mere selection of the books
on seventy camels.* This stronghold Saladin gave
to his loyal and gallant ally the Prince of Keyfa.
At this moment, news reached him that Imad-ed-din
of Aleppo had arranged an understanding with the
Franks, and was laying fire and sword to the Sultan's
lands in Syria ; so he hurried across the Euphrates at
Bira, and, taking Ayn Tab on his way, on the 21st
encamped once more on the Green Meydan before
Aleppo. Imad-ed-din did not offer a long resistance.
He was unpopular with his new subjects, and wished
to get back to his old quarters at Sinjar. On his side,
Saladin was eager to consolidate his empire by the
acquisition of the capital of northern Syria. An

---

* Ibn-Aby-Tay, in Abu-Shama, 48.

exchange was negotiated, by which in return for the surrender of Aleppo, the principality of Sinjar, with its dependent cities of Nisibin, Saruj, and Rakka, was restored to Imad-ed-din, who was to hold it as Saladin's vassal on terms of military service.

On the 12th of June, the city was formally placed in Saladin's possession. The garrison paraded on the Green Meydan and paid him homage; a great banquet was given to celebrate the event; and general rejoicings prevailed. The people had never taken kindly to their late prince; they lamented the glorious days of Nur-ed-din, and hoped for their revival under a powerful and generous king, such as Saladin promised to be. Imad-ed-din became a butt for the scorn of the crowd, who jeered about "the ass who bartered fresh milk (in Arabic, Halab, *i.e.* Aleppo) for sour (Sinjar)," and even paraded a wash-tub before him, saying: "You were never meant for a King! Try taking in washing!" He was glad to escape from the torrent of ridicule, and taking leave of Saladin on the 17th, he departed for Sinjar, richly equipped with choice horses and robes of honour presented by his generous adversary. The next day Saladin entered Aleppo. The crowd acclaimed him; poets sang his praise. The governor entertained him with splendour in the castle, and the whole city went mad with delight: was not Saladin their King? and was there any other so mighty, so just, and so generous in all the earth?

The possession of Aleppo made Saladin the most powerful ruler of Islam. From the Tigris to the Nile, and along the African coast as far as Tripoli,

many great cities and different peoples owned his
sway. His name was prayed for in the mosques
from Mekka to Mesopotamia. When he wrote to
the Pope,* he even used the style "*Rex omnium
regum orientalium,*" and of all the eastern princes
within his reach he was undoubtedly King. But to
be incontestably supreme over this wide dominion
he must still take another step. He had nothing to
fear from the east or the north: Mosil was cowed,
and the Seljuk of Konia was friendly; but there yet
remained that narrow strip of land stretching beyond
the mountains along the Syrian coast from Antioch
to Ascalon,—the cities beyond the Orontes and the
Jordan, and the barrier heights of Lebanon,—above
all Jerusalem itself, holy to Moslems and Christians
alike. That strip of hostile territory which severed
his kingdom from the great sea; those forts and
cities and holy places, which still were gripped in
the mailed hands of his enemies; that happy valley
of the Jordan where the wooden bells of Christians
harshly clashed instead of the sweet and solemn
chant of the Muezzin—all these were as a rock of
offence to "the Sultan of Islam and of the Moslems."
Until the Holy City were once more in the keeping
of the Faithful, until the rule of the Frank were
brought low, for him at least there could be no rest.

---

* Some of Saladin's despatches have been published in Latin. One
to the Pope in 1183 acknowledges the receipt of a letter through
Oliver Vitalis in reference to captives in the war. An earlier despatch
from el-Adil to Lucius III. relates to the same subject. There are
also two letters to Frederic Barbarossa and one from the Emperor to
Saladin. They may be read in Ralph de Diceto, ed. Stubbs, ii., 25-27,
56, 57, and *Itinerarium Regis Ricardi,* i. 37-42.

CHAPTER XII.

DAMASCUS.

1183–1186.

SALADIN stayed two months at Aleppo, ordering the government, awarding offices and fiefs,
and regulating the various dependent cities and
forts. On the 14th of August, 1183, he left for
Damascus, which was to be his capital and head-
quarters for the rest of his life. Much had happened during his long absence in the north. His
brave viceroy Ferrukh Shah was dead, and the
Franks had grown bolder. They had ravaged Busra
and Zora and all the country, even to Darayya, a few
miles from Damascus, destroying the crops and orchards, and laying everything waste. They had recovered the rocky fastness in the "Suhite" of which
the Saracens had been so proud. Reginald of Châtillon had even conceived the daring project to invade Arabia, destroy the tomb of "the accursed
camel-driver" at Medina, and raze to the ground the
holy Kaaba at Mekka. He transported his ships in
sections from Ascalon to the gulf of Akaba, and
sending the fleet to sack the port of Aydhab on the

African shore of the Red Sea, with two vessels he blockaded Eyla. The Egyptian fleet was soon in hot pursuit, and Admiral Lulu, after easily relieving the blockade of Eyla, came up with the main body of the expedition near el-Haura, a small port on the Red Sea, whence they intended to march on Medina. The sight of the Egyptian squadron drove them hurriedly on shore, and they made for the mountains. Lulu mounted his sailors on the horses of the Beda-wis, and catching the enemy in the Rabugh gorge cut them to pieces. Reginald escaped, but most of his men were killed ; no quarter was given, except to a few prisoners who were sent to Mekka, to be slaughtered like goats in the valley of Mina at the annual sacrifice of the Pilgrimage.* Thus should they expiate their intended sacrilege.

The Spanish Arab, Ibn-Jubeyr, was at Alexandria in May, 1183, when some of the prisoners taken from Reginald of Châtillon's expedition were brought in, lashed on camels, their faces to the tails, amid the beating of drums and the shouts of the populace. Never, he says, had there been such consternation as when the news of the raid reached Egypt. People told each other, trembling, how the accursed lord of Karak had bribed the Bedawis to carry his ships across the desert to the Red Sea ; how he had burnt sixteen Arab vessels, seized a pilgrim-ship off Jedda, landed at Aydhab and captured a caravan that had journeyed from Kos on the Nile, every soul of which was massacred ; and how, after making prizes of two ships from the Yemen, laden with stores for the holy

---

* Ibn-el-Athir, *Kamil*, 658-9 ; Abu-Shama, 41-2.

cities, he had crossed over to Arabia with the fell design of sacking Medina and dragging the blessed Prophet out of his grave! Never was such appalling news! Allah be praised, Lulu, the captain of the fleet, caught the miscreants with his swift vessels, manned by Moors from the Maghrib, and the catastrophe was averted.

Saladin's first object on his return to Syria was to punish the Franks for their temerity. He recalled the troops whom he had allowed to go home during his rest at Aleppo, and marching south by the desert route past el-Fawar, crossed the Jordan on the 29th of September, ravaged the fertile Ghaur, and finding Beysan deserted by its terrified inhabitants, sacked and burnt it. Advancing up the valley of Jezreel, he camped by the Well of Goliath (Ayn Jalud) at the foot of Gilboa. Hence his scouts, veterans from Nur-ed-din's armies, ravaged the country round, as far as Tabor and the hills above Nazareth, captured Forbelet, and encountering a body of Franks marching from Karak to join the main army at the Springs of Saffuriya, defeated them (30 September) with the loss of only one man. On this Guy of Lusignan, who commanded during the illness of King Baldwin, immediately broke up camp, crossed the hills of Nazareth into the plain of Esdraelon, and advanced to "the castle of the Bean," el-Fula, (which the Franks called Faba and La Fève,) where Saladin gave battle.

" Never, so old men said, had Palestine seen so vast an array of Crusaders ; there were one thousand three hundred knights, and over fifteen thousand well-armed foot ; among them were great nobles from Europe : Henry, Duke of Louvain, and Ralf de Maleine from Aquitaine, together with the lords of the land, Guy de Lusignan, Reginald de Châtillon, Baldwin and Balian of Ibelin, Reginald of Sidon, Walter of Cæsarea, and Joscelin de Courtenay." *

Nevertheless the battle was indecisive. It was a hand-to-hand fight, where " eye looked into eye." Saladin's vanguard of five hundred horse did much execution, but could not penetrate the serried ranks of the enemy's spears ; and eventually both armies encamped opposite each other, at Tubania and Goliath's Well, scarcely a mile apart. Here an extraordinary delay occurred. For five days the Christian army lay motionless, whilst their leaders were wrangling amongst themselves, united only in one purpose, to defy the authority of Lusignan.† Meanwhile Saladin had occupied the heights, and the Crusaders found themselves hemmed in and cut off from supplies. Their ranks were swelled by crowds of Italian merchants, Pisans, Lombards, Venetians, and Genoese, who had left their ships and hurried to join the army of the Cross, without taking thought for food, and unaccustomed to bear arms or endure privation. These were the first to feel the pressure of fatigue and want, and as no supplies could penetrate the close ring of the watchful Saracens, a grievous famine fell upon the camp. It was mid October, too, and

---

* Archer and Kingsford, *Crusades*, 262 ; Imad-ed-din gives nearly the same numbers.

† William of Tyre, xxii., 27 ; Abu-Shama, 52 ; Ibn-el-Athir, 663.

the rainy season would soon be at hand. Saladin
seems to have tried every device to bring them to the
fighting point, but in vain : they contrived at last to
escape, pursued by his arrows, and retreated in
shame to Saffuriya, whence they had set out in
glorious array but a week before.

In the same month of October the Sultan left
Damascus to settle his score with Reginald of Châtillon at Karak ; but all attempts to capture that
crafty freelance or to gain an entrance into his fortress failed, though an Egyptian army under el-Adil
co-operated in the siege. Their seven mangonels
played in vain upon the stout walls, and when
it was known that the royal forces were marching to
its relief, Saladin drew off his army (4 December)
and fuming at the repulse led it back to Damascus.
In the following summer (13 August, 1184) he made
another effort to reduce the fortress, for there could
be no peace so long as Reginald of Châtillon held it ;
but the siege—the fifth that Saladin had begun—
ended like all the rest. At first, indeed, it seemed
as if success were about to crown the perseverance
of the Saracens. The town was in no mood for
battle : it was full of dancers and musicians, making
merry for the wedding of the King's half-sister Isabella with the fourth Humphrey of Toron. The wedding feasts were like to be turned into funeral rites.
Saladin and his mamluks forced their way into the
town, and Reginald retreated over the fosse into the
castle. Even so he hardly escaped, and but for
the valour of a solitary knight, who held the bridge
like Horatius of old, whilst the garrison sawed it be-

hind him, the fort must have fallen to the Saracens.
In curious illustration of the chivalrous manners of
the time, Reginald sent Saladin meat and wine,—as
it were a piece of the bridecake,—to share in the
feast; and in return the Sultan gave strict orders,
proclaimed to the army, that the nuptial tower of
the bride and bridegroom should be scrupulously respected by his archers and artillery! *

Saladin found himself in possession of the town
and suburb, and master of every sort of festal luxury
and wedding cates; but he was as far as ever from
taking the castle. He began indeed to fill up the
fosse and to set up his engines; and his faithful ally,
Nur-ed-din of Keyfa, showed himself brilliantly in
combats with the garrison. Nine mangonels bombarded the gate and burst it open, but the enemy
held the breach. The fosse was so far filled that a
prisoner was able to jump from the ramparts and
escape. But it was labour thrown away: the rock
defied assault. Meanwhile couriers had carried the
news to Baldwin, and in September a relieving force
stationed at el-Wala, without risking a pitched battle,
supplied the castle with food and tired out the besiegers. Saladin abhorred a waiting game, and fail-
ing to draw the Christians from their entrenchments,
soon decamped from his positions at Heshbon and
Main, and went off to lay waste Samaria, pillage and
burn Nablus (Shechem) with its famous olive groves
and melons, and thence returned to Damascus on
the 16th of September, 1184.

After this there was peace between Saracen and

* Ernoul, 103.

Christian for a time. King Baldwin's misery came
to an end in the winter of 1184–5. The crown was
now on the head of a child, and Guy of Lusignan
and Raymond of Tripolis, the Regent of the infant
Baldwin V., headed rival factions. It was no time
for a Holy War, said the old Crusading houses;
better to make a truce and at least wait till a favourable occasion. So thought the Prince of Antioch,
the Counts of Tripolis and Sidon, and the brave
brothers of Ibelin. So did not think the two great
fighting Orders of the Temple and the Hospital;
nor new-comers like Guy of Lusignan, though his
only campaign had been a ridiculous farce; much
less Reginald of Châtillon, who still felt, at his stronghold of Karak, the iron of his unforgotten chains
eating into his soul, and thirsted unquenchably for
revenge. For the present the prudent policy prevailed, and at the Regent's motion a treaty was concluded with Saladin for four years. With Raymond
himself it was more than a truce; it was an offensive
and defensive alliance. Saladin was to support him
in his designs on the crown, and Raymond in return
set free all the Saracens he held captive in Tripolis,
and even supplied Damascus liberally with food
during the dearth of 1185. Nevertheless, whatever
the amity of Saladin and Raymond, the truce was
like the troubled sleep of a soldier, which might be
broken in an instant by the call to arms. It was no
real peace whilst the Patriarch Heraclius scoured
Europe to beat up recruits, whilst English knights
from the Cheviots to the Pyrenees took the Cross,
whilst the two great Military Orders were burning

to strike a blow for the faith.   The Holy War was
sleeping, but it was sure to awake.

Saladin, meanwhile, made the most of his leisure
to set the affairs of his realm in order.   Once more
Damascus had become the seat of sovereignty.
Saladin used to say that Syria was the Root and
Basis of Empire : Julian had called Damascus the
Eye of the East.   Before the beginning of history,
Damascus was a city.   From the time when Abram
took his servant Eliezer from among its citizens the
ancient Syrian capital has been renowned.   In the
days of Ezekiel its commerce was famous, and to
the port of Tyre it was written : " Damascus was thy
merchant in the multitude of the wares of thy
making, for the multitude of all riches."   In all the
ancient empires of the East, Damascus has played
its part, as the natural metropolis of its region, the
meeting-place of the people.   Through its busy
markets passed the trade of Babylonia and Persia
and furthest India, borne from immemorial days by
endless caravans, journeying from the Euphrates by
Palmyra or Aleppo, and carrying their precious bales
onward to the Mediterranean ports, or turning south
to Egypt and Arabia.   To Damascus came the
wandering nation of the Bedawis in their countless
tribes, who grazed their flocks in spring and winter
on the light fodder of the desert, roaming every year
between Arabia and the Great River along the
familiar chains of wells ; a race of cattle-dealers and
camel-drivers, carriers of other men's wealth and
sellers of their own pastoral produce in exchange for
the goods of the merchants.

Rich and populous, Damascus owed all to its central situation and its natural advantages. The Greeks called it "Most Beauteous," Καλλίστη, and the Arabs named it " The Bride of the Earth," " The Garden of the World." And looking down upon the ancient city from the Dome of Victory which crowns the near range of Antilibanus on the west, one understands the pride of the Damascene in his earthly Paradise. The famed level plain, the Ghuta, richly fertile, though it forms part of the high Syrian plateau rising two thousand feet above the sea, gains in beauty by contrast with the brown desert and the girdling rocky hills, through which the Barada, well-named " Gold-streaming " by the Greeks, forces its path, and spreading in seven streams over the plain gives it abundant life. A great green field stretches for miles from the mountains to the desert, and in its midst, in an emerald girdle of gardens and orchards, of orange and citron and jessamine, in a babel of gurgling brooks, rise the old Roman walls of the city, the yellow sea of its clay houses, a forest of minarets, and the great dome of the Omayyad Mosque, once the Church of St. John the Baptist, and before that, perhaps, the House of Rimmon.* " Though old as history itself, thou art fresh as the breath of Spring, blooming as thine own rosebud, fragrant as thine own orange flower, O Damascus, Pearl of the East ! "

Every age of its varied history has left its vestiges in Damascus :—Roman gates of polished red sand-

* The city has been well described by Kremer and Dr. Wright, and there are charming verbal pictures in Lady Burton's books.

stone, and doors plated with heavy iron; ancient walls fifteen feet thick and twenty high, built upon still older foundations of cyclopean masonry; square bastion towers, whence medieval archers drove back many a storming party by their flanking fire. The *Via Recta*, "the street which is called Straight," still leads from the east gate, as it did in the time when St. Paul was yet Saul of Tarsus; and on a wall of the Arab Mosque the pilgrim to the tomb of Saladin may still read the inscription which overhung the lintel of the older Church, and which thirteen centuries of Moslem rule have not erased:

Η· ΒΑCΙΛΕΙΑ· CΟΥ· Χ̄Ε̄· ΒΑCΙΛΕΙΑ· ΠΑΝΤΩΝ· ΤΩΝ· ΑΙΟΝΩΝ· ΚΑΙ· Η· ΔΕCΠΟΤΙΑ· CΟΥ· ΕΝ· ΠΑCΗ· ΓΕΝΕΑΙ ΚΑΙ ΓΕΝΕΑΙ

"Thy kingdom, O Christ, is an everlasting kingdom, and thy dominion endureth throughout all generations." *

The city in Saladin's time must have shown much the same mixture of colours and races as now. The dress and customs of the Moslems change very slowly, and the same peoples, clad in the same way for many centuries, must have thronged its bazars, and dwelt in the exquisitely carved and painted rooms round the shaded courts of the houses. Then, as now, the city was divided into numerous walled quarters, closed at night by heavy gates, and occupied originally by members of a separate clan. Then, as now, the clear water of the Golden Stream flowed through a network of carefully planned

* Ps. cxlv., 13.

DOME OF OMAYYAD MOSQUE AT DAMASCUS.

channels, and was brought to every street and even to the poorest houses. But invasion and fire, Tatar vandalism and Ottoman neglect, have dimmed the splendour of the mosques and palaces; and now even the noble Omayyad Mosque, where the great Caliphs of the seventh century preached as leaders of the faithful, where Moawiya held up before the trembling congregation the bloody shirt of the murdered Othman, and pinned Naila's severed fingers to the pulpit,—the mosque where Saladin worshipped the God of Battles, has been seared and ruined by a consuming fire. Its mosaics were the triumph of artists from Persia, India, and Byzantium, and exhausted the revenues of Syria for seven years, besides eighteen shiploads of gold and silver from Cyprus.

The Spanish Arab, Ibn-Jubeyr, who visited Damascus in 1184, when Saladin was living there, has left us a minute description of the wonders of this marvellous mosque, not least among which was the clock in which brazen falcons struck the hours, and a brass door shut for each hour past, whilst at night red lamps marked the time, measured by subsiding water. He mentions twenty colleges, two free hospitals, and many monasteries.

"Damascus," he adds, "possesses a castle, where the Sultan lives, and it stands isolated in the modern quarter of the city, and in it is the Sultan's mosque. Near the castle, outside the town towards the west, are two Meydans that are like pieces of silk brocade rolled out, for their greenness and beauty. The river flows between the two Meydans, and there is a grove of poplar-trees extending beside them, most beautiful to behold. The

Sultan is wont to go out there to play the game of Mall
and to race his horses ; and nothing can be pleasanter
to see than this.   Every evening the Sultan's sons go
out there to shoot the bow, and to race, and to play
Mall." *

The Spanish traveller gives us but a glimpse of
the great Sultan, playing polo on the silky lawn of
the Meydan, nor do Saladin's biographers and
chroniclers tell us much more.   We hear indeed of
evenings spent in literary discussions, of Saladin's
intimacy with the old warrior-poet Osama, of recitations of poetry, and of frequent games at chess, to
which the Sultan was passionately devoted.†   But
the echoes of these voices are faint indeed.   To gain
a picture of a Moslem ruler's life and occupations
in Crusading times we must turn to the historian of
the Mamluk Sultans, and see how Beybars, Sultan of
Syria and Egypt, kept his state in the thirteenth
century.   He was a mamluk of Saladin's family, and
he modelled his court upon the example set by his
great predecessor.

The Sultan of those days enjoyed no sinecure; he
was as hard a worker as his meanest subject.   He
sat in the Hall of Justice two days in the week to

---

* Ibn-Jubeyr, in Le Strange, *Palestine under the Muslims*, 255.
Mall or polo was an ancient Persian game, there called *chogan*, and
by the Byzantine Greeks *tzukanion* (τζουκάνιον).   Saladin was
famous for his skill at polo, but he is said to have ridden too reck-
lessly after the ball, like his father (*Kitab er-Raudateyn ;* see Quatre-
mère's admirable dissertation, *Hist. des Sultans Mamlouks*, i, 121–
132).

† Abu-Shama (Cairo text), i., 252, 264, 270 ; H. Derembourg. *Vie
d'Ousama*, 369, 396,   *Cp*. Lessing, *Nathan der Weise*, Act ii., Sc. 1.

hear the complaints and right the wrongs of his subjects. His correspondence was immense, and though
Saladin had indefatigable chancellors and secretaries
in the Kady el-Fadil, Imad-ed-din, and latterly Baha-
ed-din, he must have taken a large personal share in
the despatches. In Beybars' time there was

" a well-organised system of posts, connecting every
part of his wide dominions with the capital. Relays of
horses were in readiness at each post-house, and twice a
week the Sultan received and answered reports from all
parts of the realm. Besides the ordinary mail, there
was also a pigeon post, which was no less carefully managed. The pigeons were kept in cots at the various
stages, and the bird was trained to stop at the first post-
cot, where its letter would be attached to another pigeon
for the next stage."

Fortunately we know something of Saladin's chief
secretaries who managed his vast correspondence.
What el-Jawad was to the warlike Zengy, the
learned judge, Kady el-Fadil, was to the wider imperial administration of Saladin. El-Fadil was not
a Turk or a Persian, like so many of the statesmen
of that time, but a pure Lakhmy Arab, born at Ascalon, a member of a family of judges. His colleague
in the Council, Aluh, extols his exquisite style—then
considered a prime qualification in a Secretary of
State—in his own inflated manner:

" Sovereign of the pen and lucidity, of eloquence and
of style, his genius was resplendent, his sagacity profound, and his diction as novel as it was fascinating. . . .
He was like Mohammed's law, which annulled all others

and became the root of all knowledge. His thought was original, his ideas were new ; he showered forth brilliance, and put forth the fairest flowers. He it was who led the empire by his counsels, and threaded discourse with the pearls of style," and so forth.

In spite of fine writing, and much curious euphuism, the Kady was an admirable public servant, and Saladin frequently left him in supreme charge of the government in Egypt whilst himself absent on campaigns in Syria. Egypt, indeed, was his adopted country ; there Saladin found him in the chancery office ; and he was never happy away from his beloved Nile. " Bear me a message to the Nile," he cries in one of his poems, written during a campaign in Mesopotamia ; " tell it that Euphrates can never quench my thirst."

Another learned man, whose advice, it is said, Saladin never rejected, was el-Hakkary, the Arab jurist, who treated his master with an unceremonious familiarity which none other dared to use. His quaint figure, with the lawyer's turban surmounting a soldier's uniform, was seldom absent from the Sultan's councils. But Saladin's right-hand man in Syria, the counterpart of the Kady el-Fadil in Egypt, was the Secretary of State Imad-ed-din of Ispahan, commonly called Aluh (" Eagle "),—a poet, a master of style, a doctor learned in the law and deep in the mysteries of astrology, and a formidable gladiator in theological polemics. From being merely a professor at the college at Damascus to which he gave his name, " The Imadiya," he became President of the Council of State and Chancellor of the Syrian kingdom. His admirable skill in conducting diplomatic correspondence in Persian and Arabic, in the turgid and inflated style admired by Orientals, added to his learning and sagacity, made him invaluable to the Sultan who finally gave him his entire confidence.

Besides necessary business, state ceremonies formed a heavy burden upon the Sultan. The medieval Muslim court was minutely organised, and the selection of officers to fill the numerous household posts, the allaying of their jealousies and quarrels, the rewarding of their services with robes of honour, titles, and fiefs, cost time and thought. Everybody, from the Commander-in-Chief to the Cupbearer, Taster, and Polo-master, wanted something, or envied some-one else, and must be attended to, however summarily, in the interests of general good humour and loyalty.

Reviews of troops and state progresses were matters which involved much ceremony. The Sultan him-self (at the time of Beybars at least) rode in the midst of the procession, dressed in a plain black silk tunic with large sleeves, a turban over his steel cap, a hauberk under his tunic, and a long Arab sword at his side. In front some great noble displayed the royal saddle-cloth, covered with precious stones and gold brocade; and the Sultan's head was shaded by the state parasol of yellow silk with gold embroidery, crowned with a golden eagle, and carried by a prince of the blood, whilst another noble bore the imperial standard. The royal horse was housed in yellow silk and red atlas satin, and the regimental colours of the escort were also of yellow Cairo silk, embroidered with their colonel's badge.

"Just before the Sultan rode two pages on white horses, with rich trappings ; their robes were of yellow silk with borders of gold brocade, and a *kuffiya* or kerchief of the same. It was their duty to see that the road was sound. A flute-player went before, and a singer followed after, chanting the heroic deeds of former kings, to the accompaniment of a drum ; poets sang verses antiphonally, accompanying themselves with the *kemenga* and *mosil*. Tabardars carried halberds before and behind the Sultan, and the state-poniards were supported by the polo-master in a scabbard on the left, while another dagger with a buckler was carried on the monarch's right. Close beside him rode the macebearer, who carried the golden mace aloft, and never withdrew his eyes from the countenance of his master. The great officers of the court followed with hardly less pomp.

"When a halt was called for the night, on long journeys, torches were borne before the Sultan, and as he approached the tent, which had gone on in front and been pitched before his arrival, his servants came to meet him with wax candles in stands inlaid with gold ; pages and halberdiers surrounded him, the soldiers sang a chorus, and all dismounted except the Sultan, who rode into the vestibule of the tent, where he left his horse, and then entered the great round pavilion behind it. Out of this opened a little wooden bedroom, warmer than the tent, and a bath with heating materials was at hand. The whole was surrounded by a stockade, and the mamluks mounted guard in regular watches, inspected periodically by visiting rounds, with Grand Rounds twice in the night." *

We do not know how much of this state ceremo-

---

* S. Lane-Poole, *Cairo*, 3rd. ed., 1898, 82–90, etc.

nial was observed by Saladin, but, however simple
his own tastes might be, no Oriental sovereign could
afford to neglect those outward trappings which
have always produced a vivid impression of power
upon the popular imagination, especially in the East
where symbolism is peculiarly studied. Saladin,
though he dressed very simply in linen or wool,
doubtless maintained all the usual state of a Mohammedan King, and would be careful to display
the full court ceremonies when receiving embassies
from foreign princes. It was on such an occasion
that he first met Baha-ed-din, who afterwards became his secretary and biographer. Baha-ed-din
was a resident at Mosil when Saladin invaded Mesopotamia, and had been employed by the Atabeg to
carry an appeal for help to the Caliph at Baghdad.
When Saladin was settled at Damascus, Baha-ed-din
was again sent on a diplomatic mission. He was
empowered by his sovereign, the Atabeg of Mosil,
with the approval of the Caliph, to arrange terms of
amity with Saladin. He arrived at Damascus on the
25th of February, 1184, accompanied by Bedr-ed-
din, the " Sheykh of Sheykhs," and was received by
the Sultan with every mark of gracious hospitality.
Although unable to come to any arrangement, he
impressed Saladin so favourably that he offered him
a post in his own service. Baha-ed-din, as ambassador of a rival prince, could not accept the honour,
and the mission departed on its return to Mosil on
the 22nd of March.*

Other embassies followed, from the Atabeg's

---

* The ambassador did not join Saladin as his secretary till 1188.

nephew, Sinjar-Shah of Jezira, and from the lord
of Irbil (Arbela), who did homage as vassals of the
Sultan. The Prince of Mosil naturally resented these
defections and set about chastising the Irbil chief,
whose appeal eventually brought Saladin again into
the field. Crossing the Euphrates as usual at Bira, on
the 15th of April, 1185, he was joined by Kukbury,
and at Ras-el-Ayn he learnt that there was a general
coalition of the eastern princes to defend the Atabeg
of Mosil. Disregarding their threats, he marched onwards to Duneysir at the foot of the hill of Maridin,
the troops of which joined him, and arrived before
Mosil in June, 1185. In vain the Atabeg sent his
mother and other great ladies to humble themselves
before him and pray for peace. They were received
with all deference, but no promise was given : Saladin
was inflexible.

Prepared for the worst, the Mosilis exerted themselves with the strength of desperation, and the
siege proved as fruitless as before. A dispute in
Armenia furnished an excuse for withdrawing the
exhausted army away to the cooler climate of Diyar-
Bekr. Saladin occupied Mayyafarikin at the end of
August, and then returned to the siege of Mosil.
But now the rainy season had followed the burning
heats of summer, and neither the general nor the
troops were able to support the unhealthy climate.
Saladin became seriously ill, and was forced to remove to Harran for change of air ; scarcely able to
sit his horse, he arrived nearly dead at his friend
Kukbury's castle. His brother el-Adil hastened
from Aleppo with the court physicians, but for a

long time Saladin lingered between life and death. At one time the rumour spread that the end had come, and many a kinsman weighed his own chance of succession. Saladin himself gave up hope, and assembling his captains made them take the oath of fidelity to his sons.

At last he began very slowly to recover, and by the end of February, 1186, he was able to receive an embassy from Mosil, headed by Baha-ed-din, who came to treat for peace. Too weak as yet to dream of a campaign, and softened perhaps by suffering and danger, Saladin consented to a treaty (3 March), by which he took all the country about Shahrzur, beyond the Zab, but left the Atabeg Izz-ed-din in possession of the territory he then governed, between the great rivers, subject to his fully acknowledging the Sultan's sovereignty in the prayers and on the coinage. By this treaty the whole of northern Mesopotamia and part of Kurdistan were joined to Saladin's empire, and the Atabeg of Mosil swelled the muster of his vassals.*

Slowly returning from Harran to Damascus, Saladin paused at Emesa. He had lately given the city in fief to his cousin Nasir-ed-din, son of Shirkuh, whose kinship had been strengthened by marriage

---

* Coins in the British Museum show that Saladin's name appeared as suzerain on the currency of the following vassal lords in the years stated : the prince of Maridin (Yuluk-Arslan) in A.H., 581, 583, 584, 585, 586, or A.D. 1185–90 ; the prince of Keyfa (Sukman) in A.H. 581, 584, or A.D. 1185–8 : the prince of Jezira (Sinjar Shah) in A.H. 584, 585, or A.D. 1188–9 ; the lord of Irbil (Kukbury) in A.H. 587, A.D. 1191 ; and the Atabeg of Mosil in A.H. 585, 586, 587, or A.D. 1189–91. See the Plate of coins, next page.

13

with one of Saladin's daughters.   Nevertheless, during his cousin's illness, Nasir-ed-din had intrigued for
the throne of Syria.   Retribution followed swiftly;
for retiring, full of wine and good cheer, on the Feast
of the Victims (4 March, 1186), the pretender was
found dead in his bed next morning. *   On his way
to the city Saladin was met by the son, a boy of
twelve, whom he had appointed to his father's fief;
appropriating, however, for the purposes of State a
large part of the father's treasure.   It is related that
Saladin was kind to the boy, and interested himself
in his studies.   But when he questioned him about
his reading, and asked how far he had gone in the
Koran, the child replied, " As far as the place where
it is written, *As to those who swallow up the goods
of orphans unjustly ; verily they shall swallow down
fire into their bellies and burn at the Blaze.*" †
The Sultan marvelled at the boy's quickness, and
did not rebuke his presumption.   Leaving him in
possession of Emesa, he went on to Aleppo and
thence in April to Damascus, where he was welcomed with tumultuous rejoicings, like another
Lazarus come back from the grave.

---

* The improbable suggestion of Ibn-el-Athir that he was poisoned
by Saladin's orders hardly deserves notice.

† *Koran*, iv., 9.

$\dfrac{1}{\text{Æ}}$

THE PRINCE OF KEYFA.

$\dfrac{2}{\text{Æ}}$

THE PRINCE OF MARIDIN.

$\dfrac{3}{\text{Æ}}$

KUKBURY, LORD OF IRBIL.

$\dfrac{4}{\text{Æ}}$

THE ATABEG OF MOSIL.

COINS OF SALADIN'S VASSALS.

PART IV.

THE HOLY WAR.

1187–1191.

CHAPTER XIII.

THE BATTLE OF HITTIN.

1187.

THE great crisis was at hand. Saladin was at last in a position to attack the Franks. The object of his campaigns on the Tigris and Euphrates had been attained. He had now allies instead of enemies on his northern flank. Before this no invasion of the Christian territory could safely be undertaken without posting an army of observation to guard against an attack from the north; but now he could advance with confidence. He had also more troops at his back, and could not only command the full strength of his Syrian and Egyptian levies, but also count upon large contingents from the Mesopotamian provinces. We shall see how at the siege of Acre the great barons of these parts came to reinforce the Moslem army, and how the princes of Zengy's line, the lords of Mosil, Sinjar, Jezira, Irbil, and Harran, and the Kurds from beyond the Tigris, swelled the general muster with their vassals and retainers. This was indeed the most important result

of his northern campaigns. He had opened up new
recruiting grounds; and without this added strength
he could never have met and resisted the fresh forces
from Europe brought against him in the Third
Crusade.

The Holy War had long been a fixed resolve with
Saladin, but the immediate provocation came, as
usual, from Reginald of Châtillon. The lord of
Karak had won for himself an unenviable reputation
as a breaker of treaties. It was his delight to seize
peaceful caravans of merchants and pilgrims on their
way into Syria from Egypt or Mekka. He had done
this in 1179, in a time of truce. A caravan encamped
trustfully beneath his castle, and he took every man,
woman, and beast, with goods to the value of two
hundred thousand gold pieces; and when King Baldwin remonstrated, and sent an embassy to make him
restore the stolen spoil and captives, he flouted the
royal messengers. In 1182 he repeated this performance, also in a time of truce—"aussi com il avoit
autrefois fait en trives" *; he had even dared to push
his troops into Arabia to within a day's march of the
holy city where rest the bones of the Blessed Prophet. In 1186 there was again a time of peace.
Caravans passed freely between Egypt and Syria,
with no thought of danger from the Dead Sea castle.
Suddenly Reginald pounced upon a party of merchants and captured a rich prize. One of the Sultan's
sisters was rumoured to be travelling in the closed

---

* This is the admission of the Christian chroniclers (*e. g.*, Ernoul,
54–5, 96–7, and the *Itinerarium*, i., 5), who are confirmed by the
Moslem historians ; see above, pp. 166, 175–7.

litter under the convoy of the traders. To their remonstrances the lord of Karak jeeringly echoed the
taunts of the chief priests at Calvary: "Since they
trusted in Mohammad, let Mohammad come and
save them!" A year later he had bitter cause to
repent his jest. On hearing of the outrage, Saladin
swore a great oath that he would kill the truce-breaker
with his own hand; and the vow was kept.

"The taking of that caravan was the ruin of Jerusalem." Saladin had repeatedly sought to reduce
Karak and lay hands upon its master, and he had
always failed. He was now resolved to try no more
half-measures, but to wage a war of extermination
on the whole Christian kingdom. The winter must
first pass, when field operations were almost impossible; but in March, 1187, he sounded the tocsin for
the *Jihad.* His messengers sped to the princes of
Mesopotamia, to his vassals and viceroys and governors in the cities of Jezira, Diyar-Bekr, Syria, and
Egypt, to bid them assemble their forces for the
Holy War. Troop after troop hurried to Damascus,
and each as it arrived was posted on the frontier
against the Franks. The Sultan himself marched
out towards Karak, in April, to protect the caravan
of pilgrims returning from Mekka. After they had
safely passed, and he had laid waste the territory of
his bitterest enemy, he set up his standard at Ashtara
on the 28th of May, and marshalled his squadrons
for the great campaign.

The Franks were in no state for combined resistance. There was strife and jealousy among their
leaders. The child king, Baldwin V., had died in

the preceding September, and a faction headed by
Gerard de Rideford, the Master of the Templars,
Joscelin of Courtenay, and Reginald of Châtillon,
set on the throne Sibylla, the elder daughter of
Amalric ; and she in turn crowned her husband Guy
de Lusignan as King.   Count Raymond of Tripolis,
the regent of the late King, repudiating this irregu-
lar coronation, set up a rival sovereign in the fourth
Humphrey of Toron, the husband of Amalric's
younger daughter Isabella.   It is true, Humphrey
mistrusted the unwelcome honour, and hastened to
do homage to Sibylla and Guy ; but Raymond and
Baldwin of Ramla nevertheless refused to recognise
the new King.   It was Raymond who had made the
treaty with Saladin in 1184, and the relations between the two became exceedingly friendly now that
the Count was almost isolated from his fellow nobles.
Raymond visited Saladin, and was received with
cordiality.   It was even rumoured that the Count
would have embraced Islam but for dread of European contempt.   When Guy prepared to invade the
Count's territory and conquer his submission by
arms, it was on Saladin's promised help that Raymond relied.*   The invasion was deferred, however,
by prudent mediation, and the Count nursed his
resentment at Tiberias during the winter of 1186–7.

In the spring a fresh effort was made to restore
harmony, and Balian of Ibelin was sent to Tiberias,
with the Masters of the two Orders, to conciliate the

---

* Imad-ed-din, Abu-Shama, in Goergens, 58 ; Ibn-el-Athir, *Kamil*,
675 ; Ernoul, 141, who even states that Saladin sent a body of Saracens to Tiberias to strengthen Raymond's garrison.

sulking Achilles. Ernoul, who accompanied Balian
as his squire, has left a graphic narrative of the
expedition in his chronicle.* He tells how Balian
was detained at Nablus, whilst the others pressed on
to Faba ; how he stopped again at Sabat to visit
the bishop and hear mass ; and how when he reached
Faba he found the castle gates wide open, and his
companions' tents deserted. He sent Ernoul into
the empty fortress, and the squire went up and down
the passages shouting and hallooing, but no man answered. At last he found two sick men in a chamber, but they could tell him nothing of what had
happened. So he rode on towards Nazareth, and on
the way a brother of the Temple hailed him. When
he came up, Balian asked him "What news?" and
the Templar said "Bad." Then he told them that
the Master of the Hospital had had his head cut off,
that all the Templars with him had been killed, save
only the Master and two others, and that forty of the
King's knights were prisoners in the Saracens' hands.

It appeared that Saladin had sent forward his
eldest son, el-Afdal, to the Lake of Tiberias, where
his friend Count Raymond was still in open enmity
with the King of Jerusalem. El-Afdal, as an ally,
asked permission to cross the Jordan and make an
excursion in Raymond's territory. What his object
was is not stated † ; he may have been in want of

---

* Ernoul, 148–152.

† It is not stated by Ernoul, who is the best authority on this
point. The anonymous author of the contemporary *Libellus de Expugnatione Terrae Sanctae per Saladinum* makes it an expedition in
force, 7000 strong (ed. Stevenson, in the Ralph of Coggeshall volume,
Rolls Series, 210). Ibn-el-Athir, who was not with the army, says

forage or food, possibly he merely wished for a day's
hunting—for every prince of the land at that time
was a sportsman ; but it has more the look of a re-
connaissance in force.   Raymond could not refuse
him leave, without risking the loss of Saladin's friendship, his best protection against King Guy.   Yet to
diminish the danger of the excursion, he stipulated
that the Saracens should cross and return in a single
day, by sunlight, and that they should molest neither
town nor house on the way.   To this they agreed.
The Count sent messengers to announce the excursion and its conditions, and to warn every Christian
to keep within walls.

All would have been well but for the inopportune
arrival of the two Masters at Faba. Unluckily, as it befell, one of Raymond's messengers brought the news
to the castle at the very moment when they were
resting there, and full of righteous wrath they collected as many knights as they could, to the number
of 130, and 300 or 400 foot, and sallied forth to attack
the roving Saracens.   They, at least, would have no
pact with the " infidels."   They came up with them
at the Spring of Cresson,* whilst they were already

---

(678) that Saladin ordered el-Afdal to lay waste the country towards
Acre, and that el-Afdal did not go himself, but sent Kukbury of
Harran and two other emirs of note, with 7000 horsemen.   El-
Afdal's absence is confirmed by the statement that the battle of
Hittin was his first set battle ; but this statement also comes from
Ibn-el-Athir.   El-Afdal perhaps would not have dignified the skirmish
at Cresson by the name of *masāff* or set battle.   His presence or ab-
sence, however, does not affect the story.

* Cresson, Kerson, Kelson, Quelson, as different MSS. spell it, is
not named by the Arabic historians, who place the skirmish at Saf-

on their way back from Cana of Galilee to their own
country. It was not the first nor yet the last time
that the hot-headed zeal of the soldier-monks brought
about their own destruction. The knights rashly
attacked, in their haste, without waiting for the infantry,—and were utterly cut to pieces. The Saracens quietly continued their march to the Jordan,
and as they passed near Tiberias, Raymond could
distinguish Christian heads carried on their spears.
They had strictly kept their word. They had done
no injury to town or house or castle, and they
went back before sunset as was agreed.* This was
Friday the 1st of May, the Feast of St. Philip and
St. James.

In the face of this disaster, for which he was held
responsible, Raymond consented to waive his resentment and made outward peace with Guy. They
embraced in the presence of a rejoicing multitude
by Joseph's Pit, and concerted measures of defence.
It was ordered that a general muster of the Christian
forces should be held at the Springs of Saffuriya, about
three miles north of Nazareth, to resist the invasion
of the Saracens. The Master of the Temple made
over to Guy the money which King Henry of England had sent him, in expiation of the martyrdom
of Becket; and the men who were paid with this
treasure wore the arms of England on their shields.
The total muster may have amounted to 1200 knights,

---

furiya, nor is it found on the maps. It was probably on the road to
Tiberias.

* Ernoul, 146, 148, who was on the spot. The *Libellus de Expugn.*,
211, contradicts this

more than 18,000 foot, and a large number of light cavalry, or Turcopoles, armed in the Saracen manner.*

Meanwhile Saladin, as has been seen, returning from the Dead Sea district, had mustered his troops at Ashtara, in the Hauran, and, with the army of Aleppo and the contingents from Mosil and Maridin added to his main force, he found himself at the head of 12,000 horsemen, " all holders of fiefs and stipends," besides numerous volunteers for " the Path of God." He reviewed the troops at Tesil, and marshalled his army in the usual order of battle, with centre, right and left wings, vanguard and rearguard; Taki-ed-din and Kukbury commanded the two wings, whilst the Sultan himself led the centre. In this formation he began his march on the 26th of June, 1187. It was a Friday, at the hour of public prayer; and this was the day and the hour that he preferred above all others for warfare, that the supplications of the people and the prayers of holy men might intercede for him at the throne of God. The Saracen army camped the first night at el-Ukhuwana at the southern end of the Lake of Galilee. Here Saladin waited, whilst his scouts were collecting information as to the enemy's positions. They brought word of the great muster of the Franks at Saffuriya, and their martial spirit. A council of war was held in the Moslem camp, and it was resolved to advance and offer battle. The

---

* So the *De Expugn.*, 218, where we read of " Turcopulos innumerabiles." These may have raised the total to the 50,000 reckoned by Imad-ed-din (Abu-Shama, 70), but this estimate is probably excessive. Twenty-five or thirty thousand is more likely. The Turcopoles were evidently ineffective.

next step was to cross the Jordan to es-Sinnebra, whence Saladin moved his men to the hills at Kafar Sebt,* some six miles to the south-west of Tiberias, and commanding the road, on Wednesday, the 1st of July. Whilst waiting for the Franks to advance, he employed his troops in sacking and burning the city of Tiberias,† no longer the home of an ally. The castle itself held out under Count Raymond's wife, Eschiva, the daughter of Hugh of St. Omer. Her appeal for help reached Guy, at Saffuriya, on Thursday evening, at vespers, and caused the immediate advance of the Franks. Saladin's outposts brought news of their approach the next morning, and leaving a small force to mask the castle, he hurried up to the main army on the hills and prepared for battle.

The country where the memorable battle of Hittin was fought has been picturesquely described by an officer who knows every inch of the ground.‡

" Saffuriya," he writes, " was an unwalled town on the low hills north-west of Nazareth. The Church of St. Anne stood in the midst, and a strong tower on the hill above overlooked the brown cornfields which stretched towards the rugged mountain chain of Upper Galilee, and eastwards to the plain over Tiberias—an open and waterless plateau. The Fountain of Saffuriya lay a mile towards the south, in an open valley full of gardens, with

---

* According to an eyewitness quoted by Abu-Shama, 69, 70.

† Ibn-el-Athir, 681. Henceforward all references to this historian are to his *Kamil* (not his *Atabegs*).

‡ Lieutenant-Colonel C. R. Conder, R. E., in his *Latin Kingdom of Jerusalem* (1897), 148–150. The spelling of Arabic names has been assimilated to that used in this book.

a stream which now drives eight mills, and which, therefore, was sufficient for so large an army as that which
gathered round King Guy. The surrounding lands also
were full of villages, and gave ample provisions.

"Saladin's camp was ten miles to the east, upon the
plateau near [or rather stretching considerably south
of] the little village of Hittin. The place was surrounded with olives and fruit-trees, and a good spring
—copious and fresh—flowed on the north-west into the
gorge of Wady Hammam. There was plenty of water
in the valleys beneath, and near Tiberias, where the wife
of Raymond of Tripolis was shut up in her castle upon
the margin of the sacred lake. Just south of Hittin
rises the dark and rocky hillock famous in history as
the 'Horn of Hittin,' six hundred feet above the low-
lying village, and overlooking the western plain a hundred feet below. The highway from Acre led over the
plain, and not a single spring or stream of any size existed between the camps. It was the hottest season of
the year, and a long march for infantry divided the
hosts of Christendom and Islam.

"From the peak of Hittin the watchman looked
towards the west over a sunburnt plain, with long grey
ridges dotted with bush to north and south. Behind
him lay the Lake of Galilee seventeen hundred feet below, shut in with precipices mirrored in its shining
waters, with Hermon on the north rising snow-streaked
over the valley of the Upper Jordan. Far east the
craters of the Jaulan range stood up against the plains
which stretch towards Damascus. The towers of Safed
rose above the northern shores of the lake, and to the
south the black walls and ditches of Belvoir frowned
upon the rolling plateau. Defeat in such a position
meant disaster to the Moslem forces, hurled down the

Jacob's Ford

R. Jordan

SAFED

G A L I L E E

Eltharon

Hitten

Kara Hitin

TIBERIAS

El Ukhuwana

Siyaneby Bridge

Yarmuk R.

R. Jordan

Wady el Moallaka

Lubia

PLAIN OF TORAN

Kafar Seba

BELVOIR Kaukab

Sudmuriya

Maresella

Kana

Deburiya

Mt Tabor

PLAIN OF BUTTAUF

El Ayadiya

Tell Keysan

Mt Turan

Semunieh

Shefaïm

El Kharyuba

Nazareth

Tubaniya

Beysan

Ayn Jalud

Gould's Well

Mt Gilboa

El Kaukab

El Fula

Faba

R. Belus

R. Kishon

PLAIN OF MEGIDDO

PLAIN OF ACRE

ACRE

S A M A R I A

El Keymun

Haifa

Athlit

CAESAREA

TIBERIAS TO ACRE

Scale of English Miles

slopes and driven into the lake ; but in order to attack, the Christian army must cross the waterless plain, and after a long march would find the enemy covering all the springs and streams that flow into the lake.

"When we remember that the Franks possessed two strong outposts, at Fula [Faba] and at Belvoir ; that an advance down the Valley of Jezreel to Beysan could have been made without any difficulty as regards plentiful supply of water ; and that Saladin's position was also most dangerous, being at an angle to his line of retreat, it appears strange to a soldier that part, at least, of the Christian army was not despatched to attack the Jordan bridges, and to cut off the Moslem retreat, which could then only have been accomplished by the northern bridge guarded by the fortress of the Château Neuf.* A general like Godfrey would not have failed to take so evident a precaution, but probably the Franks were afraid of the summer heat in the Jordan valley."

The Franks were afraid of something worse than the summer heat: they dreaded the immense host which rumour said was following the standard of Saladin, and they feared to detach any portion of their force, when every man might be needed in the great battle that was before them. Nor is there any evidence that Saladin had not left a sufficient guard to defend the Jordan bridges: it was his custom to place corps of observation at dangerous points. The detaching of any considerable Christian force to cut off his retreat might have exposed the main army to

---

* Château Neuf was Hunin ; perhaps Col. Conder refers to the new castle by Jacob's ford ; but that was already destroyed (see above, p. 159).

defeat, and laid the whole of Palestine open to the invaders. The vital error of the Franks was their forgetting that their duty was to defend and not to attack. Had they chosen a strong defensive position and awaited Saladin's onslaught the issue might have been different; for the Saracens, man to man, were no match for the well-armed and high-mettled knights of the Cross, supported by steady and well-protected infantry. They threw away their advantage when, in spite of Count Raymond's urgent warning, the King yielded to the insistence of the Master of the Temple, and gave the signal for the fatal march over the waterless plain. "Better," said Raymond, "that my city of Tiberias fall, and my wife and all I possess be taken by the Saracens, than that the whole land be lost: for certes, if you go that way, lost it is." It was the counsel of a soldier, but the Master gave it the colour of treachery.

On Friday, the 3d of July, the Christian army broke up camp at Saffuriya, and began its disastrous advance upon Tiberias. Hardly had it set out, when the Saracen skirmishers were upon it. Ernoul's master, Balian of Ibelin, was with the vaward, under the command of Count Raymond, and lost many of his knights.* All that day the light horse of the Saracens harassed the troops, as they plodded along the shadeless, glaring limestone road, whilst the sun beat fiercely on the armour and headpieces, and not a drop of water was to be had. So hard pressed were the Templars and Turcopoles in the rear that they could not keep up with the King's battle in the

---

* The march is vividly described by Ernoul, 166–8.

centre, and were in sore danger of being cut off. Seeing their peril, Guy called a halt, though only half the distance to Tiberias was done; and it was decided to encamp under arms for the night. In vain Count Raymond, who was far ahead with the van, urged the vital necessity of pushing on to the water. The exhausted soldiers had no heart to face the Saracens who barred the way on the hills in front. The rearward was in difficulties. The whole army was demoralised. In desperation, Guy ordered the tents to be pitched at Marescalcia. Raymond rode in from the front in despair, crying out, "Alas! alas, Lord God! The war is over; we are dead men; the Kingdom is undone!" *

It was a night never to be forgotten. Through its long hours the one cry was for water. A raging thirst consumed man and horse. The voices of the Saracens could be heard close by as they patrolled the circle of the devoted host, triumphantly shouting, "*Allahu Akbar*, God is most great, there is no God but He." The enemy set fire to the scrub, and the smoke and fire increased the torment of the Christians. "Verily God fed them with the bread of tears and gave them to drink of the cup of repentance without measure."

The morrow came at last—the feast of the Translation of the Blessed Martin, Saturday the 4th of July.† The knights were early to horse, but the

---

* *De Expugn.*, 223.

† Baha-ed-din is misled by his fondness for Fridays into placing the date of the battle a day too soon. Imad-ed-din, Ibn-el-Athir, Abu-Shama, Ernoul, and the *De Expugn.*, all say Saturday.

14

infantry was already worn out and gaping with thirst. The Saracens, who held the wells, were fresh and confident. Saladin had posted his men in the night, and carefully distributed their rounds of arrows. Every horseman's quiver was full; seventy camels stood at hand laden with arrows to replenish them ; and there were four hundred loads of spare ammunition.* All was ready, and the anxiety of the Moslems, who had been conscious of the peril of their position, where, they said, " only God Most High could save them," was changed into jubilation when they realised the condition of the Franks. The two armies met near the village of Lubia, a couple of miles to the south-west of Hittin. Guy had been driven off the Tiberias road by the strong force of Saracens holding the hill of Kafar Sebt, and was now struggling towards the wells in the Wady Hammam to the north. The Moslems held off for a time, till the climbing sun should do its deadly work upon the weary Christians, and then they advanced, the centre a little " refused," and the wings thrown forward.†
The battle began with a cloud of arrows from the Saracen archers, " thick as a flight of locusts," which unhorsed many of the enemy. Then with a shout the Moslems charged like one man, and a hand-to-hand fight ensued. Saladin was in every part of the field, exciting, encouraging, restraining his men, as the urgency required, and using the Arab's tantalising tactics—retreat before a charge, followed by in-

---

* Imad-ed-din, Abu-Shama, 63.

† Abu-Shama, 70

stant pursuit of the retiring cavalry. Exhausted as they were, the Christian knights fought like heroes.

" But * the grip of fear was on the throats of the crowd, who went Like driven beasts to shambles evident ; They reckoned on sure disaster and dismay, And knew they would be among the visitors of the tombs next day : Yet the fury of the fight never slacked, And every knight his opposite attacked ; Till the triumph (of the Faithful) was achieved, And ruin came on those who misbelieved."

The Frank infantry, maddened with thirst, scorched by the burning sun, and blinded by the flame and smoke of the bush which the Moslems had fired, lost their formation, neglected the combination with the knights which was the only hope of victory, and wildly struggled to push towards the lake in a desperate longing for water : but Saladin barred the way. They found themselves crowded in a heap on the top of a hill, and to the King's repeated entreaty that they would come down and do their devoir for Cross and Throne, they sent word that they were dying of thirst and could not fight. Thenceforth the infantry took no part in the battle : the Saracens eventually fell upon them, cast some down the precipice, and killed or captured the rest.† Many of them threw down their arms and surrendered, coming to the Saracens, their mouths hanging

---

* Baha-ed-din rises into poetic language when he describes dramatic incidents, and he marks the occasion by the use of rhymed prose, each pair of clauses ending in the same rhyme.

† *De Expugn.*, 225, 226.

agape like thirsty dogs. Five of Raymond's knights
even went to Saladin in their despair, and said:
"Sire, why do you delay? Fall on them, they
cannot help themselves; they are all dead men." *

In truth, not only the infantry, but the Templars
and Hospitallers in the rear battle, and the King in
the centre, were so hard pressed, and in such confusion and disarray, with swarms of Saracens surging
in between them, that Guy, seeing it was hopeless to
withstand their attacks without infantry, had tried
to form a sort of lager of the tents huddled round
the Cross.† There was yet one chance, a forlorn
hope: the King called upon Raymond to charge;
the field was in his lands, and by the laws of chivalry
the post of honour was his also. The Count headed
his knights in a last desperate effort, but Saladin's
nephew was too quick for him: Taki-ed-din opened
his ranks, and Raymond's division swept through;
then, when the Christians were thus skilfully separated, the Saracens closed upon the King on all
sides.‡ The last stand was made on the Horn of
Hittin. The King and 150 of the bravest nobles
and knights had gathered on this hillock round the
royal red tent and the Holy Cross. "The Moslems
revolved about them as a globe turns round its pole,"
and the unfortunate Franks vainly tried to break
the cordon.

---

* Ernoul, 169 ; *cp.* Ralph of Coggeshall, *Chron. Anglic.,* 21.

† *De Expugn.,* 225.

‡ Ernoul, 169 ; Ibn-el-Athir, 684. The account in the *De Expugn.*
describes the flight of the vaward as a desperate case of *sauve qui
peut,* without orders from Guy (226).

Saladin's son, a lad of sixteen, himself tells the piteous story * :

"It was my first set battle," said el-Afdal, "and I was at my Father's side. When the King of the Franks had retired to the hill, his knights made a gallant charge, and drove the Moslems back upon my Father. I watched him, and I saw his dismay ; he changed colour, tugged at his beard, and rushed forward, shouting, ' Give the devil the lie ! ' So the Moslems fell upon the enemy, who retreated up the hill. When I saw the Franks flying and the Moslems pursuing, I cried in my glee, ' We have routed them ! ' But the Franks charged again and drove our men back once more to where my Father was. Again he urged them forward, and they drove the enemy up the hill. Again I shouted, ' We have routed them ! ' But Father turned to me and said : ' Hold thy peace ! We have *not* beaten them so long as that tent stands there.' At that instant the royal tent was overturned. Then the Sultan dismounted, and bowed himself to the earth, giving thanks to God, with tears of joy."

It was indeed the end. The Franks had spent their last strength in struggling to break through to the wells. The "Wood of the True Cross," which had been their gonfalon through the weary march and the hopeless battle, had fallen into the hands of the unbelievers ; the Bishop of Acre, who bore it aloft, was slain, despite his armour ; and God himself seemed to have deserted them. Tortured with thirst, parched with the heat and toil, they got off their horses and threw themselves down on the scorched grass in sheer despair. The Saracens were upon them in an instant,

* His narrative is reported by Ibn-el-Athir, 685–6.

and no defence was attempted. The knights were too weak to sell their lives dearly : they gave up their swords. The flower of chivalry was taken. The King and his brother, Reginald of Châtillon, Joscelin of Courtenay, Humphrey of Toron, the Masters of the Temple and Hospital, and many other nobles were among the prisoners. Count Raymond, after breaking through the Saracens, had seen the capture of the King, and never drew rein till he found himself safe at Tyre,—only to die of grief and shame. Legend did not deal gently with his memory. He became the Judas who betrayed Christendom, and for centuries minstrels told how Raymond basely plotted against King Guy, and sold the True Cross into the hands of the infidels. Balian of Ibelin, who had been in the advance guard, also escaped, with the Prince of Sidon. The rest of the chivalry of Palestine was under Moslem warders. Of the rank and file, all who were alive were made prisoners. A single Saracen was seen dragging some thirty Christians he had himself taken, tied together with a tent-rope. The dead lay in heaps, like stones upon stones, among broken crosses, severed hands and feet, whilst mutilated heads strewed the ground like a plentiful crop of melons.*

Saladin camped on the field of battle. When his tent was pitched, he ordered the prisoners to be brought before him. The King of Jerusalem and Reginald of Châtillon he received in his tent ; he seated the King near himself, and seeing his thirst, he gave him a cup of water iced in snow. Guy drank,

* Imad-ed-din, Abu-Shama, 65.

and passed the cup to the lord of Karak: but Saladin was visibly annoyed. " Tell the King," he said to the interpreter, " that it was he, not I, that gave that man drink." The protection of " bread and salt " was not to baulk his vengeance. Then he rose and con-fronted Reginald, who was still standing: " Twice have I sworn to kill him; once when he sought to invade the holy cities, and again when he took the caravan by treachery.—Lo! I will avenge Moham-med upon thee!" And he drew his sword and cut him down with his own hand, as he had sworn. The guard finished it and dragged the body out of the tent; " and God sped his soul to Hell."

The King, trembling at the sight, believed his own turn was now coming, but Saladin reassured him: " It is not the custom of kings to slay kings; but that man had transgressed all bounds, so what happened, happened." * The two military Orders were terribly punished for their daring and zeal for the faith. All the knights of the Hospital and the Temple that were prisoners were executed, to the number of two hundred, but the King and the chief nobles were well used and sent to Damascus. The field long bore the marks of the bloody fight where " 30,000 " Christians were said to have fallen. A year after-wards the heaps of bleaching bones could be seen from afar, and the hills and valleys were strewn with the relics of the horrid orgies of wild beasts.

---

* The accounts of Reginald of Châtillon's execution vary in details. Some represent Saladin as offering him the choice of Islam—a usual formality—and on his refusal cutting off his head. Others say he was killed outside the tent by the guard.

The scene of the battle which overthrew the Christian Kingdom of Jerusalem had been sanctified by tradition for many centuries. The Horn of Hittin was believed to be the very Mount of Beatitudes where the Saviour taught the people the blessedness of peace. The Mount now bore witness to " not peace, but a sword."

SEAL OF REGINALD OF CHÂTILLON.
FROM ARCHER'S "STORY OF THE CRUSADES."

CHAPTER XIV.

JERUSALEM REGAINED.

1187.

THE Saracens spent the night of the battle in rejoicing and giving thanks. The war-cry and the credo were shouted by thousands of triumphant voices; " God is Most Great," " There is no god but God," was echoed from mouth to mouth until the dawn. The Moslems might well rejoice. The victory of Tiberias had laid all Palestine at their mercy. The Kingdom of Jerusalem was at an end. Its King and almost all its nobles were prisoners, and hardly a leader was left to rally the broken remnant of the Crusaders. Since they entered the Holy Land ninety years before, they had never known such disaster. It was the death-blow to their dominion, and never to this day has Christendom recovered what it lost on the memorable Feast of St. Martin. In two months, from Beyrut in the north to Gaza in the south, the whole of Palestine, save a few isolated castles of the military Orders, was in the hands of Saladin, and only Tyre and Jerusalem itself remained to bear witness that there had been a Christian king-

dom. The Holy City soon suffered the fate of its
dependencies.

Saladin's first step was to take the castle of Tiberias.
He went down on Sunday, the 5th of July, and the
noble Eschiva, deserted by her husband and cut
off from all hope of relief, could only surrender;
the Sultan allowed her to depart in safety, with her
children and attendants.   Then, after one day's rest,
the Saracens began to spread over Palestine in a great
wave of conquest. It was not so much a conquest,
indeed, as a triumphal progress.   The resistance
was of the feeblest. The Moslems had but to appear before a town, and, like Jericho, the walls fell
down—the garrison surrendered.   Only a few strong
castles stood a siege, and even of these hardly one
held out a week. The leaders of the Franks were
dead or prisoners; their army was killed, captive, or
dispersed ; there were no reserves, no hope of reinforcement, no one to organise resistance.   The
people, too, the Moslem peasants and traders, were
on the side of the conquerors.   They believed after
their fashion in Saladin's religion, they admired his
courage and success, they recognised his clemency
and even-handed justice.   There were thousands of
Moslem slaves in the cities who awaited with joy
their liberation at his hands.   Even the scattered
Christian sects had less to fear from the generous
Sultan than from the rapacity and tyranny of their
Christian masters, to whom heresy was almost as hateful as Islam itself. With the people to support him,
and no one to oppose, save a desperate garrison here
and there, it is not wonderful that Saladin's progress

through Palestine was an almost uninterrupted march of triumph.

He gave the Franks no time to rally. On Wednesday, the 8th of July, 1187, four days after the battle of Hittin, he was before the strong walls of Acre; and on the Friday he celebrated the public prayers in the mosque that had been used as a church for three generations—the first Moslem prayers that had been offered on the coast of Palestine since the coming of the first Crusaders.* In Acre alone he freed four thousand Moslem captives. The treasure and stores of the great emporium and mart of the Mediterranean trade supplied him with the sinews of war and the means of rewarding and stimulating his army. He sent the troops in detachments in all directions to reduce the country, and summoned his brother el-Adil to bring the army of Egypt to aid in the subjection of Palestine. Some of his brigades occupied Nazareth, Saffuriya, el-Fula, inland; others entered Haifa and Cæsarea on the coast; another detachment seized Sebaste and Nablus; and el-Adil, marching from Cairo, took Castle Mirabel and Jaffa by assault. Saladin himself laid siege to Toron and after six days took it on the 26th of July. Returning to the coast, he next received the surrender of Sarafenda, Sidon, Beyrut, and Jubeyl, by the first week in August: Beyrut alone held out for eight days. In every case he granted honourable terms to the garrisons and people, and they learnt that the word of this Mohammedan could be trusted.†

---

* Ibn-el-Athir, 689.

† The authorities differ as to whether Toron capitulated or was

The whole of the Kingdom of Jerusalem was now subdued, with the exception of a few castles, such as Belfort and Safed still held by Templars, and Hunin and Belvoir garrisoned by knights of the Hospital; the two cities of Tyre and Ascalon on the coast; and the Holy City itself. Tyre escaped by a hair's breadth. Saladin at first had avoided testing the endurance of his army by a long siege such as this strongly fortified city might be expected to stand. He preferred to keep up the courage of his men by easier conquests. Had he attacked Tyre directly after Acre, it would have capitulated, for Count Raymond had withdrawn to Tripolis, where he had quickly died of grief and shame; and the Prince of Antioch, who succeeded to the County of Tripolis, had not reinforced the small garrison of Tyre.* Even when Saladin did venture to sit down before its walls, after the taking of Beyrut, its defenders despaired of resistance. " Reginald of Sidon and the commandant saw that all the knights were away, and that there were but few men, and little food, and they sent to tell Saladin that if he would withdraw they would surrender Tyre." † Matters had even gone so far that Saladin had sent two of his banners to be displayed on the castle the next day; when an unexpected event saved the city and changed the future of the Syrian coast.

Conrad, the young Marquess of Montferrat, who

stormed, and therefore whether the garrison was set free or made prisoners. Jaffa was severely treated, but this was by el-Adil.

* Ibn-el-Athir, 694. The historian was at Aleppo at this time, and evidently had good means of information.

† Ernoul, 179. *Cp.* Röhricht, *Regesta Regn. Hierosol.*, 660.

had won a great name in the Italian and Byzantine
wars, finding himself involved in a blood-feud at
Constantinople, escaped in a ship which was carrying
some of his followers, ostensibly on a pilgrimage to
the Holy Sepulchre. The news of Saladin's conquests had not yet reached the Golden Horn, and
when Conrad arrived off Acre he was amazed to
hear no harbour bells * and see no boats putting off to
meet him. Suspecting that something was wrong,
he did not venture to cast anchor, but lay off, awaiting events. Presently a Saracen officer of the port
came out in a boat to ask who the visitors were.
The Marquess himself answered that they were
" merchants." " Then why do you not land and
disembark ? " Conrad replied that he did not know
who was in possession of Acre. The Saracen assured him he could land, in all confidence, since the
city belonged to Saladin, who had taken the King
of Jerusalem and all his barons and put them in prison
at Damascus, and had conquered all the land except
Jerusalem and Tyre, which he was besieging. Therefore they could land in perfect safety. The grief
which the Franks could not suppress at hearing this
lamentable story betrayed them, and the Saracen
hurried to the port to arm the fleet for pursuit ; but
Conrad had the start, and arrived safely at Tyre.
His joy was unbounded at finding the place still in
Christian hands, and he was welcomed with acclamation by the inhabitants, established with his knights
in the castle, and given the supreme command. The

---

* Bells were rung at Acre when a ship came into port. Abu-
Shama, 79.

castellan and Reginald of Sidon, who were preparing
to surrender the city to Saladin on the morrow, in
great alarm took ship by night and fled to Tripolis.
Their cowardice was quickly exposed by the discovery of Saladin's banners, which the Marquess
immediately flung into the moat.　For "*the will of
God is a fixed destiny,*" * and Tyre was fated to be
saved for the Christians by means of this " man of
the Franks who border the Mediterranean, called el-
Markis,—God's curse upon him ! " exclaims the pious
Moslem historian, " for he was a devil of a man in
caution and watchfulness, and of immense bravery
withal." †

The effects of Conrad's energy were immediately
felt.　All thoughts of capitulation were abandoned,
and the garrison, inspired with new courage, set
about strengthening their defences and preparing for
a stubborn resistance.　Saladin perceived that the
opportunity was lost : he tried one argument, and
not a worthy one, by fetching Conrad's father, the
old Marquess of Montferrat, from his prison at Damascus, and bartering his life against the city.　But
Conrad professed complete heartlessness, said his
father had already lived quite long enough, and
Saladin might kill him if he liked : not the smallest
stone of Tyre should be given to save him.

The old man, however, was not sacrificed ; Saladin
was forced to raise the siege, and departed for Ascalon—the only other port of Palestine which still displayed the Cross.　His biographer alleges another

---

* *Koran*, xxxiii., 38.

† Ibn-el-Athir, 694–5 ; Ernoul, 181–3.

reason, which probably had its weight, when he states that the Sultan abandoned the leaguer " because his men were dispersed throughout the coast, each looting on his own behalf, and the army was tired of fighting and war without end." * It was also of the utmost importance to reduce both Ascalon and Jerusalem, since they barred the communications between his two great provinces of Egypt and Syria.† So he hastened to the southern frontier, occupied Ramla, Ibelin, and Darum, and sat down before Ascalon on the 23rd of August. El-Adil joined him with the army of Egypt, and the two brothers pressed the siege and directed the mangonels, whilst their foraging parties took Gaza, Beyt Jibrin and Natrun. Repeating the experiment of Tyre, Saladin had King Guy and the Master of the Temple brought from Damascus, and promised them their liberty if they could persuade the garrison to surrender ; but Ascalon, like Tyre, at first rejected the temptation. The garrison held out nearly a fortnight, but finally empowered the King to treat for them. They were allowed to depart in peace, and the Saracens occupied Ascalon on Friday, the 4th of September. It is doubtful how far Guy had contributed to this result, but Saladin kept his promise, and after some further detention at Nablus, where he was allowed a " sad interview " with his queen, the King was released, together with his brother and the other nobles, in the following summer.

On the day the Saracens took possession of Asca-

* Baha-ed-din, 99.
† Ibn-el-Athir, 696.

lon, the sun hid his face, and the day became almost as night.* An eclipse is always a sinister portent to the credulous folk of the East, and it must have held a specially ominous significance to the burghers of Jerusalem who had come at Saladin's bidding to treat for peace. The Sultan was anxious to spare the Holy City the misery of a siege. " I believe," he told them, " that Jerusalem is the House of God, as you also believe, and I will not willingly lay siege to the House of God or put it to the assault." To obtain it " in peace and amity " he offered to leave the inhabitants free to fortify the city and cultivate the land for five leagues round, and even to supply them plentifully with money and food, until the following Pentecost, on condition that when Pentecost came, if they saw a prospect of being rescued, they should keep the Holy City ; but if they saw no chance of succour, then they must surrender Jerusalem, and he would conduct them and their possessions safely to Christian soil.†

The offer was chivalrous, even quixotic, when the notorious bad faith of the Crusaders is remembered, and the lack of any security for their keeping a promise. But the delegates from Jerusalem refused it without hesitation. If God pleased, they said, they would never surrender the city where the

---

* Ernoul, 185. A total eclipse of the sun took place on the 4th of September, but its totality passed a little north of Ascalon. The expression in Muratori's edition (1725) of part of Pipino's chronicle, " *tantam passus est eclipsim, ut fere nox esset,*" suggests an eclipse which was not quite total. Ernoul says, " *qu'il sambla bien qu'il fust nuis*" ; the *Libellus de Expugn.* records, " *Feria sexta, hora nona, obscuratus est sol*" (238). † Ernoul 185–6

Saviour died for them.   So Saladin, pleased at their
devotion, promised them on his oath that he would
never take it except in the honourable way, by the
sword.   The Sultan's chivalry is the more remarkable, since Jerusalem itself had lately presented a
signal example of bad faith.   After Balian of Ibelin
had escaped from the field of Hittin, he sent to
Saladin, begging him to give him a safe-conduct to
go to Jerusalem and bring his wife and children back
to Tyre.   The petition was at once granted, on the
conditions that Balian should only stay one night in
the city, and should never more bear arms against
the Sultan.   When he arrived at Jerusalem he was
welcomed with delight as a deliverer, for there were
no knights of rank there, and he was made commander and guardian of the city by universal acclamation.   In vain he protested that he had given his
oath to Saladin and could not honourably stay or
help in the defence.   " I absolve you," said the Patriarch, " from your sin and your oath, which it were a
greater sin in you to keep than to break; for it were
a perpetual disgrace upon you to leave Jerusalem in
this strait and go away, nor should you ever have
honour again whithersoever you went."   So Balian
stayed, and since there were but two knights in the
place, who had also fled from Hittin, he knighted
thirty burghers.   The Patriarch opened the treasury
for him, and the garrison went out and bought provisions for the siege.*   Fugitives had come in from all
sides, and there were reckoned to be 60,000 men in
the city, besides women and children.

* Ernoul, 175–6.

The patience of Saladin was not exhausted even after this dishonour. Perhaps he believed that Balian could not help himself; and far from showing rancour, he gave him a fresh proof of his confidence. Balian again sent to him at Ascalon to beg him to give another safe-conduct, to remove his wife and children to Tripolis; he explained that he was forcibly withheld from keeping his former promise. Instead of reproaches, Saladin sent an escort of fifty horse, who carried out his wishes.

On Sunday, the 20th of September, 1187, the Saracens at length appeared before the walls of the Holy City. In seventy-five days they had overrun and subdued the Kingdom of Jerusalem; now they must have the capital itself, the cause and motive of the Crusades, the object of the veneration of Christian and Moslem alike. Saladin first took up his position on the west side, facing the line of walls from the gate of David to the gate of Saint Stephen. He was amazed to see the battlements packed with countless defenders, who indeed could not find room in the crowded houses and churches. He soon discovered that the ground was ill-chosen, for the great towers of Tancred and David (or the Castle of the Pisans, as it was then called) commanded his batteries, and the frequent sallies of the Christians drove back his engineers and opposed the erection of his mangonels. Moreover, the sun was in the eyes of the Moslems, and they could not see to fight till the afternoon by reason of the glare. He therefore reconnoitred the other sides of the city, and after five days transferred his army to the east, overlooking the

PLAN OF JERUSALEM.

(FROM A 12TH CENTURY MANUSCRIPT.)

valley of the Kidron, where the walls were less strong.
He moved in the evening of the 25th of September,
and the inhabitants, seeing him depart, thought he
had abandoned the siege, and ran to the churches
to pour out their thanksgivings and indulge in transports of joy. But on the morrow weeping followed
hard upon laughter : the Saracen standards were flying on Mount Olivet; already twoscore mangonels
were in position, and the engineers, who had worked
all night, were beginning to mine the barbican.* Ten
thousand Moslem cavalry masked the gates of St.
Stephen and Josaphat, and prevented sallies, and
the sappers pushed forward under a shield-wall, covered by the arrows of the archers and the stones
and Greek fire discharged from the engines. It was
impossible to keep a footing on the ramparts under
the hail of stones and shafts, for " the arrows served
as toothpicks to the teeth of the battlements "†; and
the mining went on merrily, till in two days thirty
or forty paces of the barbican wall were sapped; the
mines were stuffed with wood and fired, and a great
breach was made. The knights in vain attempted a
sortie to cut off the engineers; Saladin's horsemen
drove them in. Lamentation and despair fell upon
the city. The people crowded to the churches to
pray and confess their sins ; beat themselves with
stones and scourges, supplicating the mercy of God.
The women cut off their daughters' hair, and plunged

---

* *Libellus de Expugnatione*, 243, where the writer says he was
himself wounded in the siege.

† See a bombastic account of the siege written by Saladin's minister, the Kady el-Fadil, to the Caliph of Baghdad, quoted in Ibn-
Khallikan, iv., 520–528.

them naked in cold water, in the hope of averting their shame. The priests and monks paraded the city in solemn procession, bearing the *Corpus Domini* and the Cross, and chanting the *Miserere*. " But the wickedness and lewdness of the city stank in the nostrils of the Lord, and the prayers of the sinful people could not mount to the mercy seat."

At last the breach could not be manned ; not for a hundred gold pieces would a citizen stand there for a single night. The common people were all for surrender. The leaders took counsel together, and resolved to sally forth and meet their deaths. But Heraclius the Patriarch showed them that they would thus expose their women and children to slavery—he had his private reasons—and they were persuaded to treat for terms. Balian went to Saladin's tent, but even whilst he was entreating him, the breach was carried and the Saracen flag appeared upon the barbican. " Doth one grant terms to a captive city ? " scoffed the Sultan. Besides, he had sworn to take Jerusalem by the sword, and he must keep his vow. The city, however, was not yet taken : the garrison once more plucked up courage and drove back the assailants. Saladin wished to spare the devoted inhabitants, and sought counsel with his divines, if there might be another way to keep his vow. Balian's last visit had filled him with horror, for the baron had plainly spoken of the desperate resolution of the garrison :

" O Sultan," he said, " know that we soldiers in this city are in the midst of God knows how many people, who are slackening the fight in the hope of thy grace, believing that thou wilt grant it them as thou hast granted it to the other cities—for they abhor death and desire life. But for ourselves, when we see that death must needs be, by God we will slaughter our sons and our women, we will burn our wealth and our possessions, and leave you neither sequin nor stiver to loot, nor a man or a woman to enslave ; and when we have finished that, we will demolish the Rock and the Mosque el-Aksa, and the other holy places, we will slay the Moslem slaves who are in our hands — there are 5000 such, — and slaughter every beast and mount we have ; and then we will sally out in a body to you, and will fight you for our lives : not a man of us will fall before he has slain his likes ; thus shall we die gloriously or conquer like gentlemen." *

Balian's desperate threats, and the arguments of his own council, induced Saladin at length to modify his vow. It would be sufficiently kept, he announced, if Jerusalem surrendered at discretion, as though it had actually been taken by assault. In this case he would exercise his clemency and hold the population to ransom as prisoners of war. Each man should pay ten pieces of gold for his liberty, and two women or ten children should be reckoned as one man ; whilst of the poor, who possessed not even a gold coin, seven thousand should be set free for the sum of thirty thousand besants, to be paid out of King Henry's treasure, the remnant of which was still hoarded in the house of the Hospitallers. Forty days were allowed for the ransoming ; after that, all that remained became slaves. The articles of capitu-

* Ibn-el-Athir, 701 ; Abu-Shama, 84.

lation were signed on Friday the 2nd of October, the
Feast of St. Leger. By a strange coincidence, it was
the 27th of Rejeb, the anniversary of the blessed
Leylat el-Miraj, when the prophet of Islam dreamed
his wonderful dream, and visited in his sleep the
Holy City which his followers had now recovered
after ninety years of Christian occupation.

Balian returned to the city and announced the
terms. They were accepted, with gratitude and
lamentation. The people groaned and wept, and
would not be comforted ; they kissed the holy walls
which they might never see again, and bowing their
faces on the ground before the Sepulchre, watered
the sacred spot with their tears. To leave Jerusalem
was to tear the hearts out of them. But there was
no help for it; the Moslem flag flew overhead, the
keys were in the Saracens' hands, and in forty days
the city must be delivered up. Never did Saladin
show himself greater than during this memorable
surrender. His guards, commanded by responsible
emirs, kept order in every street, and prevented violence and insult, insomuch that no ill-usage of the
Christians was ever heard of. * Every exit was in
his hands, and a trusty lord was set over David's
gate to receive the ransoms as each citizen came
forth.

Then began a strangely pathetic scene. First Balian brought the thirty thousand gold besants, and
the seven thousand poor who were ransomed by the
King of England's treasure were allowed to shamble
out. There followed burgher after burgher, money

---

* Ernoul, 227.

in hand, with their families and sometimes with poor
dependents who could not ransom themselves. Saracen soldiers and merchants thronged the city and
bought the goods of the departing citizens, so that
each might raise the price of freedom. Kukbury
ransomed a thousand Armenians of Edessa, and
sent them to their homes; and others were not less
benevolent. There was cheating and deceit, of
course, and some of the Moslem emirs falsely
claimed lost servants and took their ransoms pri-
vately, whilst others smuggled Franks out of the
city in Saracen dress, and sucked them dry as
soon as they were clear of the guard.* The Patriarch, who had neither morals nor conscience, carried off the treasures of the churches, gold chalices
and monstrances, and even the gold plate of the
Holy Sepulchre, besides a vast hoard of his own,
which had been better spent on ransoming the poor
who still remained. When the Saracen emirs urged
Saladin not to let the old rascal make off with his
plunder, he replied, " No, I will not break faith with
him," and the Patriarch got off like the rest for his
ten besants. It was left for the Mohammedan King
to teach the Christian priest the meaning of charity.

For forty days the melancholy procession trooped
forth from the gate of David, and the term of grace
expired. Yet there still remained thousands of poor
people whom the niggardly burghers and religious
houses had left to slavery. Then el-Adil came to
his brother and said: " Sire, I have helped you by
God's grace ·to conquer the land and this city, I

* Ibn-el-Athir, 703 ; Abu-Shama, 85.

therefore pray you give me a thousand slaves from
the poor people within." To Saladin's question,
what he would do with them, he answered he would
do as pleased himself. Then the Sultan gave him
the thousand slaves, and el-Adil set them all free as
an offering to God. Then came the Patriarch and
Balian, and begged likewise, and Saladin gave them
another thousand slaves, and they were set free.
Then said Saladin to his officers : " My brother has
made his alms, and the Patriarch and Balian have
made theirs ; now I would fain make mine." And
he ordered his guards to proclaim throughout the
streets of Jerusalem that all the old people who
could not pay were free to go forth. And they
came forth from the postern of St. Lazarus, and
their going lasted from the rising of the sun until
night fell. " Such was the charity which Saladin
did, of poor people without number." *

" Then I shall tell you," says the Squire of Balian,
" of the great courtesy which Saladin showed to the
wives and daughters of knights, who had fled to Jerusalem when their lords were killed or made prisoners in
battle. When these ladies were ransomed and had come

---

* This is the report of the Christian chronicler Ernoul, who was
probably present (227–8). It is worth noting that, on the same
authority, when the poor refugees whom Saladin released came to
Tripolis, its Christian count shut the gates in their faces, and even
sent out his troops to rob the burghers of the possessions which the
Moslems had religiously respected. (*Ib.*, 234.) It is not to be
understood, however, that Saladin freed *all* the poor ; there was undoubtedly a large residue of young slaves, perhaps 15,000 : so says
Imad-ed-din, who himself received his share of women and children.
Abu-Shama, 89.

forth from Jerusalem, they assembled and went before
Saladin crying mercy. When Saladin saw them he asked
who they were and what they sought. And it was told
him that they were the dames and damsels of knights
who had been taken or killed in battle. Then he asked
what they wished, and they answered for God's sake
have pity on them ; for the husbands of some were in
prison, and of others were dead, and they had lost their
lands, and in the name of God let him counsel and help
them. When Saladin saw them weeping, he had great
compassion for them, and wept himself for pity. And
he bade the ladies whose husbands were alive to tell him
where they were captives, and as soon as he could go
to the prisons he would set them free. (And all were
released wherever they were found.) After that he
commanded that to the dames and damsels whose lords
were dead there should be handsomely distributed from
his own treasure, to some more and others less, according to their estate. And he gave them so much that
they gave praise to God and published abroad the kindness and honour which Saladin had done to them." *

Thus did the Saracens show mercy to the fallen
city. One recalls the savage conquest by the first
Crusaders in 1099, when Godfrey and Tancred rode
through streets choked with the dead and dying,
when defenceless Moslems were tortured, burnt, and
shot down in cold blood on the towers and roof of
the Temple, when the blood of wanton massacre
defiled the honour of Christendom and stained the
scene where once the gospel of love and mercy had
been preached. " Blessed are the merciful, for they

* Ernoul, 229–30.

shall obtain mercy" was a forgotten beatitude
when the Christians made shambles of the Holy
City. Fortunate were the merciless, for they obtained mercy at the hands of the Moslem Sultan.

> " The greatest attribute of heaven is Mercy ;
> And 't is the crown of justice, and the glory,
> Where it may kill with right, to save with pity."

If the taking of Jerusalem were the only fact known
about Saladin, it were enough to prove him the
most chivalrous and great-hearted conqueror of his
own, and perhaps of any, age.

SEAL OF RAYMOND II. OF TRIPOLIS.
FROM ARCHER'S "STORY OF THE CRUSADES."

CHAPTER XV.

THE RALLY AT TYRE.

1187–1188.

WHEN all the Franks had departed, and only the slaves and rescued Moslem captives remained, with the native Christians, who begged to stay and pay tribute, Saladin ordered the holy places to be purified and restored for the worship of Islam. The golden cross had been torn down from the Dome of the Rock, and all traces of the Templars' additions were removed from the Haram where stood the ancient Mosque of Omar. Doctors and divines and pilgrims hastened from all parts to share in the great consecration. Deputations thronged the Sultan's tent outside the city, chanting the Koran, reciting poems, declaiming panegyrics in his honour. The secretaries laboured to spread the good news to the ends of the kingdoms of Islam: Imad-ed-din himself wrote seventy dispatches on the day of the recapture of Jerusalem. On Friday the 9th of October an immense congregation assembled to pray with Saladin in the sanctuary of el-Aksa. The chief Kady of Aleppo preached the sermon.* He praised God for the triumph of the faith and the cleansing of his Holy House ; he declared the pure creed of the Koran, and pronounced the blessings upon the Prophet and the Caliphs, in the prescribed form of the Mohammedan bidding-prayer.

Then, "O Men," he cried, "rejoice at good tidings ! God is well-pleased with what ye have done, and this is the summit of man's desire ; he hath holpen you to bring back this strayed camel from misguided hands and to restore it to the fold of Islam, after the infidels had mishandled it for nearly a hundred years. Rejoice at the purifying of this House, *which God allowed to be raised and permitted his name to be said therein,* over which he spread his tent and wherein he established his holy rites; the house whose foundations were laid on the creed of the One God, the best of foundations, and the walls whereof were built to his glory, and stand firm upon piety from ancient times until now. It was the dwelling-place of your father Abraham, the spot whence your prophet Mohammed, God bless him, ascended into Heaven, the *kibla* to which ye turned to pray in the early time of Islam, the abode of the prophets, the resort of the saints, the grave of the apostles, the place where God's revelation came down, and where all mankind must gather on the Day of Resurrection and of Judgment. . . . It is the city to which God sent his servant and apostle, the Word which entered into Mary, Jesus, the spirit of God, whom he honoured with his

---

* The sermon is preserved by Ibn-Khallikan, ii., 634–641, from whom the following extracts are abridged. The passages in italics are quoted from the Koran.

mission and ennobled with the gift of prophecy, yet
without raising him above the ranks of his creatures :
for the Most High hath said, Christ *will not disdain to be
God's servant, nor will the angels who surround his
presence.* . . .

"Had ye not been of God's chosen servants, he had
not honoured you by this grace, wherein ye can never be
rivalled nor shall any ever share in its perfectness.
Blessed are ye, who have fought like those at Bedr,
who have been steadfast as Abu-Bekr, victorious as
Omar, who have recalled the hosts of Othman and the
onslaughts of Ali ! Ye have renewed for Islam the glorious memories of Kadisiya, of the Yarmuk, of Khaibar,
and of Khalid, the Sword of God. The Almighty recom-
pense you, and accept the offering of the blood ye have
shed in his service, and grant you Paradise, happy for
ever. . . .

"And prolong, O Almighty God, the reign of thy servant, humbly reverent, for thy favour thankful, grateful
for thy gifts, thy sharp sword and shining torch, the
champion of thy faith and defender of thy holy land,
the firmly resisting, the great, the victorious King, the
strengthener of the true religion, the vanquisher of the
worshippers of the Cross, the Honour of the World and
the Faith [SALADIN], Sultan of Islam and of the Moslems, purifier of the holy temple, ABU-L-MUZAFFAR
YUSUF SON OF AYYUB, reviver of the empire of the Commander of the Faithful. Grant, O God, that his empire
may spread over all the earth, and that the angels may
ever surround his standards ; preserve him for the good
of Islam ; protect his realm for the profit of the Faith ;
and extend his dominion over the regions of the East
and of the West. . . . Save him, O God, and his
children after him ; may they rule the land till the end

of time ; preserve his days, and his sons and his brethren, strengthen his power by their long lives ; and, inasmuch as by his means thou hast brought this lasting good to Islam, to endure whilst months and years shall roll, grant him, O God, the kingdom that never ends in the mansions of the blest, and hear his prayer that he prayeth unto thee :—*O Lord, help me to be thankful for thy favour wherewith thou hast favoured me and my fathers, that I may do that which is right and well-pleasing unto thee ; and bring me at last of thy mercy to dwell amongst thy righteous servants.''* *

This noble *khutba*, with its beautiful peroration, was pronounced with such overwhelming effect, writes the Kady el-Fadil, that " the heavens almost cracked, not in wrath, but to drop tears of joy, and the stars left their places, not to shoot upon the wicked, but to rejoice together." The delight of the Moslems at the recovery of the Sanctuary was unbounded. Saladin restored it to its former beauty and simplicity, and brought from Damascus an exquisite carved pulpit which Nur-ed-din had caused to be designed at Aleppo twenty years before. It is there to this day, and over the great niche of the Mosque may still be read the inscription :

" In the name of God, the Compassionate, the Merciful ! Hath ordered the repair of this holy *Mihrab* and the restoration of the Mosque el-Aksa, founded on piety, the servant and agent of God *Yusuf son of Ayyub Abu-l-Muzaffar el-Melik en-Nasir Salahed-dunya wa-d-din*, when that God by his hand had triumphed, in the month

* *Koran*, xxvii., 19 : the prayer is there put into the mouth of Solomon.

of the year [of the Flight] 583 : and he prayeth God to
endue him with thankfulness for this favour and to make
him a partaker in the remission of sins, through his
mercy and forgiveness." *

'   .   .   .   .   .   .

Jerusalem and Ascalon were regained ; Karak and
Mont Real in "Oultre Jourdain" and Safed and
Belvoir near Tiberias, alone of all the Crusaders'
castles south of Tyre,† still held Christian garrisons ;
but every one of these castles was masked by a sufficient force, and it was only a question of time when
they must be starved out.   Tyre was the only important place in all Palestine that Saladin had not
conquered ; and to Tyre he despatched his jubilant
army on the 1st of November, 1187.   Twelve days
later he arrived to take command.   He found the
city full of the garrisons which he had suffered to
capitulate at other places.   Conrad of Montferrat
had worked night and day, strengthening the works,
encouraging the defenders, and "directing them with
superior ability."   He had deepened and extended
the moats till Tyre became "like a hand spread upon
the sea, attached only by the wrist," an island approached by so narrow a spit that it could be easily
defended by a small force, as well as covered by the
cross-bows on the shielded Christian barges or *barbotes*.   Saladin was supported by his brother, sons, and
nephew, with their contingents from Egypt, Aleppo,

---

* Vte. de Vogüé, *Le Temple de Jerusalem*, 101 ; Le Strange, *Palestine*, 109.

† See Conrad's letter to the King of Hungary (Röhricht, *Regesta*,
670).

and Hamah ; but he was unable to bring his greatly superior strength to bear upon the enemy. He had indeed seventeen engines playing upon the walls day and night, but only a small number of men could advance at a time upon the spit of land, and these had not only to meet the frequent sallies of the Franks in front, led by the valiant Knight in Green,* but to protect themselves from the flank attacks of the barbotes drawn up on either side. Ten of the Saracen ships were brought from Acre, and soon drove the Tyrian galleys into port; but early on the morning of the feast of the holy martyr, St. Thomas of Canterbury (Dec. 29th), half the Moslem fleet was surprised and captured by the enemy, and the rest were sent to Beyrut, as they were not strong enough to hold the galleys in check. Even as they went, they were pursued by the Tyrians, and in a panic all but two of their ships went ashore, where they had to be burnt. The failure at sea was followed by a reverse on shore : the Saracens, taking advantage of the diversion by sea, had scaled the barbican wall and were attempting the main wall, when Conrad sallied out at the head of his men and drove them out with heavy loss. †

Upon this Saladin called a council of war. Some of the emirs were for retreat; they alleged, with reason, the inclemency of the season—for it was now late in

---

* This Spanish knight bore a shield vert, and a pair of stags' horns on his helmet, of the same. Saladin, says Ernoul, delighted to see the Green Knight's splendid sallies, for, be he Christian or Moslem, there was nothing he loved so much as a good knight (237–8).

† Ernoul, 242–3.

December, when rain and snow convert the plain into
a sea of mud, and damp and cold breed sickness among
the soldiers and horses ;—they spoke of the number
of dead and wounded, and the want of stores and
money ; and proposed to raise the siege, and return to
the attack in the spring.   Against these easy-going
advocates, others urged that it was of the first importance to conquer Tyre, since it was the only hope of
the Franks on that coast, and if it fell there would be
no more reinforcements coming from beyond the sea.
The timider counsels prevailed, however, and on
New Year's Day, 1188, Saladin dismissed the various
contingents to their homes in Egypt, Syria, and
Mesopotamia, and withdrew with his own personal
troops to Acre.*

The retreat from Tyre was the turning-point in
Saladin's career of victory.   It was a fatal, irremedi-
able error.   It was a fixed principle with him to
avoid long sieges whenever possible, nor was the
principle wrong.   His troops consisted largely of an
ill-disciplined feudal militia, of different races and
dialects, who were bound together more by the hope
of booty than by devotion to the Sultan or even zeal
for the Holy War.   Well led, they could fight with
success on a pitched field, and when a town or
castle could be taken by assault, the prospect of loot
and sheer love of combat would lend the storming
party a furious valour.   But a long siege discouraged
them, and opened occasions for the jealousies and
discontents inevitable in so mixed an army.   Instead

---

* Ibn-el-Athir, 707–711, unsparingly condemns the policy of retreat.

of the incitement of rapid triumphs and frequent prizes, there were the weary sapping of strong walls, the daily exposure to sharpshooters on the battlements and desperate charges from the sally-port. In the case of a regular Crusaders' castle, well garrisoned and commanded by a capable leader, the odds were against the besiegers, whose clumsy mangonels were uncertain of aim and discharged stones, ponderous indeed, but doubtfully effective against a well-constructed wall of stone twenty feet thick. Mining, though wood had to be fired instead of gunpowder or dynamite, was more successful than bombardment, but it was conducted at great risk when a determined garrison harassed the sappers, nor was the modern science of trench approaches and zigzags and other protective devices familiar to the Saracen engineers. A close blockade, ending in starving out the garrison, was the surest method ; but this involved keeping a large body of men in discontented inaction, perhaps in the trying winter season, and without a fleet it was of course useless against a coast town which could be provisioned by sea.

It is not wonderful, therefore, that Saladin avoided long sieges, for which, moreover, he did not show the same capacity that he displayed in set battles and rapid campaigns. His dislike to siege operations may account, as well as his natural clemency, for his usual practice of accepting the surrender of a fortress and letting the garrison go free, even when there was a near prospect of carrying a place by assault. He never seems to have considered that every garrison thus released went to swell the forces of the enemy,

and that even if he exacted their parole they were
certain to break it at the first opportunity for revenge. Obviously the prudent way was to hold
them prisoners of war at Damascus, or some other
distant city, until the campaign was over and peace
was made. Tyre was full of these capitulated garrisons, and Saladin had chiefly himself to reproach for
the strength of the defenders.

Nevertheless, whatever the difficulties of the siege,
Delenda est Tyrus should have been his immutable
resolve. He should have built a new fleet, destroyed
the Tyrian galleys, filled the moats, breached the
walls, if he lost half his army in so doing. The only
answer is that Saladin knew his men, and felt that he
could not count upon their endurance. But even
this does not explain his neglect to blockade the
city by sea and land, to keep off reinforcements, and
to starve its crowded population. However we look
at it, Saladin's measures against Tyre appear to be
neither soldierly nor statesmanlike. Tyre became
the rallying-point from which the Crusaders recovered part of their lost power and prestige along the
coast of Palestine; and had this one city not held
out, it is a question whether the Third Crusade would
ever have been heard of at Acre.

The effects of this serious check were not, of
course, immediately apparent. Europe took time
to assemble its forces for the recovery of the Holy
Land, and meanwhile Saladin, still ignoring the danger from Tyre, led a triumphant campaign in the
north. Hitherto he had been content with the subjection of the Kingdom of Jerusalem; he now ex-

tended his conquests in the County of Tripolis and the Principality of Antioch. Bohemond III. was its Prince, and his son Raymond had succeeded to the County of Tripolis by the will of his namesake, the unhappy survivor of the battle of Hittin. Father and son had cheerfully left Tyre to its fate, and it was no thanks to them that Conrad had beaten off the invaders. Raymond indeed sent some galleys towards the beleaguered city, but an opportune storm had enabled them to return to Tripolis with a plausible excuse for doing nothing. So fearful was Bohemond of adding to his responsibilities that he had turned away the refugees from Jerusalem lest they should exhaust his store of food, and had at the same time relieved them of such money as they carried, in order to supply his own necessities. The northern princes had long pursued a policy of conciliation towards Saladin, and this meanness was perhaps intended as a proof of good feeling, which the generous Sultan can hardly have commended. It did not, at least, prevent him from attacking the northern provinces.

The winter was spent at Acre, where Saladin occupied the Palace of el-Afdal, which had been converted into a Templars' castle. The divines were installed in the Hospital of St. John, and the bishop's palace was made a hospital : both were richly endowed by Saladin out of the spoils. Meanwhile Karakush, the fortifier of Cairo, was sent for to strengthen the defences of Acre. Leaving the coast in the spring, and after inspecting in March the blockade at Belvoir (Kaukab), the castle of the Hospitallers south of

Tiberias, which he found far too strong to be stormed, Saladin visited Damascus, and then on the 14th of May marched north.* The immediate cause was a movement of the Franks upon Jubeyl, but the direction of his march shows that his designs pointed towards Tripolis or Antioch. He camped near Emesa, whence he reconnoitred the country. Ernoul says that Saladin actually laid siege to Tripolis, but found it so largely reinforced that he withdrew. William of Sicily, first of all the princes of Europe to come to the rescue, had sent five hundred knights and a fleet of fifty galleys under his brave admiral Margaritus, whose exploits had won him the name of " the King of the Sea " and " a second Neptune," and the Sicilians brought invaluable aid to the survivors of the Crusades.† Conrad of Montferrat had also hastened to the assistance of his phlegmatic neighbour. With Conrad came the famous Green Knight, whose prowess again compelled the admiring notice of Saladin. The Sultan invited him to his tent; he came, and Saladin made him very welcome, gave him horses and jewels, and offered lands and possessions if he would take service with him. But the Green Knight refused everything; he said he had not come to the Holy Land to stay with Saracens, but to hurt and confound them; which he

---

* Before this campaign Saladin had been joined by his future biographer Baha-ed-din, who remained with him as his secretary (from June, 1188) in close intimacy until the Sultan's death. Ibn-el-Athir was also with Saladin (cp. 717) during at least part of his war against Antioch.

† *Itinerarium Regis Ricardi*, i., 13, 14; but Abu-Shama insists that the Sicilian fleet was useless for good or evil (Goergens, 100).

would do whenever he could.* So they parted in
honest respect.

Abandoning any designs he had upon Tripolis,
Saladin returned to his camp near the Hospitallers'
virgin fortress, Crac des Chevaliers (Hisn el-Akrad,
"the Kurds' Castle"), and, joined by his vassals
from Mesopotamia under the leadership of Imad-ed-
din of Sinjar, formed his army in order of battle.
He set out on his campaign on Friday, his favourite
day, the 1st of July. There was no Christian army
to oppose him, and the campaign is a monotonous
record of the storming or surrender of city after
city, castle after castle. Tortosa (Antartus) was
the first to feel the brunt of his wrath, for his un-
usually harsh treatment of the city shows that his
ill-success at Tripolis had galled him. Arriving on
the 3rd of July, he formed his army in a crescent
round the place, from sea to sea, and ordered an immediate assault. It was carried before the followers
had time to pitch the Moslems' tents ; and they
sacked, and burnt, and razed it to the ground. Of
the two castles, however, only one was destroyed ;
the Templars' Tower resisted all assaults and had to
be left, a standing support to the Christians. Valenia
was deserted by its inhabitants ; but the great fortress of Margat defied capture. Jebela opened its
gates, and its citadel surrendered on Friday the
15th of July. On the following Friday the garrison
of Ladikia capitulated; on the Friday after that,
Saone (Sahyun), the great castle of the Hospitallers
on the hills, was carried by assault, but the Sultan

---

* Ernoul, 251–2.

CASTLE OF SAHYUN (SAONE).

held the garrison and people to ransom on the same terms as at Jerusalem.* On three Fridays in August fell the twin fortresses of the Orontes, Bukas and esh-Shughr, hitherto deemed impregnable, and the town of Sarmin. The capture of six strongholds on six successive Fridays assured the Moslems that the prayers of the faithful on the day of worship had been accepted, and they remembered the sacred promise that a good deed done on Friday would be doubly rewarded in Paradise.

Barzuya, on the east of the Orontes, a fort so strong that its impregnability became a proverb, was carried by assault after hard fighting on the 23rd of August ; its defenders were made prisoners, and the Moslems were laden with the spoils. Only the governor and his relations, who were kin to the Prince of Antioch, were set free and escorted to their friends. Among them were a newly married couple whom the Saracens had ruthlessly separated. Saladin pitied their misfortune, sought them out, and sent them, reunited, to safety.† Bohemond was not likely to forget this generosity, and after the Moslems had taken Darbesak and Baghras, important frontier fortresses commanding the Beylan pass north of Antioch, and were actually marching upon the capital itself, its Prince sued for peace. Saladin's army was glutted with booty, and weary of conquest.

---

* Abu-Shama (103–4) says that Saone was protected by five walls, between which the space was filled with bears and lions ! Imad-ed-din laments the wanton destruction wrought by the Saracens in the magnificent marble buildings of Ladikia—the most sumptuous and beautiful city he had ever seen.

† Ibn-el-Athir, 729.

They had had three months of hard marching and
not a little hard fighting. The officers were eager
to go home with their spoils, and give their men
time to rest and recruit their strength. Like all
Moslem armies, it was a married army, and the
troops wanted their wives. A truce for eight months
was concluded on the 1st of October; the Prince
of Antioch released all the Saracen captives in his
power, and agreed to deliver up his city if it were
not rescued before the end of the truce.*

At Aleppo, the Mesopotamian contingents under
the Prince of Sinjar, who had been eager to depart,
were dismissed to their homes; and after ovations
in the Grey Castle, where Saladin's son ez-Zahir commanded, and at Hamah, which was under his bravest
nephew Taki-ed-din, the Sultan returned to Damascus
about the 20th of October. He had granted his
vassals and kinsmen their well-earned repose, but he
took no rest himself that winter. The month of
Ramadan was at hand, but even the holy fast must
give way to the urgent duty of fighting for the faith.
North and south of the Lake of Galilee, Safed and
Belvoir still held out against the long blockade of
the Moslems. Setting aside the thoughts of rest
and home which every Moslem cherishes during the
sacred month, and despising the rigours of a Syrian
winter, Saladin led his own guard against the Templars' fortress. The Saracens invested the rocky
hill of Safed. Rain was falling in torrents, and the
ground was a swamp, but the Sultan himself marked

---

* *Itinerary*, i., 13 ; Baha-ed-din, 117 ; Imad-ed-din, Goergens,
109.

out the places for his five mangonels, and refused to sleep till they had been erected. Orderlies went backwards and forwards all night to report the progress of the work. The siege was pressed for a month, night and day without intermission, till the garrison at last surrendered (December 6th). They were suffered to depart to Tyre with the honours of war. Belvoir was next attacked, the fastness "set amid the stars, like a falcon's nest," "the city of barking, whose dogs ever yelped and bears growled."* The siege was carried on in storms of rain and wind, with a sea of mud under foot. After heavy losses a breach was at last effected, and the Hospitallers followed the example of the rival Order and capitulated (January 5, 1189). About the same time news arrived that the fortress which had so long troubled the peace of the Moslems, and which Saladin had so often besieged, had at length been starved out : Karak had surrendered to el-Adil. The garrison had been reduced to driving out their women and children, and eating their horses, before they would abandon their trust, though they had themselves been abandoned by the Christians and no lord was there to lead them. It is worthy to record that Saladin sought out these women and children, bought them himself, and gave them back to their stoical kinsmen. Then he sent them all safely into Christian territory.†

Thus the year 1188, after a series of conquests,

---

* Abu-Shama, 113.

† Baha-ed-din, 118–9; Ibn-el-Athir, 734–8; Ernoul, 187, 255; *Itinerary*, i., 15. Mont Real held out till the following May.

closed with a triple crown of victory. Belvoir, Safed, and above all Châtillon's once dreaded eyry at Karak, would no longer menace the peaceful merchants and pilgrims on the roads from Egypt and Arabia, and along the Jordan valley. But events soon proved that even these gains did not outweigh the loss which the empire of Saladin was to suffer from the unchecked rallying of the Christians at Tyre.

SIEGE OF A CASTLE.

FROM A 13TH CENTURY MANUSCRIPT.

CHAPTER XVI.

THE BATTLE OF ACRE.

1189.

WHEN the fall of Jerusalem became known in Europe, a universal cry of dismay was heard in every court and camp and village. The black sails of the ship which bore the Archbishop of Tyre, like Theseus of old, from the dismal scene announced from afar the " mortal news."

" It is hard," says our most learned English authority on Crusading history, " at this distance of time to realise the measure of the disaster in the eyes of the western world. It was not merely that the Holy City had fallen ; that all the scenes of that Bible history, which constituted emphatically the literature of medieval Christendom, had passed into the hand of the infidel. It was all this and something more : the little Kingdom of Jerusalem was the one outpost of the Latin Church and Latin culture in the East ; it was the creation of those heroes of the First Crusade whose exploits had already been the theme of more than one romance ; it lay on the verge of that mysterious East, with all its wealth of gold and

precious stones and merchandise, towards which the
sword of the twelfth-century knight turned as instinct-
ively as the prow of the English or Spanish adventurer
turned four centuries later towards the West. . . . Palestine inspired alike the imagination, the enterprise, and
the faith of western Christendom." *

To recover what had been lost became the passionate desire of each pious knight, the ambition of
every adventurer. The Pope issued a trumpet-call
for a new Crusade, which should wash out every sin.
Richard of England, then Count of Poitou, was the
first to take the Cross. The Kings of England and
France made up their quarrel and received the sacred
badge from the Archbishop of Tyre. Baldwin of
Canterbury preached the Crusade, in which he was
later to die before Acre, and a " Saladin tax," a
tithe of every man's wealth, was collected throughout the length and breadth of the land. The eloquence of Berter of Orleans roused the enthusiasm
of France, which re-echoed with his chant—

> " Lignum crucis
> signum ducis
> sequitur exercitus,
> quod non cessit
> sed praecessit
> in vi sancti spiritus." †

The zeal of Christendom was readily kindled, but
its armies were slow to move. William of Sicily had

---

* T. A. Archer, in *Crusades*, 305–6.

† See the vigorous sketch of this Crusade in Archer and Kingsford,
305 ff., and for the Archbishop's mission, Ernoul, 244 ff.

been prompt to succour Tripolis; but England and France resumed their standing strife, and their sovereigns did not begin their leisurely Crusade till the summer of 1190. Alone among the great princes of Europe, the Emperor Frederick Barbarossa, whose seventy years had not quenched the fire of a chivalrous nature, led a vast army from Germany through the territory of the Greeks in May, 1189, but the brave old warrior met his death in the swift waters of the Salef, and only a remnant of his host slowly struggled onwards to the battle-fields of Palestine.

Meanwhile the Franks at the seat of war had not been idle. Queen Sibylla had claimed from Saladin the performance of the promise made at Ascalon; and her husband Guy with his ten fellow-prisoners at Damascus were brought before the Sultan at Tortosa in July, 1188, and after they had pledged their knightly honour never to bear arms against him, they were suffered to go free.* The Marquess of Montferrat was sent to his son at Tyre; Humphrey of Toron was restored to his mother, the widow of Reginald of Châtillon; and King Guy and his brother, with the Master of the Temple, joined Sibylla and concerted plans of vengeance at Tripolis and Antioch. They were all duly absolved from their oath,† and lost no time in rewarding Saladin's good faith and generosity after their usual manner. A number of knights and volunteers gathered round Guy's standard, and at their head the King and Queen proceeded

---

* Ernoul, 252–3 ; Baha-ed-din, 122–3.

† " The king was released by the sentence of the clergy from the enormity of his promise." *Itinerary,* i., 25.

to Tyre. Conrad of Montferrat, however, flatly refused to recognise their authority or to admit them
into his city, which, he said, God had given into his
charge. The King and Queen were forced to camp
outside, and after some successful skirmishes with
the outposts of the Saracens, who were lying before
Belfort (Shekif Arnun) some fifteen miles off, Guy
summoned the Sicilian fleet to follow him along the
coast, and boldly marched upon Acre in August,
1189.

The King's force was very inferior to the army
which Saladin could bring against him. The estimates of the various chroniclers differ, and none,
probably, can be taken as more than a very rough
guess, but the statement in the "Itinerary" is perhaps as good as any other. Guy's army, including
the Pisans of Tyre who had thrown in their lot
with the King, is there reckoned at 9000 men of all
nations, of whom 700 were knights; but in a few
days "the Morning Star visited them from on high ;
for behold fifty ships, such as are commonly called
coggs, having 12,000 men on board, are seen approaching." These were Danes and Frisians, "men
of large limbs, invincible resolution, and fervent devotion." * The total was thus 21,000. Baha-ed-din
estimated the Frank army at the same date at 2000
knights and 30,000 foot, and adds that he never
heard anyone put them at a lower figure, and that
"they were constantly reinforced by sea." It was
true, for the famous knight James of Avesnes, "a
Nestor in counsel, an Achilles in arms, and in honour

* *Itinerary*, i., 26, 27.

a Regulus," soon joined the besiegers; and so did
the Bishop of Beauvais, "who strove to be a Turpin,
if he could but find a Charles," with many others.
The Christians placed Saladin's army at a much
larger number than their own, but neither side attempts to give accurate figures.

It is time to inquire what Saladin was doing to
allow the assembling of the King's forces, and to let
him advance upon Acre. After the surrender of
Belvoir in January, 1189, the Sultan with his brother
el-Adil visited Jerusalem and kept the Feast of Sacrifice there; he then inspected Ascalon, and stayed at
Acre till March. He had placed his old officer Karakush, the founder of the citadel of Cairo, as commandant, with a garrison of tried veterans from
Egypt, and having ordered the repair of the walls
of the great coast fortress, which was to be the capital of Palestine, returned to Damascus. In April,
in an evil moment, he set out to reduce Belfort, a
strong castle of the Templars, east of Tyre, which
was the only inland fortress remaining to the Christians, except the famous Crac des Chevaliers perched
on an inaccessible crag of the Lebanon, which defied
the Moslems till 1285. If Saladin consulted an
augury in the Koran on this occasion, as was his
custom, the sacred book led him grievously astray.
The place might have been masked by a moderate
force whilst the Sultan devoted his energies to the
far more important task of crushing the King's small
army before it grew too strong. As it was, four
precious months were wasted in front of Belfort,
whilst the memory of Hittin, already two years old,

was suffered to fade from Christian minds, and the enemy waxed bolder every day.

Reginald of Sidon, one of the few survivors of Hittin, commanded at Belfort, and he rendered an invaluable service to the cause. He saw that the great thing was to gain time, and being a wily diplomatic person, he set to work to " throw dust " in the good Sultan's eyes. He spoke Arabic, and had studied the history and literature of the Moslems. His intelligence was only equalled by his fascinating manners. Using these advantages, he came to Saladin's tent, professed himself his devoted servant, and promised to surrender the castle without a blow, if only he were allowed three months to bring his family and dependents from Tyre, for whom he dreaded the Marquess's revenge. After the surrender, there was nothing he would like better than to live at Damascus, at the Sultan's gracious Court,— with a suitable maintenance. Indeed, in his many conversations, the clever rogue discovered Saladin's blind side : he began to discuss serious questions of religion, and Saladin reasoned with him, and doubtless cherished the hope, dear to the lay missionary, of bringing a convert to the true faith.

The Sultan's " intelligence department " must have been singularly incompetent not to have warned him that the governor of Belfort was a particular friend and ally of the Marquess of Montferrat, and was not in the least likely to intrigue against him. Doubts, at last, of his fascinating guest began to disturb Saladin's mind, but he was pledged to the three months' truce, and could do nothing till it expired.

THE KURDS' CASTLE, CRAC DES CHEVALIERS.

It was then discovered that Reginald had been playing with him all the time, and that while the worthy
governor had been opening his mind to theological
debate the garrison had been strengthening the fortifications;—the castle was further from capitulating
than ever. It was a melancholy disillusionment,
and Saladin showed unusual generosity in sparing
the diplomatist's life and only putting him into
chains; but in the mean while April had passed into
August, and King Guy was ready to advance upon
Acre.

There had been ample notice of the attack. The
King's movements about Tyre were no secret; Saladin had his outposts there, and early in July there
had been more than one skirmish with his troops at
the bridge over the Litany. Saladin was in the
habit of riding out every day to reconnoitre, for his
camp at Marj Oyun was within easy reach of the
coast as well as of Belfort, and he had himself witnessed one of these encounters in which the Franks
had the advantage.* He had even made a rapid ride
to Acre in July, to order further fortifications, and
enjoin the utmost watchfulness upon the garrison.
He was clearly alive to the danger of a Christian attack. Yet he kept his army before Belfort until the
guile of its governor was exposed, and it was not till
the 27th of August, after hearing that the Franks
were actually on their way, that he finally gave orders for the march to Acre. He left a sufficient
force to blockade Belfort, which surrendered seven
months later, and no doubt he might have masked

---

* Baha-ed-din, 124–5.

17

it in the same fashion three months before, and gone
to meet the enemy.*

At last, however, the Saracens were on the road
and marching night and day. They took the easy
route by Tiberias, and then struck across by the
great west road past Kafar Kenna (Cana) to el-
Kharruba,† where they picked up a division which
had come by the mountains of Toron to watch the
enemy. Detachment after detachment was sent on,
and men and stores were thrown into the threatened
fortress; and the whole army was camped on the
hills over against Acre three days after their departure from Belfort. King Guy had arrived there
two days earlier, on the 28th, the feast of St. Augus-
tine, and had established his camp on " Mount
Turon," the Hill of Prayers (Tell el-Musalliyin), now
Tell el-Fokhkhar, just opposite the city gate. Saladin's object was to outflank the enemy—to besiege

---

* Baha-ed-din, wise after the event, remembers at a later page (152)
of his history that he heard Saladin urge the council of war at Marj
Oyun to adopt his counsel and attack the enemy on the march, before
they could entrench themselves ; but the council preferred to wait till
the Franks were in position before Acre. Baha-ed-din, however,
writes as a hero-worshipper, and the story has àn *ex post facto* air.
Its repetition with variations by Ibn-el-Athir (ii., 6) is perhaps a
slight confirmation.

† El-Kharruba, an important position during Saladin's Acre campaign, is not found in the maps. The name means " the carob tree "
and may have been given to many places where such trees grew. It
was certainly a hill on the road between Saffuriya and Acre (Abu-
Shama, 121) in the mountain range which borders the plain on its
east side. The camp at Acre could be seen from this position, according to Baha-ed-din. Probably it should be placed some way
north of Shafraamm, not far from the present Abelin.

PLAN OF ACRE IN THE THIRTEENTH CENTURY.

the besiegers ; he extended his lines from the river Belus to the hill of el-Ayyadiya, placing his head-quarters on Tell Keysan ; after a month he moved further north, so as to stretch his lines as far as the coast above Acre, and making his headquarters at el-Ayyadiya.

" If a ten years' war made Troy renowned ; if the triumph of the Christians ennobled Antioch ; surely to Acre belongs eternal fame—the city for which the whole world contended." It stands on a tongue of land jutting out to the southward, behind which the Mina or harbour is sheltered from the west and north. The northern or Musart quarter was not built in Saladin's time and the city measured three-quarters of a mile by a quarter* ; strong walls and towers protected the city from the land, east and north ; the sea washed the other sides. Among the defences, the *Turris Maledicta* or Accursed Tower at the north-east angle was so named because legend connected it with the bribe of Judas ; and the har-bour was guarded by a chain and by a formidable rock fort, called the Tower of Flies, for the unsavoury reason that it had once been a famous place of sacri-fice. The ramparts of the city overlooked the great plain of Acre, twenty miles from north to south, watered by the two great branches of the river Belus, with numerous tributary streams, and bounded on the south by the Kishon running parallel with the great barrier of Mount Carmel and falling into the sea at Haifa at the extremity of the bay. Isolated hills of no great height afford military positions at a

---

* In the 11th century, Nasir-i Khusrau, ed. Schefer, 12.

distance of about five miles from the coast, and a couple of miles behind these the southern prolongation of the Lebanon range formed the eastern boundary of the plain, and served Saladin at once as a refuge from the malaria of the lowlands in winter, a retreat from superior forces, and a post of vantage and observation.

The Franks were not strong enough at this time to completely blockade the city, and the right wing of the Saracens, under the ever-valiant Taki-ed-din, easily forced their way in (15–16 Sept.). Saladin himself entered Acre and examined the enemy's position from the ramparts. Baha-ed-din also visited the fortress: " I climbed to the top of the wall," he says, " as every one did, and thence I hurled at the enemy the first thing that came to hand." The place was strongly garrisoned and well provisioned, and there was no present fear of its being stormed or starved. Perpetual skirmishing went on between the armies, and the soldiers on both sides became so accustomed to these little affairs that they would sometimes break off in the middle of an encounter and fall to talking. When they were tired of skirmishing, they diverted themselves with pitting boys of each side against each other, that they too might share in the fun, and the lads had a furious tussle whilst their elders formed the ring in a strictly sportsmanlike manner.* On the other hand we read of barbarous deeds on both sides—of wild Bedawis in Saladin's pay, who fell upon straggling Christians, cut off their heads, and brought them to the Sultan for reward ; and of Christian

* Baha-ed-din, 139.

women, dragging Turkish prisoners by the hair, shamefully misusing them, and hacking off their heads with knives.*

These varied encounters led up to a general engagement, which very nearly brought the war to an end. On the 4th of October, soon after sunrise, the Franks were in motion. Their army was extended in a semi-circle round Acre, over a line of fully two miles, from the sea to the river Belus, to match the length of the concentric Saracen line of battle. Their archers and cross-bowmen were as usual in front, and the knights and infantry were marshalled in close order behind them. They advanced in four divisions. The King commanded the right, with the Gospel borne before him under a canopy of satin. The two centre divisions were under Conrad of Montferrat and Louis, Landgrave of Thuringia, whilst the Templars mustered on the left. Saladin himself commanded the Moslem centre, with his sons el-Afdal and ez-Zafir on his right hand. On the right of the centre were the contingents from Mosil and Diyar-Bekr; and the right wing resting on the sea consisted of the fine troops of northern Syria under Saladin's best general, his nephew Taki-ed-din. The left of the centre was composed of Kurdish clans from the Tigris led by their chiefs, with the levies from Sinjar, and Kukbury's retainers from Harran; whilst the left wing was formed by picked veterans from Shirkuh's mamluks, the old conquerors of Egypt. Thus the most critical posts, the extreme right and left, were confided to the flower of the Saracen army;

---

* Ibn-el-Athir, ii., 9 ; *Itinerary*, i., 34.

but the centre, apart from Saladin's bodyguard, contained doubtful elements in the less tried levies from
Mesopotamia and Kurdistan.

The battle of Acre began at the fourth hour after
sunrise with an attack of the Franks upon the Saracens' right wing.   Instead of waiting for them, Taki-
ed-din ordered his men back, in accordance with the
usual Turkish tactics, intending to draw the enemy
on, and then manœuvre to take them in flank.   Saladin unfortunately mistook this movement for retreat, and sent part of his centre in support.   Thus
reinforced the left were able to drive the Franks in.
But meanwhile the enemy had noted the weakening
of Saladin's centre, and seizing the opportunity advanced upon it in strength, horse and foot keeping
solidly together.   When they came to close quarters,
the infantry opened out, the knights rode through,
and delivered the full shock of a mailed charge upon
the Saracens.   The brunt of this heavy attack fell
upon the men from Diyar-Bekr, who broke in disorder and fled from the field : they were next heard
from at the bridge by the Lake of Galilee, well on
their way to Damascus !   The knights, hot-headed
and undisciplined as ever, pursued the flying enemy
up the headquarters hill, rummaged the camp, and
entered Saladin's tent, where the fiery Count de Bar
disported himself in triumph.   Looking round, they
discovered that their charge had not been supported,
and that they were separated from their friends.
They had now to get back as best they could.   Saladin's left had been untouched, and still stood firm.
He rallied what remained of his centre, and held

A. King Guy   B. Conrad of Montferrat.
C. Lewis of Thuringia   D. Master of the Templars.
E. Kurds & Egyptians   F. Mesopotamians   G. Syrians.

Christians:
HORSE   FOOT
Turks:

To Tyre

0   1   2 Miles

Sally of
Garrison

Marsh of Aïz-ed-din

Plain of

Arab-el-

Ghawarneh

Hill
of
Bisr-el-
Hammar

ACRE

Mt.
Turon

Mole

Saladin's
Camp

Khan el
Ayadieh

R. Belus
(Nahr-Namein)

To Saffuria

Marshes

THE BATTLE OF ACRE, OCT. 4, 1189.

(FROM OMAN'S "ART OF WAR,")

them tight in hand till the victorious Franks were passing on their return from his camp; then with his famous battle-cry of "*Yâla-l-Islam*," he hurled his whole force on their rear, calling up his right and his left wings to join in the general charge, whilst the garrison of Acre made a well-timed sortie. The result was the utter rout of the enemy. Seeing their comrades running, the other divisions were seized with panic and fled to their camp on the hill, where they just managed to beat off their pursuers.*

In the tumult the King himself rescued his rival, Conrad of Montferrat, from imminent danger. Andrew of Brienne, the pink of chivalry, was slain whilst rallying his comrades, in the very sight of his brother, who left him to his fate. A trooper saw James of Avesnes thrown from his charger and in utmost jeopardy; he gave him his own horse to escape on, and "by his own death nobly saved his lord's life." But the most notable loss that day was the Master of the Temple. Gerard of Rideford, whose ambition and hate had stirred up strife among the Christians and brought death to many a Saracen, ended his stormy life on the field of Acre. He refused to fly, and died like a soldier. Even women

---

* The battle is described with remarkable clearness by Baha-ed-din (140–6), who was present; but he does not mention any sortie of the garrison of Acre; this may be a mistake in the confused account in the *Itinerary* (i., 29, 30), which otherwise agrees in the main outlines with the Arabic description. What happened to the Christian right and left, after the advance of the centre divisions, is not clear; but in his admirable *History of the Art of War*, ii., 336, Mr. Oman has put forward a very ingenious explanation of the defeat of the Templars on the left by the garrison of Acre.

fought manfully on horseback beside their brothers in arms, nor were they discovered till they were made prisoners.*　It was a day of Heroes and of Amazons. The Franks confessed to a loss of 1500 killed ; but Baha-ed-din, who saw their bodies being carried to the river to be thrown in,† estimated their dead at over 4000.　On the Moslems' side the loss was more by flight than slaughter.　The Diyar-Bekr contingent had vanished ; but of the rest, only the leader of the Kurds and one other emir were recorded as killed, with about 150 undistinguished warriors.　Panic will account for a good deal, but the disproportion of these estimates is inartistic.　The Christian estimate of the Moslem loss at 1500 horsemen is more consistent with the accounts of the battle.

---

* Ibn-el-Athir, ii., 13.

† He says the man in charge of the dead-carts counted 4100 odd bodies from the left wing alone of the Franks.　Imad-ed-din reckoned the total Christian loss at 10,000 (Goergens, 124), but round figures are to be distrusted.

CHAPTER XVII.

THE SIEGE OF ACRE.

1189–91.

AFTER the battle Saladin failed to push his victory home. He even allowed the panic-stricken enemy to throw up earthworks and entrench themselves more securely, whilst he let his men rest, and restored order in the rifled camp. The army, it seems, was in no mood to follow up its success. It was exhausted, and the robbing of the camp by their own followers (who left little or nothing for the pursuing Templars) had exasperated the men. A week later a council of war was held, and the Sultan addressed the generals:

"In the name of God, and praise be to God, and blessing on the Apostle of God.

"Know that this enemy of God, and our enemy, hath entered our country and trampled on the soil of Islam: but already the star of victory (if God please) hath gleamed upon us. There remains but a handful of their force, and we must diligently destroy it. By God, it is our bounden duty ! Ye know that this our army can now look for reinforcement only to el-Melik el-Adil, who is coming. As for the enemy, if it is left to hold its position till the sea is open, vast increase will come to it. My judgment is that we fight them. Each of you give his."

The council was divided, and there was much debate, but at last it was resolved to withdraw the army to the hills, to give the men rest, after fifty days under arms ; when they were refreshed and the deserters had been brought in, the attack should be renewed. Once more Saladin allowed his sound judgment to be overruled by the council. He may have been more in their hands than is acknowledged ; he certainly had a difficult task in keeping together so mixed a force and reconciling the jealousies and discontent of rival leaders and races. But the best explanation of his yielding to so unsoldierlike a decision, is that he was seriously ill. He was subject to violent attacks of what the Arab chroniclers call " colic,"—more probably the malignant Syrian fever, —and his doctors joined the emirs in counselling a change of air.* The constant fatigues and anxieties of the past two years had told heavily upon him. He was over fifty, and he had worked harder than any of his men. His long rides over the country and exposure to all weathers, the winter sieges he had undertaken, the forced march upon Acre in a sultry August, and at last the daily encounters with the Franks, where he was always in the thick of the fight, carrying heavy armour, and for days was too

* Ibn-el-Athir, ii., 14.

preoccupied to think of proper food *—all this was
enough to wear out a younger man. But for this
untoward weakness, Saladin might have insisted on
carrying out his plan, and the result could hardly
have been doubtful. Broken in spirits and crippled
by the loss of thousands of their men, shut in between the Saracen army and the well-armed walls of
Acre, the Crusaders must have suffered a second
Hittin, from which there was no recovery : they
must have been driven into the sea. The fatal error
before Tyre was repeated before Acre. The Franks
were given time to entrench themselves, and to hold
the ground till reinforcements came. The siege
might have been brought to a summary end on the
5th of October, 1189, instead of dragging on its
weary length for nearly two more years, crowned at
last by the victory of the Crusaders.

The retreat to the hills of el-Kharruba on October
16th meant more than a temporary rest. The rains
began, and nothing further was done until the spring.
The winter months were spent by the Franks in
strengthening their position by digging a great
trench, not without harassing interruption, and by
Saladin in beating up recruits. El-Adil joined him
with an Egyptian contingent, and Admiral Lulu,
coming to Acre with fifty sail from Alexandria, captured a couple of valuable prizes, and landed a naval
brigade of 10,000 sailors to harass the enemy.† Fighting soon became out of the question, as the mud
was so deep that the two armies could not get at

---

* Baha-ed-din, 137, 147.

† Imad-ed-din, Abu-Shama, 127.

one another. The Sultan visited Acre again in great
state, and looked to its defences and stores, and then,
dismissing his troops to their homes, remained at
el-Kharruba with his guard till the spring reopened
the sea and the roads. Meanwhile a fresh cause for
anxiety had arisen. News had arrived of the march
of Frederick Barbarossa through Asia Minor, and
the letter of the Armenian Catholicos—who, like the
Emperor of Constantinople, was on the side of
Saladin—announcing the tragical death of the old
Crusader, also informed the Sultan that Frederick's
son was leading the army on into Syria. Had the
extreme weakness of the remnant of the German
host been known to the Sultan, he would hardly
have crippled his fine army by sending a large division to cut off their approach. In response to his
appeal and the efforts of his secretary Baha-ed-din,
who visited the Caliph and the princes of Mesopotamia in the winter, and summoned all men to the
Holy War, the troops from Aleppo, Harran, Sinjar,
Jezira, Mosil, and Irbil, had been pouring into his
camp (now at Tell el-Ajjul near el-Ayyadiya) all May
and June. The Caliph of Baghdad had sent lances
and arrows and machines that discharged burning
shafts. But the Syrian contingents were almost
immediately sent north again to meet the imaginary
danger of the German invasion, and the more urgent
necessity of crushing the besiegers—who were really
themselves closely besieged by the Moslems—before
they could be reinforced, was neglected. The Crusading army must have been more formidable in
reality than it reads in the chronicles to have thus

intimidated the Saracens; indeed, the account of the
eight days' fighting at Pentecost shows that the two
sides must have been fairly matched.*

Saladin's mistake became painfully obvious when
Henry of Champagne effected his landing at the
end of July, with 10,000 men, and a number of
knights, nobles, and fighting prelates. Up to this
time the situation had remained unchanged; though
partly surrounded, Acre was not cut off from communication with Saladin's forces, which in turn surrounded the enemy; and the skirmishes and sallies,
the attacks on the trenches and destruction of siege-
engines, had on the whole been in favour of the
Saracens. The ingenuity of a young coppersmith
of Damascus, who possessed the secret of making a
kind of Greek fire, which burned up the enemy's
siege-towers and machines, delighted Saladin, and
still more did the young man's answer, when he offered him riches, that he would take no reward for
what he had done in the cause of God. A fleet
from Alexandria had successfully fought its way into
the harbour in June, and replenished the stores of
the besieged; and an attempt to surprise the right
wing of the Moslem camp, weakened by the departure of the troops for the north, was repulsed by
el-Adil with very heavy loss on the feast of St. James
(25th July). At least four thousand of the Christians fell on that day, by their own admission †; but

---

* *Itinerary*, i., 38; Ibn-el-Athir, ii., 18.

† Letter of Archbp. Baldwin's chaplain, 21 Oct., 1191 *(Epp. Cantuar.*, 329). Imad-ed-din rode over the battle-field in the company
of Baha-ed-din, and reckoned the number of the Christians slain to
be 10,000 (Abu-Shama, 137).

the Arabic eyewitnesses estimated the loss at more
than double.   Among the slain were some women
in armour, who had fought valiantly beside the
knights.   Imad-ed-din long afterwards recalled the
piercing screams of a woman whom he saw dying on
the field.   But Saladin evidently did not feel himself strong enough to order a general assault of
the King's entrenchments ; the Franks could not
be tempted again to risk a pitched battle ; and two
days after this engagement Count Henry arrived and
took command of the army.

   This large reinforcement, the first of several soon
to follow, changed the situation.   Saladin drew his
army off once more to the hills (1 August), and
Acre was so far cut off that communications could
only be maintained by the pigeon post, by strong
swimmers, or by swift skiffs at night.   It was small
consolation to the Sultan to receive a friendly letter
from his futile ally, the Greek Emperor Isaac, bidding him " not let the coming of the Germans weigh
heavily on your hearts : their plans and purposes
will work their own confusion " * : the French at
least were already on the spot and had put Acre
under strict blockade.   Saracen ships indeed still
forced their way in to the relief of the garrison ; one
was smuggled in under a French disguise, but generally they had to run the gauntlet.   One such adventure happened in September.   Three Egyptian
dromonds or ships of burthen opportunely arrived,
when there was not enough food in the city to last
another day.   The Christian galleys were upon the

---

* Baha-ed-din, 175 ; Abu-Shama, 144.

new-comers in a moment. The beach was lined with the Moslem army, calling aloud upon God to save the ships. The Sultan himself stood there in an agony of suspense, watching the struggle, "like a parent robbed of his child." The battle raged, but fortunately for the garrison there was a fair wind, and at last the three ships sailed into the harbour safe and sound, amid the furious shouts of the enemy and the loud thanksgivings of the Faithful.

Once in port they were protected by the celebrated Tower of Flies, which stood on a rock at the entrance to the harbour, and effectually shielded every vessel that got past it. The Crusaders retorted by a determined effort to destroy this obnoxious defence. The Pisans among them, ever adroit in seamanship, rigged up turrets on their galleys, tall enough to overlook the Fly Tower, and to bombard or set it on fire, whilst a fire-ship was sent into the harbour to destroy the Saracen vessels which might put out to interfere. The device, however, failed signally. The Pisans managed to grapple the tower, and to get their scaling ladders up, under cover of a heavy bombardment from their turrets ; but just as they were counting on success, the defenders rallied, crushed the storming party on the ladders with great rocks, and throwing their Greek fire, set ladders, turrets, and galleys in a blaze, amid the derisive shouts of the Moslems. The fire-ship went astray on a foul wind and was easily extinguished and captured.

At the beginning of October the dreaded Germans made their appearance : Frederick Duke of Suabia arrived at Acre with a bare thousand men. Incon-

siderable as was this relief, the presence of Barbarossa's son raised the spirits of the besiegers, and
his energy infused new zeal into the war. Nothing
at first would content him but an engagement with
the enemy in the open ; but Saladin's advance guard,
still posted at el-Ayyadiya, aided by the men of
Mosil, who were ordered forward from Tell Keysan,
beat back the Crusaders with little trouble. After
this failure they turned their energies to pressing the
siege with much ingenuity. For the first time they
employed a battering ram—the garrison of Acre had
evidently become very weak to allow them to get to
close quarters: it was a huge beam with an iron head
which weighed nearly three hundredweight, and had
been constructed at great expense by the Archbishop
of Besançon. Another ram, or bore, called the "cat,"
with a plough-shaped pointed head, and a penthouse
or "sow" to cover a number of men, was also set to
work; and a ship was fitted with a turret and draw-
bridge, to be dropped on to the Fly Tower. A grand
assault was made early in October; the new machines
were dragged up to the city, and the assailants
dropped into the fosse to scale the walls; when the
garrison suddenly opened a heavy fire of arrows,
fireballs, stones, and bolts from bows, mangonels,
slings, and arbalests, and sallying out in desperation
drove the Franks back; then laying naphtha to the
cat and ram they set them ablaze, and finally dragged
the flaming ram in triumph within the gate.

The rejoicing of the garrison was almost immediately damped by the arrival of more reinforcements
from Europe. At last an English fleet hove in sight.

Baldwin, Archbishop of Canterbury, Hubert Walter, Bishop of Salisbury, and the Justiciar, Ranulf de Glanville, had reached Tyre with men and stores and money in September, and coming to the army before Acre on the 12th of October, announced that the Kings of England and France were verily on their way to the Holy Land. The Archbishop's chaplain gave a sorry picture of the Crusaders' camp :

"We found our army (I say it with grief and groaning) given up to shameful practices, and yielding to ease and lust rather than encouraging virtue. The Lord is not in the camp ; there is none that doeth good. The chiefs envy one another, and strive for privilege. The lesser folk are in want and find no one to help them. In the camp there is neither chastity, sobriety, faith, nor charity —a state of things, which, I call God to witness, I would not have believed had I not seen it. The Turks are besieging us, and daily do they challenge us and persist in attacking us, while our knights lie skulking within their tents, and like conquered men let the enemy affront them with impunity. Saladin's strength is increasing daily, whereas our army daily grows smaller." *

The coming of the English put some spirit into the "skulking knights." The churchmen stirred up their zeal, if they could not mend their morals ; the venerable Archbishop himself raised the standard of the holy martyr, St. Thomas of Canterbury, and sent the army forth with his blessing to do battle ; whilst the Bishop of Salisbury and many other priests and

---

* *Epp. Cantuar*, ed. Stubbs, 328–9 ; Archer, *Crusade of Richard I.*, 18.

prelates manfully took part in the fight.*   A general
action near the Spring Head (or source of the southern
branch of the river Belus), about six miles south of
Acre, began on "the morrow of St. Martin's," the
12th of November.   The enemy's object was to
bring in provisions from Haifa, for they were running very short of food.   Seeing them advancing in
force, the Saracen outpost, after a sharp skirmish,
withdrew from their usual station at el-Ayyadiya to
Tell Keysan, and on the 13th, the army formed up
in two positions almost facing each other and en-
closing the enemy who nevertheless advanced to the
Spring Head.   Saladin's left wing stretched across
from near the sea to the Belus, facing north-east,
whilst the right, posted on the hills, faced west towards the river, which it touched on the east bank
near the bridge of Da'uk.   The centre was thrown
forward beneath Saladin's reserve, which with his
headquarters were on the summit of Mount Kharruba, whence he could view the whole plain below;
and he also held the hill of Shafraamm, once a Templars' stronghold.   This situation was maintained on
the 14th, when the Franks, hearing that there was no
food at Haifa, turned back by the east bank and
made for the bridge of Da'uk.   They were closely
hemmed in by the Saracens all the way, whose light
horse assailed them at close quarters with mace,
sword, and lance, striving to break the solid and
orderly formation†; and Saladin continually sent

---

* *Itinerary*, i., 62.

† The best account of the engagement at the Spring Head is by
Imad-ed-din ; *see* Abu-Shama, 162–4, and Baha-ed-din.

down supports from the hills behind; but they
pluckily forced their way to the bridge, camped
there for the night, and cutting it behind them on
the morrow, retired much exhausted but in good
order, and carrying many wounded, to their entrenchments. Here they were covered by their reserves, who came out under Godfrey de Lusignan,
and drove back the Moslems' pursuit. Conrad and
Henry of Champagne had themselves led the expedition, but the Franks had suffered heavily. Among
the killed was a knight whose appearance astonished
Baha-ed-din : he rode a charger with housings of
chain mail to its hoofs. Saladin's picked guard had
also lost severely.

Indecisive as the action was, it encouraged the
Saracens, who wished immediately to follow it up.
It was evidently a critical test, of doubtful issue, for
Saladin had sent his baggage for safety to the rear,
towards Nazareth ; and the fact that he was himself
again ill with colic or fever, and could not take part
in the battle, added to his anxiety. Yet he kept his
invincible spirit ; and when some one spoke of the
sufferings and deaths of the Moslems from the unhealthy state of the plain, he quoted the Arab
proverb, " Kill me and Malik ; kill Malik with me,"
alluding to a famous historical combat in which the
hero called upon his comrades to kill the adversary
struggling with him on the ground, even if they also
killed himself. Saladin was ready to die, with all
his host, if only the Franks died too.* Yet when
some Crusaders of rank were taken in an ambush

---

* Baha-ed-din, 196–201.

a little later, Saladin received them with stately
courtesy, clothed them in robes of honour, gave
them furs to keep out the bitter cold, allowed them
to write to the camp for anything they wanted, and
sent them in high good humour to Damascus. It
was better to be the guest of Saladin than to shiver
and starve in a Christian tent.

The winter of 1190–1, which stopped all active
operations, was passed in great misery by the Crusaders. Many of their chiefs were dead. They had
lost their Queen, Sibylla; Ranulf de Glanville, the
earl of Ferrers, the earl of Clare's brother, among the
English, were no more; and the aged Archbishop of
Canterbury died in November, grieved unto death at
the licence around him. Conrad of Montferrat had
attained the first step in his ambition by his unscrupulous marriage with Isabella, now the heiress to the
crown of Jerusalem, whose divorce from Humphrey
of Toron he had successfully contrived; he then
withdrew to Tyre to nourish schemes of kingship,
leaving the army before Acre to its fate. The English "Itinerary" is full of curses upon the Marquess
for his callous indifference to the perishing people,
whom he might perhaps have relieved. For famine
and disease were working havoc behind the entrenchments. Corn was selling for a hundred pieces of
gold the sack, and a single egg cost six deniers.
The greedy merchants kept up the prices, and the
camp was starving. Blood horses were slaughtered
for food, nor did the hungry people despise even the
entrails of animals that died from age or disease.
They ate grass like cattle, fought over the bakers'

ovens, gnawed the bare bones abandoned by the
dogs. Even nobles were reduced to stealing, and a
pitiful story is told of how two friends, having come
to their last coin, spent it on the purchase of thirteen
beans, and then, finding one bean bad, went a long
way back to the seller to insist on his replacing it
with a good one. A few even sought relief by going
over to Islam. The prelates and some of the better
nobles made contributions for the poor, but it was
little they could do. This state of wretchedness, ag-
gravated by the sickness and ague bred by perpetual
rains, lasted until Lent, 1191, when at last the sea
became navigable to the timid seamen of those days,
and a cornship saved the camp from starvation.*

Meanwhile Saladin had dismissed most of his
army to their homes, and remained only with his
own guard. The Mesopotamian princes were the
first to leave in November: they had been with difficulty induced to stay so long. It was not to be
expected that the vanquished descendants of Zengy
should show much enthusiasm in their supplanter's
service; but apart from such natural jealousy, Oriental troops cannot endure being long separated
from their wives and homes. The provisioning of
Acre was Saladin's chief occupation during the winter. The Christian galleys had gone to escort Conrad to Tyre for his wedding, and the city was open
to the sea. An Egyptian convoy failed to get in in
December, but el-Adil, stationed at Haifa, contrived
to send in stores, and Saladin in February introduced
a fresh garrison under a new commander. The new

---

* *Itinerary*, i., 67 ff.

garrison, however, was smaller than the old; many
more came out than went in; nor were the new-
comers adepts in siege-work, and Saladin was accused
of imprudence and carelessness in leaving too much
to incompetent or interested subordinates.* Probably he was still suffering from the effects of illness.
The relieving of Acre was not accomplished without
assaults from the Franks, whose misery did not
wholly paralyse their energy, for the famine was not
then at its worst. On the other hand the garrison
repulsed their attacks, and Saladin captured a few
stray ships, aided by some deserters from the enemy's
camp.†

So the weary winter months passed by. The
spring found the contending forces in the same
position: the city well garrisoned, and for the present sufficiently provisioned; Saladin on the hills,
waiting for the return of his troops; the Christians,
between the two, weakened, dispirited, and demoralised, but holding their entrenched camp unmolested,
save for occasional sallies of the garrison or skirmishes with Saladin's outposts. The summer
brought a complete revolution in the relations of
the two forces, and the Saracens were soon to find
themselves no longer the besiegers of the besiegers,
but the attacked. The Crusade of Richard Cœur
de Lion was at hand.

---

* Ibn-el-Athir, ii., 33; Imad-ed-din, Abu-Shama, 165.
† Baha-ed-din, 207.

PART V.

RICHARD AND SALADIN.

1191–2.

CHAPTER XVIII.

THE LOSS OF ACRE.

1191.

RICHARD of England and Philip of France were at last approaching the Holy Land. They had set out in the summer of 1190, but their advance was as leisurely as a yachting cruise. The long delays at Messina and at Cyprus, the subjection of the one and the conquest of the other, and the marriage with Berengaria, are commonplaces of history, but they nearly allowed the destruction of the army before Acre. A honeymoon at Cyprus was a strange manner of rescuing a starving camp. The King of France was the first to arrive. He was welcomed at Easter " with hymns and songs and floods of tears, as if he were an angel of God." He at once set up his siege-engines, and in May the city was assailed with renewed energy. Saladin's Chancellor records in a letter how the Franks attacked with wooden towers, stone-slings, rams, and other engines; how they strove by day to break the walls, and by night toiled in the trenches, filling up the

moat, setting up scaling ladders, desisting neither by
day nor night.   They began to build an earthen dyke,
which was like a wall, with round towers, and was
heightened with wood and stones.   It started from
their camp, and as it progressed they dug the earth
from behind it and cast it in front, and so pushed it
forward to within half a bowshot of the ramparts.
Neither stones nor fire had the least effect on it.*
But whilst pressing the siege with vigour, Philip
courteously awaited Richard's arrival before beginning the general assault.

How Cœur de Lion at last sailed from Cyprus to
Acre, and how the siege was crowned with success,
may best be read in the contemporary " Itinerary of
Richard," which, however biassed in favour of England's hero, presents the most detailed and picturesque narrative of the great siege that we possess.†

" And so, having concluded these matters, Richard
straightway turned his thoughts towards his passage
across [to the Holy Land] ; and, when he had arranged
his baggage, set sail with a favourable wind. . . . And
lo ! there now went abroad a report that Acre was on the
point of being taken ; upon hearing which the king with
a deep sigh prayed God that the city might not fall
before his arrival, ' for,' he said, ' after so long a siege
our triumph ought, God willing, to be one of excep-
tional glory.'   Then with great haste he went on board

---

* Letter from Kady el-Fadil, Abu-Shama, 173.

† The translations here extracted from the *Itinerary*, Bk. ii., c. 42,
to Bk. iii., c. 18, are quoted by permission from Mr. T. A. Archer's
admirable *Crusade of Richard I.*, in the series entitled " English
History by Contemporary Writers " (1888).

one of the best and largest of his galleys at Famagusta ;
and being impatient of delay, as he always was, he kept
right ahead, though other and better appointed galleys
followed him from every side.   And so, as they were
furrowing the sea with all haste, they caught their earliest
glimpse of that Holy Land of Jerusalem.   The castle of
Margat was the first to meet their eyes ; then Tortosa,
set on the sea-shore, Tripolis, Nephyn, Botron, and not
long after the lofty tower of Gibeleth.   At last on this
side of Sidon near Beyrut they descried afar off a
certain ship filled with Saladin's choicest warriors, the
pick out of all his pagan realm, and destined to bring
aid to the besieged in Acre.   Seeing that they could not
make direct for Acre on account of the nearness of the
Christians, the Saracens drew back to sea a little and
waited their time to make a sudden rush into the harbour.   Richard, who had taken note of the ship, calling
up one of his galley-men, Peter des Barres, bade him
row hastily and enquire who commanded it.   Word was
brought back that it belonged to the king of France ; but
Richard, as he drew near eagerly, could neither hear any
French word nor see any Christian standard or banner.
As it approached he began to wonder at its size, its firm
and solid build.   For it was set off with three masts of
great height and its smoothly wrought sides were decked
here and there with green or yellow hides.*   Added to
which it was so well rigged out with every fitting appointment and so well furnished with provisions of every
kind as to leave no room for improvement. . . .

  " At the king's command a galley started after the
strange ship at full speed.   Seeing this, its sailors began

_____

  * The hides were generally saturated with vinegar to protect the
wood from Greek fire and naphtha.

to hurl arrows and darts against the crew of the galley,
as it drew up alongside of them without offering any
greeting. Noting this, Richard gave the word for an
immediate onset. On either side the missiles fell like
rain and the strange ship now went on at a slower rate,
for the oarsmen had to slacken their efforts and there
was not much wind. And yet, frequently as our galley-
men made their circuits round the enemy, they could
find no good opportunity of attacking ; so strongly was
the vessel built and so well was it manned with warriors,
who kept on hurling their darts without a pause. . . .
Our men began to falter and relaxed their efforts, won-
dering what the peerless courage of the unconquered
king Richard himself would deem the best course under
these circumstances. But he boldly called out to his
own men as follows :

'What ! are you going to let that vessel get off untouched and unharmed ? Shame upon you ! After so
many triumphs will you let sloth get hold of you now
and give way like cowards ?

> Never, so long as any foes
> Remain, are you to seek repose.

Well do you know, all of you, that you will deserve to
be hung on a gallows and put to death if you suffer
these enemies to escape.'

"On hearing these words our galley-men, making a
virtue of necessity, plunged eagerly into the sea and
getting under the enemy's ship bound the helm with
ropes so as to make the vessel lean to one side and
hinder its progress. Others, pushing alongside with
great skill and perseverance, grasped hold of the cordage
and leapt on board. The Turks were ready for these
and slew them promptly, cutting off one man's arms,

another man's hands or head, and pitching the dead
bodies out to sea. This sight roused the other Christians
to greater valour . . . so that scrambling over the ship's
bulwarks they hurled themselves upon the Turks and
gave no quarter to those who offered any resistance.

"But the Turks emboldened by despair used every
effort to repel the galley-men, and succeeded in cutting
off a foot here, a hand or head there; whilst their opponents, straining every nerve, drove the Turks back to
the very prow of the ship. Upon this other Turks came
rushing up from the hold of the vessel and, massed into
one body with their fellows, offered a stout resistance,
being determined to die bravely or repulse their advers-
aries like men. For these were the very flower of the
Turkish youth—a band skilled in warlike exploits and
well armed. So the fight continued and warriors fell
everywhere on either side till at last the Turks, pressing on
with greater vigour, forced our men back and compelled
them to quit the ship. Our galley-men accordingly betook themselves to their own galleys and again began to
row round the ship, looking out for a place suitable for
attack.

"Meanwhile the king, noting the danger of his men,
and seeing that it would be no easy thing to take the
Turkish vessel with all its arms and stores intact, gave
orders for each of his galleys to prick the enemy with its
beak. Accordingly the galleys, after drawing back a
space, are once more swept forward under the impulse of
many oars to pierce the enemy's sides. By these tactics
the ship was stove in at once,* and, giving an inlet to the

* Baha-ed-din confirms the loss of the great ship from Beyrut, with
her 650 soldiers, stores, provisions, and machines of war; but he says
her captain himself sank her, when he saw she must be taken, so that
the enemy got nothing of her cargo (220–1).

waves, began to sink ; while the Turks, to avoid going down with their vessel, leapt overboard into the sea, where they were slain or drowned. The king, however, spared thirty-five of them, to wit the emirs and those skilled in the making of warlike engines. All the others perished ; the warlike gear was lost, and the serpents were drowned or tossed about here and there on the sea waves.

"Had that ship got safe into Acre the Christians would never have taken the city. Thus did God bring disaster upon the infidels, while to the Christians who trusted in him he gave help at the hands of king Richard whose war-like endeavours prospered without intermission. . . .

"After destroying this ship, king Richard and all his company hastened with joy and eagerness towards Acre, where he longed to be. Thanks to a favourable wind on the very next night his fleet cast anchor off Tyre. Early next morning he hoisted sail once more, and had not gone very far before he caught sight of that place we have mentioned before—Scandalion ; thence passing by Casal Imbert the lofty tower of Acre rose up in the distance, and then by degrees the other fortifications of the city.

"Acre was then girt round on every side by an infinite number of people from every Christian nation under heaven—the chosen warriors of all Christian lands, men well fitted to undergo the perils of war. . . . Beyond them lay an innumerable army of Turks swarming on the mountains and valleys, the hills, and the plains, and hav-ing their tents, bright with coloured devices of all kinds, pitched everywhere. Our men could also see Saladin's own pair of lions and those of his brother Saphadin,* and Takadin the champion of heathendom. Saladin him-self was keeping a watch on the sea-coasts and harbours

---

* " Saphadin " is Seyf-ed-din el-Melik el-Adil.

without however ceasing to contrive frequent and fierce attacks upon the Christians. King Richard too, looking forth, reckoned up the number of his foes; and as he reached the harbour the king of France, together with the chiefs of the whole army, all the lords and mighty men, welcomed him with joy and exultation; for they had long been very eager for him to arrive. It was on [June 8] the Saturday before the feast of the blessed Barnabas the apostle, in Pentecost week, that king Richard with his followers reached Acre. On his arrival the whole land was stirred with the exulting glee of the Christians. For all the people were in transports, shouting out congratulations and blowing trumpets. He was brought ashore with jubilant cries; and there was great joy because the desired of all nations had come. . . ."

Since the opening of the season Saladin had again taken up his position on the hill of el-Ayyadiya (5 June), whence he made daily attacks upon the enemy's trenches. The garrison was closely pressed; the daily labour of clearing the fosse of the bodies of horses and men with which the Franks filled it, added to the constant struggle to repulse the storming parties and destroy the machines, had tired them out; and Saladin's main object was to draw the enemies' attention to the rear by ceaselessly harassing the camp entrenchments, night and day, so as to relieve the garrison. He had not yet his full strength, though the North Syrian troops had rejoined him early; but at the end of June he received large reinforcements both from Egypt and from Mesopotamia. He was untiring in beating up recruits, and his despatches are full of reproaches for the lukewarm support of the Holy War by the Mohammedan princes. He even sent an embassy to the Almohade Caliph of Marocco to invite his assistance.

Hardly had Richard landed when he was taken ill with the fever of the country, which the Franks called "Arnoldia" : but "none the less did he during the whole course of his illness continue the construction of his stone-slings and mangonels and the erection of a castle before the city gate"—like the "Mate Griffon" or "Kill Greek" tower which he had successfully set up against Messina and had now brought to Acre. Philip also fell sick in the same manner, but he was the first to recover.

"When the king of France got well from his sickness he devoted himself to preparing his engines and setting up his stone-slings in fitting places, from which he kept them working night and day. He had one very good engine of war called 'The Bad Neighbour'; and, within the city, the Turks had another which they called 'The Bad Kinsman,' by whose assistance they frequently managed to destroy the 'Bad Neighbour.' The king of France on his part kept rebuilding the latter machine till by constant blows he had partly overthrown the chief wall of the city and shattered the Accursed Tower. On one side the stone-sling of the duke of Burgundy used also to work, and not without effect ; on the other that of the Templars wrought the Turks vast injury, whilst that of the Hospitallers—equally dreaded by the Turks—kept plying always. Besides all these there was a certain stone-sling, built out of common funds, which they used to call 'God's stone-sling.' Close by it a certain priest, a man of the greatest integrity, was always

preaching and at the same time begging money for its
reconstruction or for the payment of those who collected
the stones it discharged. By its blows the wall near the
Accursed Tower was shaken for a length of two perches.
The count of Flanders, too, had a peculiarly choice
stone-sling, to say nothing of a smaller one. King Richard took possession of the former on the count's death.
These two stone-slings kept plying at a tower near one
of the gates, much frequented by the Turks, till it was
half smashed in. Moreover king Richard had made
two other new stone-slings of remarkable material and
workmanship, and these hit the mark at an incredible
distance. He had also built an engine of the strongest
construction of beams. It had steps fitted to it for getting up, and was commonly known as the belfry. This
engine was covered with closely-fitting hides, with ropes,
and strong planks of wood, so as not to be destroyed by
the blows of the stone-slings or even by Greek fire.
[Richard] had also got ready two mangonels—one of
them of such power that it could hurl its charge into
the very middle of the city market.

"King Richard's stone-slings were plying night and
day, and it is a known fact that a single stone discharged from one of this king's engines slew twelve
men. This stone was sent to Saladin for him to look at.
The messengers who carried it said that that devil the
king of England had brought from the captured city of
Messina [a store of] such sea-flints and most lustrous
stones for doing execution on the Saracens. Nothing,
they went on, could resist the blows of these stones
without being shattered or ground to powder. Meanwhile the king, whose fever was getting worse, lay on
his bed, chafing sorely when he saw the Turks challeng-
ing our men, whilst his sickness prevented him from at-

tacking them. For the constant onsets of the Turks caused him keener pangs than the most fiery throes of his fever.

" Acre seemed a city very hard to take, not only because of the natural strength of its position, but also because it was defended by the very choicest Turkish troops. It was all to no purpose that the French had spent so much pains on constructing engines of war and implements for pulling down the walls ; because the Turks by a sudden volley of Greek fire would destroy everything their enemies had prepared, no matter at what expense, and consume it utterly with fire. Now among the other engines made by the king of the French was one which he had constructed with the utmost care. It was intended for scaling the walls, and for this reason was called " The Cat," because after creeping up in the manner of a cat it got a grip of the wall and stuck fast to it. He had also finished another contrivance of hurdles very strongly fastened together with twigs, and this the people used to call the *circleia.* Under this little hurdle, covered with raw hides, the king used to take his seat anxiously discharging bolts from his crossbow and watching his opportunity to strike any unwary Turk on the battlements of the city."

These engines worked havoc in the defences of Acre ; the walls began to crumble, and the garrison, worn out with incessant vigils, sent despairing messages to Saladin in the extremity of their danger. In response he seems to have lost no opportunity of attacking the camp of the enemy and drawing their attention from the city. The garrison would beat their drums to give notice that they were being

assailed ; Saladin's drums would instantly reply, and
his troops would forthwith charge the Franks' entrenchments. We read of such attacks on the 14th
and 17th of June; the Saracens rushed the earthworks and plundered part of the camp ; the enemy
hurried back from the city walls ; the engagements
lasted till night, when each side retired to its position.* The most furious attempt upon the camp, however, took place on the 2nd and 3rd of July,† when
the garrison were actually threatening to surrender
unless Saladin could save them. It is described
in the " Itinerary " :—

" Now it chanced one day, while the French were
drawing too close to the walls in their eagerness to bring
up the *cat*, that the Turks cast a heap of dry wood over
the walls on to the *cat*. Then, without any delay, they
discharged a quantity of Greek fire down upon the *circleia*
that had been prepared with such great care. After
this they set up a stone-sling, taking aim at the same
place, when lo ! suddenly everything is in flames or
destroyed by the blows of the stone-sling. Upon this
the king of France, madly wrath, began to curse with
horrid oaths at all who were under his rule and to chide
them with shameful reproaches for not taking vengeance
against the Saracens who had done him such a wrong.
In the heat of his anger, as evening drew on, he proclaimed an attack for the morrow by herald's voice.

" Early next morning chosen guards were set at the
outer ditches to keep off sudden attacks of the Saracens
[outside]. For Saladin had bragged that on the same

---

* Baha-ed-din, **222–4.**

† Id., **229–32.**

day he would cross the trenches in full force and shew
his valour, to the destruction of the Christians. But he
did not keep his word ; for he did not come himself,*
but his fierce and persistent army, under his lieutenant
Kahadin [Taki-ed-din], hurling itself in great masses
against the trenches, was valiantly opposed by the
French. There was no small slaughter on either side.
The Turks, dismounting, advanced on foot. The fight
went on at close quarters with drawn swords, daggers,
and two-headed axes, not to mention clubs that bristled
with sharpened teeth. The Turks press on ; the valorous
Christians drive them back ; each side rages with a
twofold fury ; for it was the time of summer heat.

"That part of the army destined to take the city
continued hurling darts, undermining the walls, pound-
ing away with engines or creeping up to scale the walls.
The Turks, dreading the courage of these assailants,
signalled to their fellows outside by raising aloft the
standard of Saladin in the hopes that [their friends]
would come to their aid at once or draw off the enemy
by an attack [in the rear]. Seeing this Kahadin and
his Turks, pressing on with all their vigour, filled the
ditch, but were resisted and driven back by our men,
who, thanks to God, stood like an impenetrable wall.
Meanwhile the king of France's diggers gradually bur-
rowing by subterranean passages reached the very
foundations of the walls and filled the chasm they had
made with logs, to which they set fire. Then, when the
fire had consumed the beams upholding the wall, a great
part of it gave way, sloping down by degrees, but not
falling flat. Very many Christians ran up to this spot
in the hope of entering, whilst the Turks came up to

---

* Baha-ed-din says Saladin commanded in person.

drive them back. Oh! how many banners might you then see and devices of many a shape, not to mention the desperate [valour] of the Turks as they hurled Greek fire against our men. Here the French brought up ladders, and attempted to scale the wall that was not quite prostrate ; there the Turks on the other hand used ladders to defend the breach. . . ."

During this attack, el-Adil had led two gallant charges in vain, and Saladin himself had gone from battalion to battalion, shouting his war-cry, and urging on his men. Looking towards the city he saw the terrible crisis and danger of the struggling garrison, and his eyes filled with tears, as he charged again and again. All that day he took no food, and nothing passed his lips but the doctor's stuff which he was forced to take.* Meanwhile the assault became fiercer and fiercer.

"King Richard . . . had a kind of hurdle-shed (commonly called a *circleia*) made and brought up to the ditch outside the city wall. Under its shelter were placed his most skilful cross-bowmen ; whilst, to hearten his own men for the combat and to dispirit the Saracens by his presence, he had himself carried there on silken cushions. From this position he worked a crossbow, in the management of which he was very skilful, and slew many of the foes by the bolts and quarrels he discharged. His miners also, approaching the tower against which his stone-casters were being levelled, by an underground passage dug down towards the foundations, filling the gaps they made with logs of wood, to which they would set fire, thus causing the walls, which had

---

* Baha-ed-din, 230.

already been shaken by the stone-casters, to fall down
with sudden crash.   .   .   .

" At last when the tower had fallen prostrate before
the blows of our stone-casters and when king Richard's
men began to stop digging, our men-at-arms, in their
greed for fame and victory, began to don their arms.
Amongst the banners of these were the earl of Leicester's ; that of Andrew de Chavigny and of Hugh Brown.
The bishop of Salisbury also came up, equipt in the
noblest fashion, and many more.   It was about the third
hour, *i. e.*, about breakfast time, when these valorous
men-at-arms began their work, going forth to storm the
tower, which they boldly scaled at once.   The Turkish
watchmen, on seeing them, raised a shout, and lo ! the
whole city was soon in a stir.   The Turkish warriors,
hurriedly seizing their arms, came thronging up and
flung themselves upon the assailants.   The men-at-arms
strove to get in ; the Turks to hurl them back.   Rolled
together in a confused mass they fought at close quarters, hand against hand, and sword against sword.   Here
men struck, there they fell.   Our men-at-arms were few,
whereas the numbers of the Turks kept on increasing.
The Turks also threw Greek fire against their enemies,
and this at last forced the men-at-arms to retreat and
leave the tower, where some of them were slain by
weapons, others burnt by that most deadly fire.   At last
the Pisans, eager for fame and vengeance, scrambled
up the tower itself with a mighty effort ; but, bravely
as they comported themselves, they too had to retreat
before the onset of the Turks, who rushed on as if mad.
Never has there been such a people as these Turks for
prowess in war.

" Though its walls were partly fallen and partly
shaken, though a great part of the inhabitants were

slain or weakened by wounds, there still remained in the city 6,000 Turks. With these were the leaders, Mestoc [el-Meshtub], and Caracois [Karakush], who began now to despair of receiving aid. . . . So, by common consent and counsel, the besieged begged a truce while they sent notice of their plight to Saladin, hoping that, in accordance with their Pagan ways, he would ensure their safety—as he ought to do—by sending them speedy aid or procuring leave for them to quit the city without disgrace. To obtain this favour, these two noble Saracens, the most renowned [warriors] in all Paganism, Mestoc and Caracois, came to our kings, promising to surrender the city, if Saladin did not send them speedy aid. They stipulated, however, that all the besieged Turks should have free leave to go wherever they wished with their arms and all their goods. The king of France and almost all the French agreed to this ; but king Richard utterly refused to hear of entering an empty city after so long and toilsome a siege. Wherefore, perceiving king Richard's mind, Caracois and Mestoc went back to Acre without concluding the business. Saladin, meanwhile, having received envoys from the beseiged, bade them hold out stoutly in the certainty that he would shortly send them efficient aid. He declared that he had certain news of the approach of a mighty host of warriors from Babylon [*i. e.* Cairo] in ships and galleys."

The succour had already come. Saladin received frequent reinforcements at the end of June and the beginning of July. On the 25th came the levies from Sinjar ; then a strong force from Egypt ; the next day the lord of Mosil arrived with his division ; on the 28th more troops from Egypt ; on July the 9th came

the Prince of Sheyzar with his Arabs, on the 10th
Dolderim with a large squadron of Turkmans in Saladin's pay; on the 11th, the young Prince of Hamah.
Yet, with all this host of Saracens about it, Acre
surrendered on the 12th. After a magnificent defence for nearly two years, the garrison laid down its
arms in the sight of a great and unbeaten army of relief! Nay, the very spirits of dead heroes seemed in
vain to lend mysterious aid to the beleaguered city.
A mighty noise, like the tramp of many armed men,
was heard at night within the walls. The Christian
outposts sprang to arms, and wonderingly perceived
as it were a regiment entering the gates, clothed in
green robes; for such is the aspect of the martyrs of
Islam who dwell in Paradise. Even the souls of the
Faithful could not put faith into the panic-stricken
people.

The story of this surrender, however, is not hard
to understand. The large forces and improved siege-
engines brought to bear upon the city by the Kings
of England and France made the place untenable:
it could only be rescued from without. Saladin's
army seemed numerous enough for anything it might
be called upon to do; yet it evidently could not fight
against earthworks. A few bold leaders might force
their way among the tents, but the enemy's entrenched camp was never really carried by the Saracens. Some of Saladin's men even mutinied, refused
to attack, and accused him of "ruining Islam." *

Convinced that Saladin could not break through
the iron ring that held them, the garrison foresaw

* Baha-ed-din, 233–4.

nothing but a massacre. To hold out much longer was impossible. Three leading emirs succeeded in making a cowardly escape by night. A panic ensued. Some of the frightened people threw themselves from the battlements; others fled to the enemy's camp and begged to be baptised. Karakush, the governor of the city, and el-Meshtub (" Le Balafré ") the commander of the garrison, resolved to make terms. They went to the Christian camp on July 4th, but were refused a capitulation. Saladin was no party to this: he urged resistance and promised relief. On the next morning, the 5th, he had his army ready for the effort, but the garrison failed to do its part. On the 7th a swimmer brought a despairing message: "We have sworn to die together; we will fight till we are slain; and we will not deliver up this city so long as we live. Look you to distract the enemy from us and prevent his attacking us. . . . Our turn is over." It was a last appeal. Still no relief came, and on the 12th, despite their desperate resolve, the same swimmer brought the message that the garrison had capitulated. Saladin was in the very act of preparing a reply, denouncing * the terms of the treaty, when the banners and crosses of the Franks suddenly glittered upon the city walls and towers. The deed was done; Acre had surrendered without its sovereign's consent.

" Thus, on Friday after the translation of the Blessed

---

* The *Itinerary* (iii., 17) says that Saladin had previously consented to the surrender; but every other evidence points to the contrary conclusion.

Benedict [July 12], the wealthier and noble emirs were
proffered and accepted as hostages, one month being
allowed for the restoration of the Holy Cross and the
collection of the captive Christians. When the news of
this surrender became known, the unthinking crowd was
moved with wrath ; but the wiser folk were much rejoiced
at getting so quickly and without danger what previously
they had not been able to obtain in so long a time.   Then
the heralds made proclamation forbidding any one to insult the Turks by word or deed.   No missiles were to
be hurled against the walls or against the Turks if they
chanced to appear on the battlements.   On that day,
when these famous Turks, of such wonderful valour and
warlike excellence, began strolling about on the city walls
in all their splendid apparel, previous to their departure,
[our men] gazed on them with the utmost curiosity.
They were wonder-struck at the cheerful features of men
who were leaving their city almost penniless and whom
only the very sternest necessity had driven to beg for
mercy ; men whom loss did not deject, and whose
visage betrayed no timidity, but even wore the look of
victory. . . .

   " At last, when all the Turks had quitted Acre,* the
Christians entered the city in joy and gladness, glorifying
God with a loud voice and yielding Him thanks for
having magnified His mercy upon them and brought re-
demption to His people.   Thus did the kings set their
banners and varied ensigns on the walls and towers ;
while the city, together with all it contained in the way
of victuals and arms, was equally divided among them.

---

   * This is a mistake.   The inhabitants of Acre were detained
prisoners (Ernoul 274), as hostages for the execution of the treaty, as
appears further on.

The captives too they reckoned up and halved the lot.
To the king of France fell the noble Caracois and a
great host of other folk ; to king Richard, Mestoc and
many more.   Morever, the king of France had the noble
palace of the Templars with all its appurtenances, while
the royal palace fell to king Richard, who established
the two queens there with their maidens and attendants.
Thus each king had his own part of the city in peace,
whilst the army was distributed over its whole area, en-
joying pleasant rest after so long and continuous a siege."

SEAL OF RICHARD I. (1195.)

FROM ARCHER'S "STORY OF THE CRUSADES."

CHAPTER XIX.

THE COAST MARCH.

Aug.—Sept., 1191.

THE surrender of Acre took Saladin by surprise, but his anger was roused more by the terms that had been arranged behind his back, than by the act itself. He had evidently realised that the city could not hold out much longer, and that his army could neither break through the enemy's entrenchments, nor draw them into a pitched battle. So long as he had to deal with Guy de Lusignan and the Palestine Franks he had never thought of a truce; but the coming of the two Kings changed the situation, and he prepared to negotiate. The first overture, however, came from Richard. The King of England had sent very soon after he landed to request a personal interview. It was like his frank soldierly character to wish to be face to face with the man with whose courage and greatness of heart even the Christian camp was ringing. But Saladin declined the meeting: it was not well, he said, for kings at war with each other to meet in friendly converse until a treaty of peace was actually afoot.* Possibly he feared being won too far by the manly presence and chivalrous manner of the hero of whose exploits he too had heard so much : more probably his reply was thrown out as a feeler towards peace.

Other envoys came from the English camp during the King's illness. A meeting was arranged between Richard and el-Adil ; it was to take place in the middle of the plain between the two camps, but the King's sickness postponed the interview. Some passages of wit were exchanged between the ambassador and the Sultan's brother, about a present of falcons which Richard wished to offer to Saladin, and the fowls which he required in return, and each tried to discover what the other was aiming at. On the 1st of July Saladin himself received the envoy and his Maghraby interpreter. "All these interviews," says Baha-ed-din, "were designed to find out our temper of mind, our strength and our weakness." It was doubtless to promote these *pourparlers* that the Franks stopped the bombardment for three days.†
The ambassadors came again on the 4th, asking for fruit and snow ; and the Master of the Knights of St. John was himself announced as coming on the morrow to treat for peace. Three envoys arrived instead, and had an hour's conference with el-Adil, but nothing was settled. There was a further discussion on the 6th, but the Christian terms were too

---

* Baha-ed-din, 223–4 ; who extols Richard as a King " of mighty strength, vast courage, and firm will : great battles had he fought, and daring was he in war."

† Baha-ed-din, 234 ; Ernoul, 274.

hard. Saladin kept his army in battle array, and menaced the Franks as far as he dared, to induce them to lower their demands. But up to the 11th,

"they stood resolute, not to make peace nor to grant a capitulation to the citizens, unless all the prisoners in the hands of the Moslems were released, and the cities of the coast-land were restored to them. It was proposed (on our part) to surrender the city and everything in it, save only its defenders, but they would not ; and we offered besides the Cross of the Crucifixion, but they would not."

The next day came the news that the garrison had capitulated on these terms : (1) Acre to be surrendered with all its contents, ships, stores, and material of war ; (2) 200,000 pieces of gold to be paid to the Franks ; (3) 1500 prisoners, together with 100 prisoners of rank, to be delivered up ; (4) the True Cross to be restored to them ; (5) 4000 gold pieces to be paid to the Marquess of Montferrat. On these conditions, the inhabitants were to go free, and without molestation, taking with them their families and such private possessions as they could carry.*

Conditions such as these were naturally repugnant to the Sultan, still at the head of a strong army which had not lost a battle since the rout at Ramla fourteen years before. The terms had been made by Saladin's officers, and he did not repudiate them ; but it was the greatest reverse he had ever experi-

* Baha-ed-din, 227, 228, 234–237 ; the 1500 prisoners are stated at 500 in one place by an obvious slip.

enced, and his grief was unconcealed. Having now
no further need to guard the city, he at once moved
his army to Shafraamm, and awaited the commissioners who should arrange the execution of the humiliating treaty. Agents passed between the two camps,
and visited Damascus, drawing up full lists of the
prisoners and paving the way for a permanent treaty
of peace. This went on for a month, during which
the outposts of the two armies faced each other in no
friendly mood, and once even indulged in a regular
set-to, when the Franks were driven to their trenches.
Meanwhile the smothered quarrel between Philip and
Richard had broken out again ; the King of France
was ill of a fever, such as had just carried off the
Count of Flanders, and he made it an excuse to desert the Crusade and return home, there to stir up
" confusion in Normandy." But if, in the words of
Cœur de Lion,* Philip did " against the will of God
and to the eternal dishonour of his kingdom, so shame-
lessly fail in his vow," he at least left behind him the
greater part of his army under the Duke of Burgundy
to carry on the Crusade. The French, unfortunately,
were a source of weakness rather than strength, for
they opposed the King of England at every step,
and in this they were cordially abetted by Conrad
of Montferrat, who withdrew to Tyre on the 1st of
August, when he found that his schemes for the crown
of Jerusalem received no countenance from Richard.

"While the king of France was hastening home, king
Richard was paying heed to the repair of the city walls,

* *Roger of Howden,* iii., 128.

building them higher and stronger than before. He himself was always making the round of them, encouraging the workmen and masons, just as if his sole business were to regain God's heritage. He was still awaiting the end of the time fixed upon between himself and the Turks, occupying himself in the meanwhile with collecting his mangonels and baggage ready for carrying them away. After the period agreed upon for the return of the Holy Cross and the captives had been overpassed by three weeks [*sic*] to see if Saladin would keep his word ; when the Saracens kept demanding a further delay, the Christians began to enquire when the Holy Cross was coming. One said ' Already has the Cross come ! ' Another said : ' It has been seen in the Saracens' army.' *

---

* The fate of the " True Cross " is obscure. When it was taken at the battle of Hittin the sacred wood is described as mounted in red gold and adorned with pearls and precious stones. It was sent first to Damascus and then to Baghdad, where the Caliph buried it (4th of June, 1189) under the threshold of the Bab en-Nuby to be trodden under Moslem feet : a bit of the gold could be seen. Yet Baha-ed-din says the " True Cross " was exhibited in Saladin's camp at Acre and included in the first instalment of the proffered indemnity. When the negotiations were broken off, this Cross was sent to Damascus and exposed to contempt in the Omayyad Mosque. It should be noted that as the Moslems hold the story of the Crucifixion to be an unworthy fable, contempt for what they regard as a superstitious forgery involves no disrespect towards the honoured name of Jesus, whom they reverence. From Damascus the Cross is said to have been sent as a gift to Isaac the Emperor of Constantinople. Yet the Bishop of Salisbury is reported to have seen it at Jerusalem by permission of Saladin in September, 1192. Ernoul, moreover, has a curious story of a Frank soldier who undertook to find it on the field of Hittin at the spot where he had buried it with his own hands during the battle ; but after three nights' digging he gave up the search. Another presumed fragment was shown to Richard by the Abbot of St. Elias at Beyt Nuba. There were doubtless several " True Crosses "—and imitations.

But each was deceived, for Saladin was not even setting about its restoration ; nay, he neglected the hostages, in the hope that he would get better terms if he kept it in his possession. And all the while he kept sending frequent presents and envoys, while he made it his aim to waste time in long talks and ambiguous words." *

The Holy Cross (or a convincing imitation) was actually in Saladin's camp, for Baha-ed-din says it was shown to some English officers, who devoutly prostrated themselves in the dust. Whether Saladin was prolonging the negotiations merely to gain time can neither be proved nor disproved ; but his secretary's account seems genuine, and does not confirm the insinuation of bad faith. By this account * these English officers brought, on the 2nd of August, Richard's acceptance of Saladin's proposal to deliver up the prisoners and money specified in the treaty, in three separate instalments, at intervals of a month each. The first of these instalments was ready at the end of the first month. The officers sent by the Franks certified that the numbers were correct, except that certain prisoners specified by name were not yet included. On the 11th of August they came to exact their full due, and Saladin, to meet the difficulty, said "*Either* give us up our comrades (the captives at Acre) and take what has been agreed upon for this instalment, and we will give you hostages for the fulfilment of the remaining terms ; *or* take what we offer you now, and give us hostages to hold until our comrades in your hands shall re-

* *Itin.*, iv., 1.

† Baha-ed-din, 241-2.

20

join us." The commissioners replied, " We will not do that: but do you give us what is due for this term, and take our pledge that your people shall be given up to you." To this Saladin would not consent; he had already had too much experience of what a Christian oath was worth. Obviously neither side trusted the other, and Saladin's natural demand for some guarantee that his fulfilment of the treaty would be followed by a corresponding release of the captives at Acre was regarded by the Christians as an evasion. If we believe Baha-ed-din's statement, there was no reason for this suspicion; but, believe it or not as we may, there is no imaginable excuse or palliation for the cruel and cowardly massacre that followed. The horrible scene is described by the admiring chronicler :

" Orders were then given to cut off the heads of the hostages with the exception of a few of the nobler prisoners, who perhaps might yet be relieved or exchanged for captive Christians. King Richard, always eager to destroy the Turks, to confound the law of Mahomet utterly, and vindicate that of Christ, on the Friday after the Assumption * bade 2700 Turkish hostages to be led out of the city and beheaded. Nor was there any delay. The king's followers leapt forward eager to fulfil the commands, and thankful to the Divine Grace that permitted them to take such a vengeance for those Christians whom these very [captives] had slain with bolts and arrows." †

---

* 16th Aug. ; Baha-ed-din and Howden date the massacre on Tuesday, the 20th.

† *Itin.* iv. 2. In explanation of this atrocious crime it has been suggested that Richard could not safely leave so large a number of

When the Saracen outpost over against Acre saw
their countrymen being butchered in cold blood beneath their very eyes, they rushed madly forward to
prevent the slaughter; but though they fought till
night they could not save them. "Only those had
been spared who were of note or were strong to
work"; and the aged and weak, apparently even
women and children, had been ruthlessly put to the
sword. After Saladin's almost quixotic acts of
clemency and generosity, the King of England's
cruelty will appear amazing. But the students of
the Crusades do not need to be told that in this
struggle the virtues of civilisation, magnanimity, toleration, real chivalry, and gentle culture, were all on
the side of the Saracens.

Immediately after the massacre, Richard prepared
to march down the coast to Ascalon, on his way to
the Holy City where Saladin had so conspicuously
taught the lesson of mercy. There was great difficulty in getting the Crusaders to move. No less
than 300,000 men were under the King's command,
but they left the city "slowly and surlily." "The
people, given up to sloth and luxury, were loth
to leave a city so rich in comforts, to wit, in
the choicest of wines and the fairest of damsels.
Many, by a too intimate acquaintance with these
pleasures, became dissolute, till the city was polluted

---

prisoners behind him when he marched south. One would rejoice
to discover a less contemptible excuse for his barbarity. Another
reason is alleged by Roger of Howden, who says that Saladin had
already massacred his Christian captives two days before. There is
nothing to support this in any other authority.

by their luxury, whose gluttony and wantonness put wiser men to the blush." *   Richard's order that no women, save washerwomen, "who could not be an occasion of sin," were to follow the army, hardly encouraged the zeal of these worthy warriors.   He managed to collect 100,000 however, and these he marshalled on the eve of St. Bartholomew.

On the surrender of Acre, Saladin had at once fallen back upon his line of retreat, and massed his main army on the hills which commanded the two great roads, the one leading east to Tiberias and Damascus, the other south-east through Nazareth to Jerusalem.   The hill of Shafraamm overlooked both routes.   Richard, however, did not gratify his adversary by attempting to force the passes ; daring as he was, he would not risk an advance through hills completely held by the Saracens.   He chose the longer but safer route by the old Roman road which skirts the coast, where if he had the enemy on the hills on his left, he had also the protection of the sea and the support of his fleet on his right.   His plan was to descend the coast as far as Jaffa and Ascalon, and after making a fortified base, to strike across to Jerusalem.   The distance to Jaffa, in a straight line, was a little over sixty miles ; but there were eight rivers to be forded, the road was often difficult through brushwood and long grass, the season was the hottest in the year ; and the whole route was commanded by a range of low wooded hills, which offered vantage ground for the Saracens,

* *Itin.* iv., 7.

and, if Saladin had possessed field artillery, would have made the march utterly impossible. As it was, only the firm resolution of Richard in keeping his men in close order and pushing doggedly on, without attempting to follow the Moslems into the hills, saved him from disaster.

On Friday, the 22nd of August, the Franks crossed the Belus and encamped on the southern side. At daybreak on Sunday Saladin saw the fires of the enemy, which announced that they were breaking camp. He instantly loaded up his baggage and set out for the hill of Keymun, a spur of the Carmel range, which commanded the main southern road from Acre and Haifa into the interior of Palestine. The detachments he had sent out to harass the Franks brought word that the enemy had crossed the Kishon and camped at Haifa. Apparently they were not going to march inland. A line of troops was posted for the night to watch their movements, and next morning, leaving a strong detachment close to the enemy, under Jurdik, a trusty emir of Shirkuh's old Egyptian staff, Saladin himself rode across the hills towards Cæsarea, where the shoreland woods began, and where the Franks, if they kept the coast, must make their next camp. Here he examined the lie of the land to find a good position for a pitched battle. " He came back to the camp very tired after the time of evening prayer," and announced that the Franks were still at Haifa, and that nothing could be done till their movements were decided. The next day he reviewed his troops, and put them in heart by presents and compensations to those who had lost their goods and horses. On the 27th he rode out thrice towards the coast, searching for a suitable place to engage the enemy, who were slowly rounding the shoulder of land formed by the jutting spurs of Mount Car-mel; and on the following day he moved the army on, so as to cover Cæsarea. Prisoners were brought in, who told him that the Franks were waiting for the fleet which carried their supplies. All prisoners, except women, were sternly executed: the King of England's cruelty was not to pass unavenged, even by Saladin. Eighteen Franks were thus put to death in one day.

At last, on the 30th, the news came that the enemy were at hand. The Saracens were still near Cæs-area, and Saladin at once formed them up along the line of advance. Baha-ed-din was with his master close to the enemy, and describes the first engage-ment. He says that the Moslem archers could do little against the armour of the Franks:

" their infantry drawn up in front of the horsemen stood firm as a wall, and every foot-soldier wore a thick gam-beson and a hawberk, so dense and strong, that our arrows took no effect, whilst their cross-bows wounded both our horses and their riders. I saw soldiers with from one to ten arrows sticking in them, still marching on."

The divisions nearest the shore, being unexposed to the Saracen attack, relieved in turn the fighting battalions on the left, and the knights were kept in the centre protected by the infantry, and were not permitted to charge. In this formation the Christ-

ians marched steadily on, fighting on the left all the
way.   " The Moslem archers harassed them and tried
to induce them to break the ranks, but the men controlled themselves admirably, and went on, without
hurry, their ships following along the coast." *

This engagement is typical of the whole march.
The Franks pressed doggedly on, whilst the Moslems, " like mountain torrents, raining down from
the heights," worried them at every step.   They
came on in small parties, trying to tempt the Crusaders to break their impenetrable formation, but
Richard's orders were strict.   Yet we read in the
" Itinerary " how

" the Duke of Burgundy and his French who were in the
rear followed at less speed, and thanks to their delay,
came near to suffering a most terrible loss.   The army
was marching having the sea on its right, whilst from the
mountain heights on the left the Turks kept a watch on
all our movements. . . .   The army had now reached a
narrow passage along which the provision wagons had to
go.   Here on account of the narrowness of the way there
was some confusion and disorder, which the Saracens
noting swept down upon the packhorses and wagons,
cutting off unwary men and steeds, plundering much of
the baggage, breaking through and dispersing those who
offered any resistance, and driving them in flight and
slaughter to the brink of the sea.   There both sides
fought with manful courage for dear life.   On this occasion when a Turk had cut off the right hand of a certain Everard, one of the Bishop of Salisbury's men, he
without changing countenance seized his sword with the

* Baha-ed-din, 250–2.

left hand and closing with the Turks stoutly defended himself against them all, brandishing his weapon."

Then King Richard came to the rescue, and

" thundered on against the Turks, slaying them right and left with his sword. Nor was there any loitering, but right and left as of old the Philistines fled from the face of the Machabee, so now did the Turks scatter and flee from the face of king Richard till they gained the mountain heights, leaving, however, some of their number headless in our hands."

Richard, of course, was always to the fore in these emergencies, " thundering on like a wild boar," and taking heads as a Red Indian took scalps. Nor was Saladin behind-hand : he was often seen riding between the front ranks, with the arrows flying about his head and only a couple of grooms with spare horses as his escort. But it was not his habit to fight in person, and he certainly never encountered Richard on the field of battle. The days were now intolerably hot, and both sides suffered severely ; the unseasoned Franks fell fainting by the way, and many died of sunstroke. But they kept up their courage, and every night as they were turning in to sleep, a herald went through the camp crying in the midst " Help us, Holy Sepulchre ! "

" On hearing these words the whole multitude would take up the cry, stretching out their hands to heaven and, with copious tears, praying God for aid and mercy. Then a second time would the herald repeat the same words, calling out as before, 'SANCTUM SEPULCHRUM

ADJUVA,' after which the words were repeated by the
whole host ; likewise, when he cried aloud for the third
time, all imitated him with the utmost sorrow of heart
and bursts of tears."

Meanwhile Saladin had at last chosen a site for a
set battle.   It was near Arsuf, where the downs
shelve gently to the seashore ; the dense woods of
oaks offered shelter to within a couple of miles
of the beach, yet there was space for the exercise
of cavalry.   Here, if anywhere, the Christian array
might be broken and their advance stayed.   The
news that a Saracen army, magnified by rumour to
the size of 300,000 men, was waiting for battle
seems to have shaken the fortitude of the invaders,
who reckoned their own numbers more modestly at
100,000.   For on the 5th of September, Richard asked
for a parley.   He was weary of the daily fighting
and grieved at the sufferings and losses of his troops.
El-Adil went to meet him ; but when the King proposed that peace should be made on the basis of the
Saracens' restoring all Palestine and retiring into
"their own country," Saladin's brother scornfully
broke off the conference.   Nothing remained but to
leave the issue to the battle.   The Franks were now
at Rochetaillie, the "Stream of the Cleft" (Nahr el-
Falik), halfway between Cæsarea and Jaffa.   There
they rested a day, protected by the great bog of
Ramadan, and on the 7th they began the six miles'
march along the road to Arsuf.*   The Saracens were
posted on the downs on the left, between Rochetail-

---

* See the careful description in Oman, *Art of War*, ii., 308–316,
whence I have been permitted to borrow the plan of the battle-field.

lie and Arsuf. The battle is finely narrated in the
" Itinerary ":

"On Saturday [Sept. 7] the eve of the Nativity of the
Blessed Mary, at earliest dawn all prepared themselves
most carefully as though the Turks were going to attack
immediately ; for they knew the enemy to have fore-
stalled our path, and that the insolence of the Turks
would not abate before a very severe contest had taken
place. Indeed the Turks were already setting their men
in order, and always drawing a little nearer. For this
reason all our men looked to their own affairs very carefully, and the ranks were ranged with the utmost precaution. King Richard, who was very skilful in military
matters, drew up the squadrons according to a special
scheme, arranging who had better lead the vanguard,
and who bring up the rear. With this intent he
appointed twelve squadrons ; and arranged [his whole
army] into five battalions, assigning to each men of
great skill in warfare—warriors whose betters were not
to be found on earth had their hearts only been firmly
staid in God. On this day the Templars led the first
rank ; after them went the Bretons and the men of Anjou
in due order ; next went king Guy with the men of
Poitou ; in the fourth rank were the Normans and the
English, with the royal banner under their charge. Last
of all went the Hospitallers in due rank. This last array
of all was made up of choice knights divided into squadrons, and its members marched so close together that an
apple could not be thrown to the ground without touching the men or their horses. Our army occupied the
whole space between Saladin's and the sea-shore. . . .
Count Henry of Champagne kept guard on the side of
the mountains : as did also the followers on foot. Last

THE BATTLE OF ARSUF, SEPT. 7, 1191.

(FROM OMAN'S "ART OF WAR.")

of all were drawn up the bowmen and the cross-bowmen
closing the rear. The packhorses and wagons carrying
provisions, baggage, &c., journeyed between the army
and the sea so as to be safe from attack. Thus did the
army advance at a gentle pace so as to guard against
separation. . . .

" The third hour was now drawing on, when lo ! a host
of Turks, 10,000 in numbers, swept rapidly down upon
our men, hurling darts and arrows, and making a terrible
din with their confused cries. After these came running
up a race of dæmons very black in colour ; for which
cause, because they are black, they are not unfittingly
called the negro pack (*nigreduli*). [Then too came on]
those Saracens who live in the desert and are commonly
called Bedawis, rough, darker than smoke, most pestilent
foot-men with their bows and round targets—a people
light of foot and most eager for battle. These were ever
threatening our army. And beyond those we have mentioned, you might see along the smoother ground well-
equipt phalanxes of Turks advancing with their several
ensigns, banners, and emblems. They seemed to number more than 20,000 men. On steeds swifter than
eagles they thundered down upon us, till the whirling
dust raised by their rapid flight blackened the very air.
Before the emirs there went men. clanging away with
trumpets and clarions ; others had drums, others pipes
and timbrels, rattles, gongs, cymbals, and other instru-
ments fitted to make a din. . . .

" That day our own losses and the sufferings of our
horses, who were pierced through and through with arrows and darts, shewed how persistently the enemy kept
up the attack : and then indeed we found out the use of
our stalwart cross-bowmen, our bowmen, and those
closely-wedged followers who at the very rear beat back

the Turkish onset by constant hurling of their weapons so far as they could. Yet for all this, the enemy in a little while rushed on them again like a torrent of waters, redoubling their blows and so drunk with fury that at last many of our cross-bowmen could hold out no longer, but, throwing away their bows and cross-bow, in sheer dread of death, gave way before the intolerable onset of the Turks and forced a path within the close ranks of our main army, lest they should be cut off from their comrades. But the better men and bolder, whom shame forbade to yield, faced about and strove against the Turks with unflagging valour. So they marched backwards in their anxiety to keep themselves from the danger they would run by advancing too confidently in the ordinary method ; and all that day they went on, picking their way rather than marching, with their faces turned toward the Turks, who threatened at their rear. Ay ! in the stress and bitter peril of that day there was no one who did not wish himself safe at home, with his pilgrimage finished. . . .

"The Turks pressed on so stoutly that they nearly crushed the lines of the Hospitallers, who sent word to king Richard that they could bear up no longer unless their knights were allowed to charge the enemy :

> But he, forbidding, bids them wait
> In closer line and patient state.

Wherefore, for all the peril they were in, they endured on ; though with many a heavy gasp, since they were not suffered to breathe freely. So they pursued their way, the excessive heat adding to their toil. Men might well augur that ill things were in store for so small an army hemmed in with so great a host. And now our assailants smote on the backs of our men as they advanced, as if

with mallets ; so that it was no longer a case for using
arrows and darts from a distance, but for piercing with
lances or crushing with heavy maces at close quarters :
for hand to hand attacks with drawn swords, whilst the
blows of the Turks resounded as if from an anvil. The
battle raged most severely in the rear rank of the Hospitallers because they might not repay the enemy, but
had to go along patient under their sufferings, silent
though battered by clubs, and, though struck, not striking in return. At last, unable to bear up against so vast
a host, they began to give way and press upon the
squadron ahead of them. They fled before the Turks,
who were madly raging in their rear. . . .

" At last more than 20,000 Turks made a sudden confused rush, battering at close quarters with clubs and
swords, redoubling their blows against the Hospitallers
and pressing on in every way, when lo ! one of this
brotherhood, Garnier de Napes, cried out with a loud
voice, ' O illustrious knight St. George, why dost thou
suffer us to be thus confounded ? Christendom itself is
now perishing if it does not beat back this hateful foe ! '
Thereupon, the Master of the Hospital going off to the
king said, ' Lord king, we are grievously beset and are
likely to be branded with eternal shame as men who
dare not strike in their own defence. Each one of us
is losing his own horse for nothing, and why should we
put up with it any longer ? ' To whom the king made
reply, ' My good master, it must needs be endured,
[seeing that] none can be everywhere.' So the Master
returned to find the Turks pressing on and dealing death
in the rear, while there was no chief or count who did
not blush for very shame."

At last two of the Knights of the Hospital could

bear it no longer; calling on St. George, they spurred
out against the Saracens; the rest would not be denied, and squadron after squadron wheeled round,
until there was a general cavalry charge from end to
end. Baha-ed-din witnessed this wonderful charge,
which burst out when the Franks reached the woods
and gardens of Arsuf.

" I myself saw their knights gather together in the middle of the infantry ; they grasped their lances, shouted
their shout of battle like one man, the infantry opened
out, and through they rushed in one great charge in all
directions—some on our right wing, some on our left,
and some on our centre, till all was broken." *

The charge had anticipated Richard's signal, but
the movement was not ill-timed, and he hastened to
direct it.

" King Richard, seeing the army in confusion, put
spurs to his horse and flew up to the spot, not slacking
his course till he had made his way through the Hospitallers, to whose aid he brought his followers. Then he
bore on the Turks, thundering against them and mightily
astonishing them by the deadly blows he dealt. To
right and left they fell away before him. . . . Fierce
and alone, he pressed on the Turks, laying them low ;
none whom his sword touched might escape ; for wherever he went he made a wide path for himself, brandishing his sword on every side. When he had crushed this
hateful race by the constant blows of his sword, which
mowed them down as if they were a harvest for the
sickle, the remainder, frighted at the sight of their

* Baha-ed-din, 258–9.

dying friends, began to give him a wider berth ; for by
now the corpses of the Turks covered the face of the
ground for half a mile.   . . .

" But still the Christians pounded away with their
swords till the Turks grew faint with terror, though the
issue is doubtful yet. Oh ! how many banners and
standards of many shapes, what countless pennons and
flags might you see falling to earth ; aye, and just as
many good swords lying everywhere, lances of reed tipt
with iron heads, Turkish bows and clubs bristling with
sharpened teeth. Twenty or more wagon loads of quarrels, darts, and other arrows and missiles might have
been collected on the field. There you might see many
a bearded Turk lie maimed and mutilated, but still
striving to resist with the courage of despair until, as our
men began to prevail, some of the enemy, shaking themselves free from their steeds, hid among the bushes or
climbed up the trees, from which they fell dying with
horrid yells before the arrows of our men. Others leaving
their horses strove to slip off by circuitous ways toward
the sea, into which they plunged headlong from the
promontories, some five perches high."

The rout of the Saracens is confirmed by their
own historian. Baha-ed-din saw centre, left, and
right wing all flying pell-mell, till only seventeen
men stood by the standard, where the Sultan's
drum still beat to action. Three separate charges
he records, and each drove the Moslems further up
the hillocks : but as each retired the Moslems rallied.
Saladin remained immovable by his standard, trying
to check the panic and bring the men back to the
battle. At last he managed to collect a large number

round the flag, and it is clear from the following passages from the " Itinerary " that the Saracens returned more than once to the attack.

" The Normans and English chosen to guard the Standard drew up gradually and with cautious steps towards that part of our army that was fighting, keeping no great distance from the battle, so that all might have a sure place of refuge. At last, having finished their slaughter our men paused, but the Turks continued their flight till, seeing our slackness, they regained their courage, and immediately more than 20,000 strong fell upon our men in the rear, threatening them with clubs in the hope of releasing our captives. With deadliest effect they kept launching forth their darts and arrows ; smashing, lopping, bruising the heads, arms, and other limbs of our knights, till these bent stupidly over their saddle bows. At last our men recovering their courage, fierce as a lioness robbed of her whelps, rushed upon them again, forcing a way through them as if they were merely tearing through meshes. . . .

" Over this host of Turks there was a certain Emir, a kinsman of Saladin. This warrior had a banner marked with a wonderful device, to wit, a pair of breeches.* These he bore—a device well known to his men. This Tekedin pursued the Christians with a peculiarly fierce hatred ; and he had with him on this occasion more than 700 choice and sturdy Turks attached to his person. They were selected from Saladin's special followers. Each squadron of this body carried a yellow banner in

---

* The chronicler has misinterpreted a well-known *renk* or heraldic badge, copied from an ancient Egyptian hieroglyphic cartouche. The use of armorial bearings was common among the Saracens, especially the Turkman mamluks.

front with a pennon of a different colour. And now, coming on at full speed, with noise and pride they fell upon our men who began to turn off from them towards the Standard. . . . Then the king, sitting on his peerless Cyprian steed, with his chosen band made towards the hills, routing all the Turks he met; helmets clinked as the enemy fell before him, and sparks leapt out from the battery of his sword. So fierce was his onset this day that the Turks very soon all turned off from his irresistible attack, and left a free passage to our army. Thus at last, despite their wounds, our men reached the Standard, the ranks were formed again, and the host proceeded to Arsuf, outside which town it pitched its tents.

"Whilst busied in this work a huge mass of Turks fell upon our rear. Hearing the din of conflict king Richard, calling his own folk to battle, gave reins to his horse, and with only fifteen comrades rushed against the Turks, crying out with a loud voice 'GOD AND THE HOLY SEPULCHRE AID US.' This cry he uttered a second and a third time and, when the rest of his men heard his voice, they hurriedly followed him, fell upon the foe, and drove them in headlong rout right up to the wood of Arsuf, whence they had formerly come. . . .

"Then the king returned to his camp, and our men, wearied with so fierce a combat, rested for the night. Those who were eager for spoil went back to the battle-field and got as much plunder as they desired. Men who in this way returned used to say that they counted thirty-two emirs whom they found lying dead— all cut off on this day. These they reckoned to be men of the greatest authority and power, from their splendid arms and costly gear; and the Turks afterwards begged leave to carry them off because of their rank. In addition they brought back news of 7,000 Turkish corpses, to say nothing of the wounded, who, straggling here and there out of the fight, died later on, and lay scattered over the fields. But thanks to God's protection, hardly a tenth or even a hundredth of this number fell on our side."

No emir of the first rank fell, except Musik the Kurd ; but the Christians lost that peerless knight James of Avesnes, whose body was found in a circle of fifteen dead Saracens. One Christian was taken prisoner, and beheaded. Saladin was so overwhelmed at the reverse that he would not listen to the well-meant consolations of his secretary. He sat under the shade of a cloth—for his tent had gone on—attending to the wounded, and giving his own horses to the men who had lost their mounts. Then the army passed on, and encamped on the green fields beside the river of Jaffa, some few miles from the enemy's camp under the walls of Arsuf.

The victory of the 7th of September was Richard's greatest achievement in Palestine, though it was brought on against his orders by a breach of discipline. But the Crusaders did not follow it up. Far from being crushed by the disaster, Saladin, recovering from his momentary depression, marched his whole force the very next day back to Arsuf, drew them up in order of battle before the enemy, and challenged a renewal of the fight. He waited all day, but the Franks would not stir. On Monday he repeated his challenge, and harassed the enemy with his archers, but they preserved their former stubborn reserve, and succeeded in getting into Jaffa

without a general engagement. Once there, they
had walls to their back, and Saladin drew his army
off to Ramla, a dozen miles to the south-east, to
hold the road to Jerusalem, and await events. The
coast-march had been accomplished, slowly and painfully, but with consummate generalship and final
success.

COPPER COIN OF SALADIN STRUCK IN 1187–8.

CHAPTER XX.

IN SIGHT OF JERUSALEM.

Sept., 1191—July, 1192.

THE Franks were in no haste to follow up their victory. They declined Saladin's offers of battle, and shut themselves up at Jaffa for two months. They had succeeded, with much difficulty and at the rate of three miles a day, in pushing their way from Acre sixty miles south, and they set about fortifying their base before venturing to leave the coast and the fleet which had hitherto served them with intermittent supplies and reinforcements. The pleasant orchards of Jaffa were a refreshing change, after a diet of dead horses, and the weary troops showed little eagerness for the advance upon Jerusalem. "The army rested a long time in ease and pleasure; while day after day its manifold sins increased, to wit, drunkenness and luxury. For the women from Acre began to return to the army, and were a source of iniquity to corrupt the whole people, whose love for pilgrimage diminished as its religious zeal abated" *; indeed, a number of them began

* *Itin.*, iv., 26.

flocking back to Acre, " where they spent their time
in taverns." Richard at least lent no countenance
to this sloth and immorality. He sent King Guy to
Acre to recall the deserters, and when this appeal
proved unavailing, he went himself and preached " a
most moving discourse," exhorting the backsliders
to gird up their loins for the holy work.

By these exertions the army was restored to even
more than its former strength. But up to the middle of November, beyond strengthening Jaffa, and
restoring two or three fortified posts in the plain, a
few miles out on the road to Lydda, this large and
well-appointed army accomplished nothing.* There
were some brisk skirmishes with the Saracen outposts, who did not allow them to rebuild the " Casal
of the Plains " unmolested, and Richard indulged his
love of adventure and deeds of " derring-do," whilst
roving about the country. Once, when out hawking,
he was surprised by the Saracens whilst asleep, and
might have been taken prisoner but for the devotion
of William de Préaux, who calling out in Arabic that
he was the " Melik," passed himself upon the unsuspecting enemy as the King of England, and was carried off in triumph. But as for the object of the
Crusade, the Franks never went further than one
good day's march on the road to Jerusalem all the
time they were in Palestine.

One reason for the inaction of the Crusaders is
found in the negotiations for peace which were going
on throughout October and part of November. Sal-

---

* According to Baha-ed-din (280) the outposts of the Franks had
only advanced to Yazur, $3\frac{1}{2}$ miles from Jaffa, by the 30th of October.

adin's strength, despite his losses at Arsuf, was un-
broken, and his army held the road to Jerusalem.
He had shown that he would spare no sacrifice to
worst his enemy, for immediately after his retreat
to Ramla he had begun to raze the fortified city of
Ascalon, to prevent its forming a support to the
Franks. "'Fore God," he said to Baha-ed-din, "I
had sooner lose all my children than throw down a
single stone of it; but it is the will of God, and the
safety of the Moslems hangs upon it." The work
of demolition and burning took a whole month,
amid general lamentations, and the people were
transported to Egypt and other lands. The position of Ascalon, as a great port close to the Egyptian frontier, and a powerful base of operations by
sea and land for southern Palestine, justified Saladin's precaution; but the Christians felt that the
man who could destroy so noble a city would shrink
from nothing.

But even before the razing of Ascalon was known
at Jaffa, Richard had made overtures for peace.
The example of Acre suggested a possible repetition
of a similar bloodless success. Within a week of the
battle of Arsuf, he sent Humphrey of Toron, to feel
the way towards an arrangement. Saladin was then
busy dismantling Ascalon, but his brother, el-Adil,
who commanded the advance guard at Lydda, had
full powers to treat, and from that time forth generally conducted the negotiations. According to Baha-
ed-din, on whom we have mainly to rely for this
diplomatic history, the Sultan was anxious for peace,
in view of the worn-out state of his army; and indeed

the haste with which he levelled Ascalon, and afterwards dismantled Lydda, Ramla, and Natrun, lest
they should be taken and garrisoned by the enemy,
seems almost a sign of panic. Thus Saladin, almost
as impetuous as Richard, was for accepting terms,
even though they included the surrender of all the
coast to the invaders; but el-Adil was a more cool-
headed diplomatist, and resolved to prolong the
pourparlers in the orthodox manner, so as at least
to give time for the thorough demolition of Ascalon.

Whilst thus engaged, a new factor complicated
the negotiations, entirely to the advantage of the
Saracens. On the 3rd of October Conrad of Montferrat opened from Tyre a separate correspondence
with Saladin. He offered to break with the rest of
the Crusaders, become the Sultan's ally, and retake
Acre for the Saracens, on condition that Sidon and
Beyrut were added to his dominion. Another ambassador from Richard arrived on the same day.
Here was indeed a diplomatic godsend: el-Adil, evidently perfectly at home at such manœuvres, began
to play the Marquess off against the King. All
through October messages were passing between
the camps. Richard scented the treachery of Montferrat, and became pressing in his attentions to el-
Adil, called him " my true friend and brother," and
urged a lasting settlement of the quarrel. " Both
Moslems and Franks," wrote the King, according to
the Arabic paraphrase,

" are worn out ; all their cities are being destroyed ;
lives and wealth are perishing on both sides. This mat-

ter has gone far enough. The only question is about the Holy City, the Cross, and the land. As for Jerusalem, we are firm ; we will not recede, no, not if there were but a single man of us left. As for the land, give us back to the further side of Jordan. As for the Cross, to you it is only worthless wood, but to us it is priceless ; let the Sultan then be gracious to us concerning it, and there shall be peace, and we shall rest from this weary toil."

To this appeal Saladin made answer :

" Jerusalem is holy to us as well as to you, and more so, seeing it is the scene of our Prophet's journey, and the place where our people must assemble at the Last Day. Think not that we shall go back therefrom, or that we can be compliant in this matter. And as for the land, it was ours to begin with, and ye invaded it ; nor had ye taken it but for the feebleness of the Moslems who then had it ; and so long as this war lasts God will not permit you to set up a stone in it. And as for the Cross, our holding it is a point of vantage, nor can we surrender it except for the benefit of Islam." *

The secretary has doubtless infused into these despatches the tone which he considered appropriate to each side, and they are not to be implicitly accepted as literal copies; but they probably preserve the general sense of the correspondence. His next revelation, however, is more astonishing. He says that on the 20th of October el-Adil acquainted him

---

* Baha-ed-din, 275 ; compare the *Itinerary*, iv., 31, for a different version.

with the latest proposals of the King of England. Richard offered peace on these terms : el-Adil was to marry his sister Joan, the widowed Queen of Sicily, who should be dowered with the coast cities, Acre, Ascalon, and Jaffa, and live at Jerusalem ; Saladin, on his part, was to endow el-Adil with the rest of Palestine, besides what he already held in fief, and the wedded pair should reign together over the land ; the Cross was to be surrendered ; prisoners to be freed ; the Templars and Hospitallers to be given establishments ; these conditions settled, Richard would return to England.* El-Adil thought the scheme excellent, and sent Baha-ed-din to Saladin to obtain his consent ; the Sultan said *"Na'm"* (" yes ") energetically three times over, in the presence of witnesses. The secretary adds that Saladin took it as a bad joke on Richard's part, and the whole affair evidently caused much merriment in diplomatic circles. The fantastic humour of the notion struck Sir Walter Scott, who in the *Talisman* modified it into a projected alliance between Saladin and the imaginary Edith Plantagenet ; whilst Lessing in *Nathan der Weise* adopts the true version.

The suggestion is not inconsistent, perhaps, with the character of a knight-errant ; but it was plainly impossible for so strict a Moslem as Saladin to entertain it seriously. There is no doubt, however, that Richard struck up a warm friendship with el-Adil. Joan, it is true, is reported to have indignantly refused to marry a Mohammedan, and her brother's next idea, that el-Adil should turn Christian, was

* Baha-ed-din, 277.

scarcely more practical. But he invited him to his camp, on the 8th of November, entertained him sumptuously at dinner in his own tent, and after a day of great festivity they parted in renewed love. This meeting is the only part of the negotiations which is alluded to by the English author of the " Itinerary," who deplores the successful manner in which el-Adil (or as he calls him " Saphadin," *i. e.*, Seyf-ed-din)

" so imposed upon the unsuspecting king with his cunningly-fashioned speeches, that they seemed to have contracted an intimate friendship with one another. For the king consented to receive Saphadin's presents, and messengers were always running between them bearing little gifts from Saphadin to king Richard. The king's conduct seemed very blameworthy to his men, and it was a common saying that friendship with the Gentiles was a heinous crime. But Saphadin declared himself to be anxious to establish a fixed and lasting peace. So the king deemed himself acting wisely in making an open and fair peace for the enlargement of the bounds of Christendom." *

Richard's desire for peace was certainly not diminished by the knowledge that at the very moment when he was entertaining el-Adil, Conrad's ambassador was actually in Saladin's camp a few miles away. The Marquess was eager to secure the Sultan's support in his claim upon the crown of Jerusalem, against Richard's friend and vassal, the nominal King Guy, who had been playing a very minor part in recent

* *Itin.* iv. 31

events.   His ambassador for this purpose was the
same ingenious Reginald of Sidon who had passed
so scurvy a trick upon Saladin at Belfort two years
before. The Sultan, however, bore him no malice,
received him hospitably, and provisionally approved
the Marquess's renewed proposal of an alliance
against the Crusaders, but postponed a definite reply.
That same evening Humphrey of Toron arrived with
fresh suggestions from Richard, in which he reiterated
his wish to see el-Adil made King of Palestine, but
insisted on the Christians having a share in Jerusalem.   To him also Saladin was all complaisance
and good will.   He then called a council and set the
two treaty proposals before the emirs.   He found
them of opinion that, if peace must be made, it were
better to make it with Richard than with the Marquess, because experience had taught them that it
was impossible to trust the good-faith of the Syrian
Franks.   The conditions thus accepted were those
by which el-Adil was to marry Joan and be ruler of
all Palestine, as previously proposed.   The ex-queen's
refusal does not seem to have been regarded as final.
Richard, in his last communication to el-Adil, confessed that the Christians were all blaming him for
wishing to give his sister to a Moslem ; but he would
try to get the Pope's dispensation ; and if that failed,
he would give el-Adil his niece instead of his sister.
The niece was declined, but otherwise on this basis
negotiations went on, and the sight of Reginald of
Sidon riding beside el-Adil on the hills between the
camps gave temporary wings to the slow-footed
messengers of diplomacy.   But nothing seems to

have been definitely concluded when winter interrupted the negotiations.*

The seasons play an important part in Syrian campaigns. The beginning of the rains drove Saladin
into winter quarters. Hitherto he had kept his advance guard at Lydda, but the main army had been
camped on the hills, latterly at Tell Jezer, west of the
Ramla road, for the sake of forage. These troops
were now withdrawn to Jerusalem, whence after a
time the more distant contingents were gradually
dismissed to their homes as soon as they could safely
be spared. Saladin had great faith in the protection
of mud, but Richard had yet to learn the virtue of a
Syrian winter. In December the Crusaders made
their famous march upon the Holy City, the goal of
all their pilgrimage. They ventured as far as Ramla,
no less than eleven miles from their base at Jaffa,
and after waiting six weeks there, in a ruined city, exposed to constant attacks from Saladin's outposts,
they plucked up courage to penetrate seven or eight
miles further, as far as Beyt Nuba ; and then, almost
in sight of Jerusalem, they turned about and went
back again.

The " Itinerary " † tells the tragical story. After
describing the delay in the ruined city of Ramla, and
the hazardous adventures of the Earl of Leicester
and other knights, it continues :

---

* All these separate stages in the negotiations are very precisely described, with dates, by Baha-ed-din (265, 270-9, 283-93), but the
date of the council, " 11th Shawwal," is, as the context shows, a slip
for 21st.

† Bk. iv., 34 ; v., 3.

" Our army in due order set forth for the Casal of Betenoble [Beyt Nuba], where we were discomforted by
heavy rain and unwholesome weather, owing to which
very many of our beasts of burden died. Indeed, so
great was the tempest and such the downpour of rain and
showers, coupled with the blasts of violent winds, that
the stakes of [our] tents were torn up and whirled away,
whilst our horses perished of cold and wet. A great
part of our food and biscuit was also spoiled ; and the
swine flesh, commonly called bacon, grew rotten. Our
armour and breastplates became fouled with rust and
could not be restored to their original brightness by any
amount of rubbing ; clothes began to wear out and very
many people, from long sojourn in a foreign land, lost
health and were afflicted with great ills. This comfort
alone sustained them : the hope that they were at last on
the point of visiting the Lord's Sepulchre ; for beyond
measure did they desire to see the city of Jerusalem and
finish their pilgrimage. . . .

" But the wiser set of men did not fall in with the too
hasty zeal of the common folk. For the Templars, the
Hospitallers, and the *Pullani*,* having a sharper view of
the future, dissuaded king Richard from going towards
Jerusalem at that moment ; because, they said, if he were
to lay siege and set himself with all his might to take
Saladin and all the Turks cooped up in the city with
him, the Turkish army that lay on the mountain heights
outside would be making sudden attacks. Thus there
would be a double danger in every fight from the enemy
in Jerusalem and the enemy outside. Nor, they continued, if they were successful in capturing the city
would their success avail much unless they had very

---

* Half-breeds, Franco-Syrians ; or perhaps, in a wider sense, creoles—Franks born in Syria.

stout warriors to whose care they might entrust the city.
And this they did not think was likely to be the case,
for, in their opinion, the people were showing all eagerness to get their pilgrimage finished, in order that they
might get home without delay, being already unspeak-
ably wearied at what they had undergone."

These prudent counsels prevailed, to the " great
grief of the common people ; all groaned and sighed
at finding the dear hope of their heart to visit the
Lord's Sepulchre so suddenly cast away. . . .
They cursed the delay and those who brought about
such untoward things." But the decree had gone
forth, and the multitude was sorrowfully led back in
snow and hail to the wretched ruins of what once
was Ramla. This was before the feast of St. Hilary,
which falls on the 13th of January.

" Now, whilst the army was staying at Ramla in the
utmost grief, very many began to desert, either through
a distaste for the tiresome march or indignation. Owing
to this the army was diminished in no small degree ; for
the greatest part of the French went off in anger to Jaffa,
and there abode at their ease. Some also went off to
Acre where there was no lack of food. Some also accepted the urgent invitation of the Marquess of Tyre ;
whilst some, in their wrath and indignation, accompanied
the Duke of Burgundy when he turned off to the Casal
of the Plains, at which place he dwelt eight days."

In order to retrieve this deplorable failure, and put
heart into the army, Richard hit upon the plan of
rebuilding Ascalon, and restoring it to its former
power as a great Christian stronghold. At another

season the policy had been admirable, but a winter march was not the most encouraging expedient that could have been devised. Richard and Henry of Champagne led the downhearted and diminished army to Ibelin.

" So marshy and clayey did they find the ways that at the time of pitching their tents they could think of nothing but how best to rest their wearied heads. At Ibelin he stayed for one night, outworn with grief and toil such as no tongue nor pen can describe. At earliest dawn the army went forward in due order, preceded by those whose business it was to pitch the tents. But the misery of the previous day was as nothing to this day's march. For, as our men plodded on wearily, bitter snow drifted in their faces, thick hailstones rattled down, and pouring rain enveloped them. The marshy land too gave way beneath their feet ; baggage, horses and men sank in the swamps, and the more men struggled the deeper they became involved. . . . So battered, so weary, and so worn, cursing the day on which they were born, and smiting themselves, they at last reached Ascalon—only to find it so levelled by the Saracens that they could barely struggle through the gates over the heaps of stones."

The re-building of Ascalon, and difficulties with the French and with Conrad of Montferrat, occupied the next four months, and no attempt was made to molest the Saracens. There was civil war at Acre ; the Duke of Burgundy and the French again deserted ; and to crown all, the Prior of Hereford arrived from England with the news that the kingdom was being ruined by the oppression of John, who was plainly usurping the sovereignty. At this Richard declared he must go home and see to his own realm; but since no one would stay to carry on the Crusade unless there were a leader, and there were two claimants to the crown, he made the people choose their King. Without hesitation, one and all chose the Marquess of Montferrat, and Richard gave his reluctant assent. The unpopular widower of Sibylla, who had hitherto held if not enjoyed the title, was compensated with the kingdom of Cyprus. His supplanter was less fortunate. Hardly had Conrad attained his ambition when he was suddenly murdered by two emissaries of the Sheykh of the Assassins (27 April).* Henry of Champagne succeeded as King by general acclamation.

Whilst these things were happening on the coast, Saladin had spent the winter quietly at Jerusalem, after sending his army away to their homes. The Franks were still in correspondence with him, for Conrad had not broken off his negotiations during the winter months. An offensive and defensive alliance was actually concluded in April, the details of which are of little interest, since the Marquess-King was murdered immediately afterwards. But the treaty, as epitomised by Baha-ed-din,† contains a reference to an understanding already existing between Saladin and Richard which probably explains

---

* The French accused Richard of prompting the murder, and Ibn-el-Athir charges Saladin with bribing the Assassins to kill Richard and Conrad. Neither charge deserves any more consideration than the forged exculpation ascribed to the Sheykh of the Assassins.

† P. 295 ; compare the *Itinerary*, v., 24.

a certain mysterious visit of Stephen of Turnham to Jerusalem.   Stephen was astonished to see the envoys of the Marquess, Balian of Ibelin and Reginald of Sidon, "two miserable go-betweens," coming out of the city.   It was apparently a case of Greek meeting Greek.   The worthy Stephen was probably himself a "go-between," for the Arabic secretary mentions a message that was received about March from the King of England asking for an interview with "my brother" el-Adil, with a view to a treaty.

El-Adil set out on this mission on the 20th of March, with definite instructions.   He was empowered to conclude a treaty of peace including a division of the country, the surrender of the Cross, with the right of pilgrimage to Jerusalem and of establishing priests in the Church of the Resurrection; if the King insisted on the cession of Beyrut, he must have it, but only on condition that it was destroyed. Thus far might el-Adil make concessions.*   When he reached the plain of Acre, Richard was on the point of returning to Ascalon, but the conditions of the treaty were settled through an intermediary, Abu Bekr the chamberlain, and el-Adil returned at the beginning of April, having apparently succeeded in his mission.   Jerusalem was to be divided between the Christians and the Moslems, but the latter were to retain the sacred Dome of the Rock.   That the treaty was not ratified is obvious from subsequent events; but a proof of the extraordinary amity then existing is found in the amazing words of the " Itin-

---

* Baha-ed-din, 293.

22

erary " : " On Palm Sunday [March 29] King Richard
amid much splendour girded with the belt of knighthood the son of Saphadin, who had been sent to him
for that purpose."

It is hard to believe that, after so unprecedented
—almost incredible—a mark of friendship, the King
took advantage of a rumour of Saladin's temporary
difficulties with a rebellious nephew in Mesopotamia,
to postpone the conclusion of peace, in the hope of
witnessing a civil war among the Saracens.* There
is, however, no disputing the fact that in May, in
spite of an all but ratified treaty, Richard again
assumed the offensive, and sailing down the coast
laid siege to the castle of Darum, where the Crusaders unhappily proved that they had lost nothing of
their usual savagery in dealing with vanquished
Moslems :—

" Those Turks whom our men found holding out on
the battlements they hurled down into the ditch there to
be dashed to pieces. The number of Turks slain in the
different parts of the castle was sixty. Those who had
taken refuge in the tower, seeing that they were lost . . .
surrendered themselves to perpetual slavery on the Friday before Whit-Sunday. . . . On the Friday night
the king made his men keep watch over the Turks who
were still in the Tower till early on the Saturday morning. Then on Whitsun Eve the Turks, coming down
from the Tower at the king's command, had their hands
bound so tightly behind their backs with leathern thongs
that they roared for pain. They were three hundred in
number, not reckoning little children and women. Thus,

* Baha-ed-din, 296.

COVER OF CASKET OF EL-ʿADIL.

CASKET OF EL-ʿADIL.

before the French came up, with the aid of his own men only did king Richard *nobly* get possession of Darum after a siege of four days." *

The capture of Darum so inspirited the Crusaders, unaccustomed of late to success, that they ventured to make a raid across the plain as far as Ibelin of the Hospitallers (Beyt Jibrin), and in June resolved to advance once more upon Jerusalem. Leaving Ascalon on the 7th, Richard marched by way of Blanche Garde and "Toron of the Knights" (Natrun), and camped once more near Betenoble, where he was joined by the French. Here the whole army waited a month for the new King, Henry, and during the delay Richard scoured the country in search of adventures. Once, "on the morrow of St. Barnabas," whilst hotly pursuing some Saracens on the hills, he raised his eyes and on a sudden beheld the Holy City afar off; or, as others say,† he *would not* see it, but holding his coat-of-arms before his face, wept and prayed, "O fair Lord God, I pray thee let me not see thy Holy City, if I may not deliver it out of the hands of thine enemies." But Jerusalem was not to be delivered by his sword. Whilst the Crusaders were lingering at Beyt Nuba, their enemy was daily gathering strength. Saladin's provincial contingents began to return from their homes after the breaking of winter, and were joining his colours in thousands. Dolderim, the lord of the old Courtenay fortress of Turbessel, was the first to arrive with his Turkmans at

---

* *Itin.*, v., 39.
† Joinville, 108.

the end of May ; others followed close on his heels.
Careful preparations were made for the defence of
Jerusalem, and the light troops were taken out by
Saladin himself to skirmish with the enemy.   Both
sides scored successes in these affairs, but on the 23rd
of June the loss of an important caravan from Egypt,
laden with treasure and stores and arms, was the
worst blow the Moslems received.   After this, with
thousands of fresh baggage animals at their command, Saladin made no doubt that the Crusaders
would march without delay on the Holy City, and he
set about destroying the wells and cisterns in the
neighbourhood, till there was not a drop of water left
fit to drink.   But the enemy still hesitated.

An anxious council was held at Jerusalem on
Wednesday night, the 1st of July.   Even Abu-l-
Heyja "the Fat" attended, though he walked with
difficulty and had to be given a chair in the Sultan's
tent.*   Baha-ed-din was ordered to address the
assembled emirs, and he "spoke as God prompted
him," urging to the Holy War.   Saladin remained a
long time deep in thought ; then he made a short
earnest appeal to the soldiers :   " The lives and
children and possessions of the Moslems rest upon
you," he said ; " if *you* fail, which God forfend,
they will roll up the land like a scroll.   .   .   .   The
Moslems over all the country hang upon your

---

* This emir's corpulence was so phenomenal that his stomach
touched his horse's neck.   When he was a governor in Mesopotamia,
the potters of Mosil paid him the compliment of modelling a capa-
cious jolly sort of bowl after his person, and these were known in
commerce as " Abu-l-Heyjas."   Abu-Shama (Goergens), 39 *n*.

valour. *Wa-s-Selam.*" Then the Balafré, lately
ransomed from his prison at Acre, spoke up :

" O Maulana, we are thy mamluks and thy slaves. Thou
hast been gracious to us, and made us great and powerful ; thou hast given to us and made us rich ; we have
only our necks to offer, and they are between thy hands.
By God, not a man of us will turn back from helping
thee till we die ! "

All the emirs said the like, and Saladin was
comforted.

Thursday was spent in strenuous exertions, that
no means of defence might be neglected, and after
they had said the evening prayer together, Saladin
and his secretary spent the night in anxious consultation. The Sultan was very uneasy; there were
divided opinions among his officers as to the best
way of meeting the attack; and the Kurds and
Turks were not working well together. Dawn found
him still deliberating. It was Friday, and in the
mosque he prayed more earnestly than ever, in a low
voice, his tears falling on the carpet. At any moment,
he felt, the enemy might be at the gate, and Jerusalem
might fall—"the Holy City for which he had an
ineffable care."

That evening came a despatch from old Jurdik,
who commanded the advance guard : "The enemy
has ridden out and taken up a position on the hill,
and then returned to camp." The next morning
(Saturday the 4th) another message came : Jurdik's
scouts had learnt that there was dissension in the
Christian camp ; some were for pushing on, others

for going back; the French declared that they had left their country for the sake of Jerusalem, and they would not return without recovering it; the " Inkitar" (Englishman) had pointed out that all the wells were fouled, and there was no water to be had; finally a jury was appointed to decide the issue.

The scouts spoke truth: another spell of fatal vacillation had come over the purpose of the Crusaders, and in the mist of divided counsels the decision had been committed to a jury chosen equally from the knights of the Temple and Hospital, the French, and the Syrian Franks. They decided * to abandon the advance upon Jerusalem, which was now almost in sight, and recommended a march upon Cairo— 250 miles away, across the desert! The French knights protested in vain.

The next day they were in full retreat.† The Sultan rode out at the head of his men to see the wonderful sight. The rejoicing passed description. The danger was over, and Saladin felt that his prayers had indeed been heard. The Holy City was saved.

---

* *Itin.*, vi., 2.

† I have followed the chronology of Baha-ed-din, who was present and is generally accurate. It agrees with the statement in the *Itinerary* (vi., 9) that the Crusaders reached a castle near Lydda on the 6th of July. The previous statement (vi., 7) that " the feast of St. John was close at hand" (*i. e.*, 24th June) must be taken to refer, as the context shows, to a time before the decision of the jury to abandon the advance.

CHAPTER XXI.

THE LAST FIGHT AT JAFFA.

1192.

HARDLY had the Crusaders retired, when an ambassador to Saladin was announced from Henry "King of Jerusalem." He sent to inform the Sultan that the King of England had given him all the lands he had conquered on the coast: "Give me back, therefore, my [other] lands," was his modest request, "that I may make peace with thee, and become as one of thy children." Saladin was so furiously indignant at this demand, coming hard after an ignominious retreat, that he could hardly keep his hands off the ambassador. He controlled himself with an effort, and sent the envoy away on the 6th of July with the reply that, as the successor of the Marquess, Henry must conform to Conrad's agreement, and that nothing beyond Tyre and Acre could be the subject of discussion. Three days later another but very different message came from Richard himself, recommending "his sister's son Count Henry" to Saladin's good graces, and urging an

343

arrangement in a friendly and conciliatory spirit.
The Sultan's council were all for peace, and an
amicable answer was returned : Saladin would treat
Henry "as a son," give up the Church of the Resurrection to the Christians, and divide the country ; the
coast would belong to the Franks, the hills to the
Saracens, as then, and the lands between would be
shared equally between them ; but Ascalon would
be demolished, and belong to neither side. Yet a
third and a fourth embassy arrived within a few
days, with a present of falcons from Richard ; their
object was to discuss details and above all to retain Ascalon. Saladin, however, remained firm ; he
offered Lydda in exchange, but Ascalon must in-
evitably be dismantled. On this rock the negotiations foundered. Richard refused to let a single
stone of Ascalon be pulled down.

The King of England and most of his army had
retired to Acre, where they were eagerly preparing
to return to Europe, heartily sick of campaigning.
Richard intended to embark at Beyrut, which he
proposed to seize by a *coup de main*. Saladin, hearing more of the meditated raid upon his city than of
the sailing that was to follow, took the opportunity
to make a dash upon Jaffa. Leaving Jerusalem on
the 27th of July, he was before the walls of Jaffa
the same day. He met more resistance than he
expected, but after three days' hard sapping and
bombarding, in which Saladin himself took a vigorous
part, the curtain was breached and the Saracens
rushed forward to the assault. They were met by a
wall of steel ; when one man fell, another took his

place. The constancy and courage of the garrison
filled the Moslem chronicler with admiration. What
soldiers they were, he cries, how undaunted and
valiant! At last, however, there was no hope of
keeping out the besiegers, and a capitulation was
arranged on the same terms as at Jerusalem five
years before. But the Moslems were hot with battle;
they were in no mood for quarter; and Saladin confessed that he could not hold them. " Retire to the
Citadel," he told the besieged, " and give up the
town, for nothing will stop the Moslems going
in."

It was indeed no time for peaceful citizens to be
about. The town was full of wild Kurds and Turkmans, ranging the streets sword in hand, and plundering every house they entered: " stores of fine
stuffs, corn in plenty, even the remnant of the plunder of the Egyptian caravan—all fell into their
hands." It is no wonder that a few stray citizens
were killed " by mistake." * In an orgy of victory
such mistakes are apt to occur. The Sultan meanwhile had received news which made it urgently
necessary to get his troops in hand. The officers
commanding the corps of observation near Acre †
sent word that on the very eve of his departure King
Richard had heard of the perils of Jaffa and was on
his way to the rescue. It was now essential to gain
possession of the citadel, without which the town

---

* Baha-ed-din, 328.

† Throughout the war Saladin constantly kept bodies of troops
watching the chief places of the enemy, Acre, Tyre, Antioch, and
others when necessary (Ibn-el-Athir, ii., 10).

could not be held; but the difficulty was to get the
garrison and refugees away. Though they had surrendered,* they were not likely to leave the safety of
its walls without strong pressure, and the Moslems
were gorged with spoil and weary with looting, and
paid no attention to Saladin's repeated orders. He
tried to get a force up to the citadel till late in the
evening, but he spoke to deaf ears.

All night that worthy man, the secretary Baha-ed-
din, lay sleepless with anxious forebodings. At daybreak Richard's trumpets were heard at sea. The
King was at Acre, actually on the point of embark-
ing for England, when breathless messengers arrived
from Jaffa, rending their garments, and bewailing
the extremity of their city. Richard did not wait
to hear them out, but burst forth, "As God lives
and by His help, I will set out and do what I may";
the herald sounded the assembly; knights ran to the
summons; and with such force as he could hastily
gather the King instantly set sail. It was the trumpets on his galleys that roused the Saracens on that
Saturday morning.

There was no time to be lost. Saladin at once
sent for Baha-ed-din. The man of peace, who had sur-
veyed so many bloody fights from his mule's back,
not always at a safe distance, was now entrusted with
an aide-de-camp's task. While Saladin despatched

---

* According to the *Itinerary*, Saladin had accorded the garrison a
day's delay; but this is contradicted by Baha-ed-din. The Latin
statement is, however, very circumstantial, and though it is almost
inconceivable that Saladin broke his word, there may have been a
misunderstanding.

troops to the shore to oppose Richard's landing,
Baha-ed-din was to help to secure the citadel and
bring out the garrison. He was to take three emirs
and pick up the prince ez-Zahir, on the way. The
prince was found asleep in his armour, wrapped in
his wadded gambeson; and, still but half awake, he
mounted his horse and joined the others. They rode
through the glutted streets and reached the citadel.
On their summons to surrender, the garrison, who
were ignorant of Richard's arrival, obeyed, and prepared to leave. Had they been allowed to go forth
at once, the issue might have been different. But
one of the emirs, old Jurdik, who had served with
Saladin in the invasion of Egypt nearly thirty years
before, was a man of bowels, and he declared that he
could not let the people go out from the citadel into
the gathering crowd of Moslems, where they would
be robbed and roughly handled. He began beating
back the crowd to carve a safe retreat for the garrison, but the troops were in very ill-humour and out
of control. At last forty-nine of the garrison were
gotten out, with their horses and wives; but so much
time had been lost in the hustle that it was now
nearly noon, and as they marched out, the fleet of
Richard, consisting of as many as thirty-five ships
and fifteen swift galleys, could be descried close in
shore. This cheering sight gave the rest of the defenders new courage, and one of them came up to
Baha-ed-din and courteously informed him that they
had changed their minds. In a few minutes the
walls of the citadel were manned again; and the
next thing was a charge of the garrison, which drove

the Moslems out of the town. They were soon
chased back to the fortress, and the place was furiously attacked ; indeed so desperate was the situation, so slow the succour, that they had jurt sent
again to Saladin to beg for the same terms as before,
when the face of fortune changed.

At this very moment the English galleys suddenly
fell to their oars. Richard had waited and wondered
to see Moslem banners floating from the towers, and
feared that the citadel was already taken. The noise
of the sea, the yells of the combatants, the shouts of
the Moslem battle-cries, drowned the appeals of the
men at bay. To land in face of the Saracen army,
if nothing was left to be rescued, was an adventure
too foolhardy even for Cœur de Lion. In this uncertainty and dismay, his quick eye caught sight of
a man who plunged boldly from the castle into the
sea and swam lustily towards the fleet. He was soon
pulled on board, and proved to be a priest. " O noble King," he panted, " the remnant hunger for thy
coming. They are borne down by the brandished
swords of yonder butchers ; their necks are stretched
out as sheep for the slaughter ; they will perish on
the spot unless God helps them, through thee." And
he showed the King where the garrison still stood at
bay " in front of yonder tower." That was enough
for Richard : " Perish the hindmost ! " he shouted,
and the King's red galley pulled hard for the shore.
Ere it was beached, Richard was up to his middle in
the sea ; his knights leaped after him, and they set
upon the Saracens with might and main. Right and
left the King laid men low with swinging blows

from his famous Danish axe.* The Moslems scattered in all directions, the beach was cleared:— "under my very eyes," says the astonished secretary, "they drove us out of the harbour." Up a stairway of the Templars' house the King rushed alone, and in an instant the English flag was waving on the walls, a signal of salvation to the garrison. Down they came at the charge, and meeting their deliverer hacking with his sword, as only Richard knew how to do, they all joined together and soon there was not a live Moslem in the streets.

What Saladin was about to allow all this can only be guessed. He may have been deceived by the long inaction of the fleet, and believed they dared not land in face of his troops. At the critical moment he was called away, and it was the man of peace who warned the general of his danger. "I galloped to the Sultan," writes the secretary, "and found him with the two envoys," who had even then come from the garrison to treat for terms. A whisper told Saladin what had happened, but he went on talking lest the envoys should guess the truth. Crowds of fugitives running headlong past the tent left no further doubt, and the Sultan formally ordered the retreat that was already a rout. The great bales of booty were abandoned; the army vanished to Yazur; only Saladin himself remained on the spot with a division of light cavalry.

Thus was Jaffa taken and re-taken in two days. The gallant rescue crowned Richard's Crusade with

---

* Ernoul, 281 ; Ralph of Coggeshall, 43. The *Itinerary* says Richard brandished a cross-bow.

a glow of setting glory.   He had routed a Moslem
army with a handful of heroes, and had put them to
flight, with three horses! *

The flight was over, but not the fight.   Richard
knew this as well as anyone.   Abu-Bekr the chamberlain went to visit him—evidently with proposals
for a truce—the very night of the rout, and brought
back a quaint tale.   He found the King, he said,
conversing in his jovial way with some of the Moslem emirs—prisoners, probably—and reported his
talk, half serious, half rallying: " Why did this
mighty Sultan of yours run off at the mere sight of
me ?   By God, I was not even in armour or ready for
fight—I had only my boating-shoes on!   Why did
you bolt ? "   Then he went on, " Great God, I thought
he could not have taken Jaffa in two months—and
he did it in two days! "   Addressing Abu-Bekr he
said, " My compliments to the Sultan and say that I
beg him in God's name to make peace.   There must
be an end to all this.   My country over the sea is in
a bad way.   There is no use to us or to you in going
on with this." †

Saladin did not reject the overture, but he narrowed
the limits of negotiation to the coast between Tyre
and Cæsarea.   It was not the attitude of a beaten
general.   Richard then proposed that the Sultan
should fief him Jaffa and Ascalon, whereby he would

---

* Ralph of Coggeshall, who took his account from an eyewitness,
Hugh Neville, puts Richard's strength at 80 knights and 400 cross-
bowmen, and Saladin's army at 62,000.   (*Chron. Angl.*, 44.)   He
evidently does not reckon the Genoese and Pisans who swelled
Richard's forces to between two and three thousand.   (*Itin.*, vi., 20.)

† Baha-ed-din, 334.

become his " man," after the custom of the Franks,
and he and his troops would be at Saladin's service.
As the King was soon going away, the proposed
vassalage (even if truly reported) could hardly be of
much value, but Saladin did not wholly reject it; he
offered to give Jaffa and keep Ascalon. On Sunday
an ambassador came to Ramla, reiterating the demand for Ascalon. Saladin's reply was given without
hesitation : we cannot give up Ascalon, he said, and
your King cannot go away as he proposes without
leaving *all* the country he has won to fall into our
hands. If *he* can spend a winter here, far away from
his country and his people, when he is still in the
midst of his youth and pleasures, how much more
can I stay here, both winter and summer? " I am
in the heart of my own country," he added, "my
children and folk are about me, I can obtain all I
wish. And I am an old man; the pleasures of this
world are nothing to me—I have enjoyed them to
the full and have renounced them utterly. . . .
I believe in my soul that I am doing the best of good
works, and I will not desist until God grants the
victory to whomsoever he willeth."

This negotiation split upon the rock of Ascalon,
like its predecessor. Possibly it was merely intended
to gain time, for on the Monday there was a report
that reinforcements were marching from Acre to the
King's support. Saladin sent his baggage into the
hills, and taking only his cavalry went out to meet
the new danger. The Franks, he found, had already
reached safety at Cæsarea; and leaving them there,
he turned back and resolved to make another attempt

upon Jaffa. The Saracens were now well aware of
the weakness of the force from which they had fled
on Saturday, yet even so, they preferred to seek the
advantage of a surprise. A certain Genoese prowling
about at daybreak on Wednesday (5 Aug.) heard the
neighing of horses and the tramp of men, and saw
the glitter of steel in the slanting rays of the sun.
Running back to the camp he gave the alarm, and
the knights sprang out of their beds. They had no
time to gird all their armour on. Richard and
many others went forth with no guards to their eyes;
some had no breeches and the keen morning air
struck cold upon their naked thighs; each picked up
the weapon nearest to hand and sallied forth.

The King had only fifty-four knights in all, of
whom only fifteen had horses, and some two thousand stout soldiers; but at their head stood Henry
of Champagne, the Earl of Leicester, Bartholomew
de Mortimer, Ralph de Malo-Leone, Andrew de
Chavigny, Gerard de Furnival, and many another
trusty sword. The Saracens came on at the gallop
in seven divisions, each of a thousand horsemen;
but their spears rattled upon an iron fence. Behind
a slight palisade, hastily set, of tent-pegs, to hamper
the cavalry, the Franks were formed up on one knee
to receive cavalry, the butts of their spears firmly
planted in the earth, their shields locked before
them. Between each pair Richard placed an archer,
who plied his cross-bow over the shields; another
man stood behind to stretch and load a spare bow.
Squadron upon squadron came thundering on, only
to be brought up sharply by the wall of spears.

For a time they sat like paralysed men, locked spear to spear, able only to shout and curse, and at such close quarters that no one loosed a bowstring; then they sullenly wheeled off. Five or six times the charge was repeated, with the same result; but at last, at three in the afternoon, Richard made his cross-bowmen pass through to the front and deliver a volley of bolts at the galloping line. The spear-men then let the archers pass between them, and following up the attack completed the discomfiture of the enemy. At the moment of retreat, Richard sallied out with his fifteen mounted knights, and fell upon the Saracens with his incomparable fury, cleaving heads and chopping off limbs in every direction. In the heat of battle, he must have had his horse killed; for suddenly a Turk rode up to him on a foaming charger, leading another; seeing the King unmounted, Saladin had sent him two swift Arabs, thinking it shame that so brave a warrior should fight on foot.* Richard accepted them in the same spirit, and the battle went on. Meanwhile the Moslems tried to seize the town behind, but Richard with a handful of knights drove them out; the craven galley-men made off in alarm, but the King brought them back to hold the town; the day is one long record of Richard's exploits. " Velut leo ferocissimus invadit, invadendo prosternit, prostratos interficit." † Nor

---

* The story is told in a different form by Ernoul, 281–2, who makes el-Adil the generous, or, as some suggest, the treacherous, giver; but as el-Adil was lying sick near Jerusalem at the time this version is clearly wrong.

† See the vivid account, from an eyewitness, in Ralph of Cogge-shall, 45–50.

23

is this the coloured imagination of the Christian chronicler. Baha-ed-din admits the total failure of the Moslem attack, which he ascribes to the clemency shown to the garrison of Jaffa; some of the soldiers, he says, even taunted the Sultan—" Make your slaves charge who beat off our people on the day we took Jaffa!" Whatever the cause, Saladin could not get his men to return to the attack, and his secretary tells, in admiration and disgust, how the King of England rode along the whole front of the Saracen army, lance at rest, defying them, and not a man attempted to touch him!* Saladin at last left the field in a fury, and on the Friday he was in Jerusalem ordering fresh fortifications. He had now no faith in Richard's going away without taking the Holy City.

The next day the Sultan was back at the camp near Ramla, praying for reinforcements: he could not trust the men who had twice failed him. Supports came in the nick of time—troops from Mosil, from Egypt, the old mamluks of Shirkuh, the levies from northern Syria: in a few days he had a new army to shame the men who had skulked before Jaffa. But they were not needed. The King of England was seriously ill; health, as well as troubles at home, urged a speedy move; the other Crusaders were impatient to be off; the new King of Jerusalem and even the two Military Orders refused to be responsible for the conquered cities on the coast unless Richard were there to lead them: "they rejected his proposals and walked with him no more."

---

* Baha-ed-din, 338.

With so small a following, and so many friends
estranged; lying on a sick bed with "swarming
hordes of Turks" all round; the King could only
make terms with Saladin and go.   The second failure
at Jaffa had taught the Sultan a lesson, and even
with his fresh troops he was not eager to carry on the
war *à outrance*.   There had been enough of fighting,
in all conscience, and no one could say that for five
years the Moslems had not trodden "the path of
God" with the zeal and endurance of martyrs.   The
illness of the King softened the hearts of Saladin and
el-Adil, always disposed to friendship with so frank
and soldierly an adversary.   In his burning fever
Richard craved for cooling fruit, and Saladin constantly sent him pears and peaches and refreshing
snow from the mountains.   It is said that el-Adil
was afflicted at the King's danger, and Richard of
Devizes * relates a pretty tale of one of his visits to
the sick man's tent:—

"Meanwhile there came down to see the king, as was
his wont, a certain gentle Saffadin, Saladin's brother, an
old soldier, very courteous and wise, and one whom the
king's magnanimity and munificence had won over to
his side.   When the king's servants received him with
less glee than usual, and would not admit him to speech
with their master, he said : ' By the interpreter I perceive
ye are in great sorrow, nor am I ignorant of the cause.
My friend your king is sick, and it is for this reason
ye close the door against me.'   Then bursting into tears,
' O God of the Christians,' he said, ' if thou indeed be

* *Chronicon*, 88–92.

God, thou canst not suffer such a man, and one so need-
ful, to die so early."

It is a pity, but it is quite certain that el-Adil was
never at Jaffa during the King's illness.

It was to el-Adil, nevertheless, though he lay ill at
Mar Samwil, that Richard turned in his distress;
he begged him to make " the best terms he could " *
with Saladin. "Ask my brother, el-Adil," he urged
Abu-Bekr the chamberlain, " to see how he can bring
the Sultan to make peace, and beg him to leave me
Ascalon." But Ascalon was not to be his. Diplomacy was busy from Friday the 28th of August
to the following Wednesday; a swift courier sped
between el-Adil and the two camps; and finally the
treaty of peace for three years was signed on the
2nd of September, 1192. The coast cities he had
conquered from Acre to Jaffa were given to the
King of England; Ascalon was to be demolished;
Moslems and Christians were to pass freely in each
others' territories, and pilgrims might visit the Holy
Sepulchre at Jerusalem. When the messenger placed
the draft treaty in his hands, the King was very ill
and said, " I have no strength to read it, but here
is my hand on the peace." When the embassy came
for the signing, Richard gave his hand to each, and
they all pledged their word to him. He would
not take an oath himself, saying that it was not the
way of kings, but Henry of Champagne, King though
he was, Balian of Ibelin, the knights of the Temple
and Hospital, and all those present, took the oath.
In the evening the Franks sent their ambassadors

---

* *Itin.* vi., 27.

for the Sultan's ratification, and the next morning
Saladin gave his hand on it, and the peace was proclaimed throughout the camp. " It was a joyful
day : God alone knoweth the measureless delight of
both peoples."

King Richard went on board his ship at Acre on
the 9th of October : but before he sailed away he sent
a message to his chivalrous adversary that when the
three years' truce was over he would come again and
rescue Jerusalem ; and Saladin said in answer that,
if he must lose his land, he had liefer lose it to Richard than to any man alive. And so they parted, and
the land had rest.

COIN OF IMAD-ED-DIN OF SINJAR STRUCK IN 1188 (OBVERSE).

CHAPTER XXII.

AT REST.

1192–1193.

THE Holy War was over; the five years' contest ended. Before the great victory at Hittin in July, 1187, not an inch of Palestine west of the Jordan was in the Moslems' hands. After the Peace of Ramla in September, 1192, the whole land was theirs, except a narrow strip of coast from Tyre to Jaffa. Saladin had no cause to be ashamed of the Treaty. The Franks indeed retained most of what the Crusaders had won, but the result was contemptible in relation to the cost. At the Pope's appeal, all Christendom had risen in arms. The Emperor, the Kings of England, France, and Sicily, Leopold of Austria, the Duke of Burgundy, the Count of Flanders, hundreds of famous barons and knights of all nations, had joined with the King and Princes of Palestine and the indomitable brothers of the Temple and Hospital, in the effort to deliver the Holy City and restore the vanished Kingdom of Jerusalem. The Emperor was dead; the Kings

had gone back; many of their noblest followers
lay buried in the Holy Land; but Jerusalem was
still the city of Saladin, and its titular king reigned
over a slender realm at Acre.

All the strength of Christendom concentrated in
the Third Crusade had not shaken Saladin's power.
His soldiers may have murmured at their long
months of hard and perilous service, year after year,
but they never refused to come to his summons and
lay down their lives in his cause. His vassals in the
distant valleys of the Tigris may have groaned at
his constant requirements, but they brought their
retainers loyally to his colours; and at the last
pitched battle, at Arsuf, it was the division of Mosil
that most distinguished itself for valour. Throughout these toilsome campaigns Saladin could always
count on the support of the levies from Egypt and
Mesopotamia, as well as from northern and central
Syria; Kurds, Turkmans, Arabs, and Egyptians,
they were all Moslems and his servants when he
called. In spite of their differences of race, their
national jealousies, and tribal pride, he had kept
them together as one host—not without difficulty
and twice or thrice a critical waver. But, the shirk-
ing at Jaffa notwithstanding, they were still a united
army under his orders in the autumn of 1192, as
they had been when he first led them "on the
Path of God" in 1187. Not a province had fallen
away, not a chief or vassal had rebelled, though the
calls upon their loyalty and endurance were enough
to try the firmest faith and tax the strength of
giants. The brief defection, quickly pardoned, of a

young prince of his own blood in Mesopotamia only emphasises, by its isolation, Saladin's compelling influence over his subjects.   When the trials and sufferings of the five years' war were over, he still reigned unchallenged from the mountains of Kurdistan to the Libyan desert, and far beyond these borders the King of Georgia, the Catholicos of Armenia, the Sultan of Konia, the Emperor of Constantinople, were eager to call him friend and ally.

To such allies he owed nothing: they came not to aid but to congratulate.   The struggle was waged by Saladin alone.   Except at the last, when his brother came prominently to the front, one cannot point to a single general or counsellor who can be said to have led, much less dominated, the Sultan.   A council of war undoubtedly guided his military decisions, and sometimes overruled his better judgment, as before Tyre and Acre, but in that council it is impossible to single out a special voice that weighed more than another in influencing his mind.   Brother, sons, nephews, old comrades, new vassals, shrewd Kady, cautious secretary, fanatical preacher,—all had their share in the general verdict, all helped their Master loyally according to their ability, but not a man of them ever forgot who was the Master.   In all that anxious, laborious, critical time, one mind, one will was supreme, the mind and the will of Saladin.

When the struggle at last was ended, when the Franks had been driven to the seashore, and the places holy to Moslems as well as to Christians were once more in his own keeping, Saladin may well have dreamt of wider empire, larger schemes. The memories of the first great tide of Saracen victory, even the late example of Seljuk triumphs, might awaken thoughts of other worlds to conquer. But such imaginings were not ripe to trouble his newly found peace. Saladin's first concern was for the repose of his weary troops. Hardly had the Treaty been signed when he dismissed them to their homes, and on the 10th and 11th of September the long procession of the men of Mesopotamia began the glad march to their villages by the great rivers and in the upper highlands. His next care was for the crowded caravans of Christian pilgrims who were at last to content their souls' craving to see the place where the Lord died. There were rough Saracen soldiers at Jerusalem, hungry for vengeance upon the slaughterers of their kindred upon the plain of Acre; but Saladin's escort on the road, and honest Jurdik's humane rule in the city, brought the pilgrims through all dangers.

The Sultan himself was in Jerusalem in September, when Hubert Walter the Bishop of Salisbury brought the third of the pilgrim caravans to the Holy Places.

" To this bishop, on account of his uprightness, his reputation for wisdom and his wide renown, Saladin sent, offering him a house free of cost. But the bishop refused on the ground that he and his company were pilgrims. Then Saladin bade his servants shew all kinds of courtesy to the bishop and his men. Saladin also sent him many gifts of price and even invited him to a conference in order to see what kind of a man he was in appearance. He had the Holy Cross shewn him, and they sat together a long time in familiar conversation. On this occasion Saladin made enquiries as to the character and habits of the king of England. He also asked what the Christians said about his Saracens. To him the bishop made answer, ' As regards my lord the king, I may say that there is no knight in the world who can be considered his peer in military matters, or his equal in valour and generosity. He is distinguished by the full possession of every good quality. . . . If any one could give your noble qualities to king Richard and his to you, so that each of you might be endowed with the faculties of the other, then the whole world could not furnish two such princes.' At last Saladin, having heard the bishop patiently, broke in : ' I know the great valour and the bravery of your king well enough ; but, not to speak too severely, he often incurs unnecessary danger and is too prodigal of his life. Now I, for my part, however great a king I might be, would much rather be gifted with wealth, so long as it is alongside of wisdom and moderation, than with boldness and immoderation.'

" After a long interview by means of an interpreter Saladin bade the bishop to request any gift he liked and it should be granted him. For this offer the bishop gave many thanks, begging to have a space of time—till the morrow—granted him for deliberation. Then, on the next day, he begged that two Latin priests and two Latin deacons might be permitted to celebrate divine service with the Syrians at the Lord's Sepulchre. These priests were to be maintained out of the offerings of the pilgrims. For, in visiting the Lord's Sepulchre, the bishop had found only the services half celebrated after the barbarous fashion of the Syrians. He made a similar request for Bethlehem and Nazareth. This was a great petition to make, and, as is believed, one very pleasing to God. When the Soldan consented, the bishop, in accordance with his request, established priests and deacons in each place, thus inaugurating a fitting service to God." *

Four months before these Latin priests were installed, an ambassador from the Greek Emperor had preferred a similar request to Saladin on behalf of the priests of the Orthodox Church, and had been refused. It is curious to discover in the twelfth century the same contest over the Holy Places which was among the Russian pretexts for the war with Turkey in 1854.

When he was assured that the King of England had really taken ship and left the country, Saladin began a progress through the land which had been won and held at so great cost. He visited all the strongholds and chief cities, examining their defences, giving orders for fortifications, and placing in each a strong garrison of horse and foot. At Beyrut, on the 1st of November, he received the Prince of Antioch, Bohemond the Stammerer, who participated in the treaty of peace; the meeting was cordial, and the Prince was presented with lands in the plain of Antioch to the value of 15,000 gold pieces a year. At Kaukab—no longer to be called Belvoir—he found his ancient servant of early days, Karakush the builder of the walls of Cairo, who had languished in prison at Acre ever since the surrender. There were no reproaches, but only the welcome due to old and tried devotion. On the 4th of November

---

* *Itin.*, vi., 34.

Damascus once more acclaimed its Sultan. He had
not been within its gates for four years, and his public levee the next day was thronged with old friends
and joyous subjects. The poets had no words rare
and rich enough for the great occasion.

Once more Saladin was at home among his children. We see him sitting in his summer-house in
the castle grounds, with his younger children about
him. Envoys from the Franks were announced, but
when they came into his presence, their shaven chins,
cropped hair, and strange clothes frightened little
Abu-Bekr, who began to cry. The father, thinking
only of the child, dismissed the ambassadors with
an excuse, before they had even delivered their
message. Older sons were there, grown men who
had fought in his battles, and with these and his
brother, el-Adil, he went day after day hunting the
gazelle in the spacious plains about Damascus. He
had thoughts of going to Mekka on pilgrimage, the
supreme duty of the pious Moslem; he wished to
visit again that Egypt which had been his stepping
stone to power; but the time passed, and the pilgrims came back from Arabia, and Saladin was still at
Damascus, revelling in the delights of a peaceful home.

On Friday the 20th of February, he rode out with
Baha-ed-din to meet the caravan of the Hajj. He
had not been well of late, and it was the wet season;
the roads were streaming after heavy rains, and he
had imprudently forgotten to wear his usual quilted
gambeson. That night he had fever.* The next day

---

* It was probably an acute remittent fever, of the bilious type,—
the " yellow fever " of Arabic writers,—due to blood poisoning. His

he could not join his friends at dinner, and the sight of the son sitting in the father's seat brought tears to many eyes—they took it as an omen. Each day the Sultan grew worse, his head was racked with pain, and he suffered internally. On the fourth day the doctors bled him; and from that time he grew steadily worse. The fever parched his skin, and he became weaker and weaker. On the ninth day his mind wandered; he fell into a stupor and could no longer take his draught. Every night Baha-ed-din and the chancellor el-Fadil would go to see him, or at least to hear the doctors' report; and sometimes they would come out streaming with tears, which they strove to command, for there was always a multitude outside the gates waiting to learn from their faces how the Master was. On Sunday, the tenth day of the illness, medicine gave some relief, the sick man drank a good draught of barley water, and broke into a profuse perspiration. "We gave thanks to God . . . and came out with lightened hearts." It was but the last effort. On Tuesday night the faithful secretary and chancellor were summoned to the castle, but they did not see

---

previous malarial attacks and exposure to constant and intense fatigue and hardships, and recently to wet and cold, may have produced organic complications. The symptoms, recorded very fully by Baha-ed-din,—suppression of the excretions with retention of the poison, which increased until it burst through the skin in exhausting perspiration, followed by death,—are common to various forms of virulent fever. So I am informed by Sir William Gowers, M.D., F.R.S., who kindly interested himself in the subject of Saladin's fatal illness, and consulted the local experience of Dr. F. J. Mackinnon, of the Victoria Hospital, Damascus, who confirmed his diagnosis.

the Sultan, who was sinking fast. There was a divine with him, repeating the confession of faith and reading the Holy Word; and when he came to the passage " He is God, than whom there is no other God,—who knoweth the unseen and the seen,—the Compassionate, the Merciful," the Sultan murmured, " True "; and when the words came, " In Him do I trust," the dying man smiled, his face lighted up, and he rendered his soul to his Lord.

Saladin died on Wednesday, the 4th of March, 1193, at the age of fifty-five.

They buried him the same day in the garden house in the Citadel of Damascus, at the hour of the *asr* prayer. The sword which he had carried through the Holy War was laid beside him : " he took it with him to Paradise." He had given away everything, and the money for the burial had to be borrowed, even to the straw for the bricks that made the grave. The ceremony was as simple as a pauper's funeral. A striped cloth covered the undistinguished bier. No poet was allowed to sing a dirge, no preacher to make oration. When the multitude, who thronged about the gate, saw the bier, a great wailing went up, and so distraught were the people that they could not form the words of prayer, but only cried and groaned. All eyes were wet, and there were few that did not weep aloud. Then every man went home and shut his door, and the empty silent streets bore witness to a great sorrow. Only the weeping secretary and those of the household went to pray over the grave and indulge their grief. The next day the people thronged to the tomb, praying, lamenting, reciting the Koran, and invoking the blessing of God upon him who slept beneath.

It was not till the close of a second year that the body of the Sultan was interred by a son's loving care in the oratory on the northern side of the Kellasa, beside the great Omayyad mosque, where it lies now. Over it the faithful chancellor, who was soon to follow his master, wrote the epitaph: "O God, accept this soul, and open to him the gates of heaven, that last victory for which he hoped."

"I entered into this oratory," says a later biographer, "by the door which gives on the Kellasa, and after reciting a portion of the Koran over the grave, I invoked God's mercy on its dweller. The warden showed me a packet containing Saladin's clothes, and I saw among them a short yellow vest with black cuffs, and I prayed that the sight might be blessed to me." *

The wise physician Abd-el-Latif wrote, somewhat cynically, that to his knowledge this was the only instance of a King's death that was truly mourned by the people. The secret of Saladin's power lay in the love of his subjects. What others sought to attain by fear, by severity, by majesty, he accomplished by kindness. In the memorable words which he spoke, not long before his death, to his best-beloved son, ez-Zahir, on dismissing him to his provincial government, he revealed the source of his own strength.

"My son," he said, "I commend thee to the most

* Ibn-Khallikan, iv., 547.

high God, the fountain of all goodness. Do His will, for that way lieth peace. Abstain from the shedding of blood ; trust not to that ; for blood that is spilt never slumbers. *Seek to win the hearts of thy people,* and watch over their prosperity ; for it is to secure their happiness that thou art appointed by God and by me. Try to gain the hearts of thy emirs and ministers and nobles. I have become great as I am because I have won men's hearts by gentleness and kindness."

Gentleness was the dominant note of his character. We search the contemporary descriptions in vain for the common attributes of Kings. Majesty ? It is not mentioned, for the respect he inspired sprang from love, which " casteth out fear." State ? Far from adopting an imposing mien and punctilious forms, no sovereign was ever more genial and easy of approach. He loved to surround himself with clever talkers, and was himself " delightful to talk to." He knew all the traditions of the Arabs, the " Days " of their ancient heroes, the pedigrees of their famous mares. His sympathy and unaffected interest set every one at his ease, and instead of repressing freedom of conversation, he let the talk flow at such a pace that sometimes a man could not hear his own voice. Old-fashioned courtiers regretted the strict propriety of Nur-ed-din's levees, when each man sat silent, " as if a bird were perched on his head," till he was bidden to speak. At Saladin's court all was eager conversation—a most unkingly buzz. Yet there were limits which no one dared to transgress in the Sultan's presence. He suffered no unseemly talk, nor was any flippant irreverence or disrespect of per-

TOMB OF SALADIN, DAMASCUS.
(FROM A PHOTOGRAPH BY BONFILS.)

sons permitted. He never used or allowed scurrilous language. He kept his own tongue, even in great provocation, under rigid control, and his pen was no less disciplined: he was never known to write a bitter word to a Moslem.

The Baghdad physician has left a record, far too brief, of his first impressions of Saladin, in which we see the Sultan in his social aspect.

"I found him," wrote Abd-el-Latif, "a great prince, whose appearance inspired at once respect and love, who was approachable, deeply intellectual, gracious, and noble in his thoughts. All who came near him took him as their model. . . . The first night I was with him I found him surrounded by a large concourse of learned men who were discussing various sciences. He listened with pleasure and took part in their conversation. He spoke of fortification, touched on some questions of law, and his talk was fertile in ingenious ideas. He was then [1191-2] absorbed in strengthening the defences of Jerusalem, and personally superintended the work, even carrying stones on his own shoulders; and everybody, rich and poor, followed his example, even Imad-ed-din the Katib, and the Kady el-Fadil. He was on horseback before dawn, superintending the work till noon, . . . and again from afternoon prayer till he returned by torchlight. Then he would spend a great part of the night in arranging the morrow's labours."

His whole life was simple, laborious, ascetic. When he was shown a beautiful pavilion that had been built for him at Damascus, he scarcely glanced at it: "We are not to stay here for ever," he said. "This house is not for one who looks for death.

We are here to serve God." Luxury and self-indulgence he despised. When he found that one of his sons was neglecting his duties in his passion for a slave-girl, he sternly upbraided the voluptuary, and separated the girl.

" Our Sultan," says Baha-ed-din, " was very noble of heart, kindness shone in his face, he was very modest, and exquisitely courteous." The histories are full of his goodness. He could not bear to have his servants beaten, in an age when the beating of servants was a matter of course. If they stole his money, he dismissed them ; but the whip he abhorred. His indulgence and patience knew no bounds, and he never set store by his own dignity. Baha-ed-din relates with horror how, when they were riding together into Jerusalem on a rainy day, his mule splashed the Sultan with mud ; but Saladin only laughed, and would not let the abashed secretary ride behind. Another time a servant threw a shoe and almost hit the Sultan, but he turned smiling to the other side, as though he had not noticed it. An old mamluk importuned him with a petition when he was worn out with fatigue, but he fetched the ink-horn himself and granted the request without a sign of irritation. Petitioners would so crowd him when he sat in audience, that they even trampled his divan, but he always took their petitions with his own hand and attended to their grievances, and none went empty away. Every day he received these troublesome documents, and set apart a certain time to go through the papers with his secretary and endorse them with the proper answers.

On Mondays and Thursdays he sat on the judgment seat, with the Kadis and jurisconsults, in the
court of law, and administered justice to all comers.
He claimed and allowed no privileges before the
court, and if a man had a suit against one of the
royal princes, or even against the Sultan himself, they
had to appear before the Kady like any ordinary de-
fendant and submit to the law. But if Saladin won
the case, he would clothe the defeated suitor in a
robe of honour, pay his expenses, and send him away
happy and astonished. From such a judge people
could not fear sternness. Yet in the war for the
Faith he could be stern, almost implacable, and the
list of executions, especially of Templars, shows how
religion may embitter even the gentlest of men.
But it was not always so. It is related how a Frank
prisoner was brought trembling before Saladin, and
then cried out, " Before I saw his face I was sore
afraid, but now that I have seen him I know he will
do me no harm." He went off a free man.

These pages have recorded instances of his
clemency and tenderheartedness, but many might be
added. There is the touching story of the woman
who came from the Crusaders' camp at Acre seeking
her baby, who had been carried off by the Saracen
soldiery. The pickets let her pass and led her to the
Sultan, to whom she had appealed,—" for he is very
merciful," they said. Saladin was touched by her
anguish; the tears stood in his eyes; and he had the
camp searched till the little girl was safely restored
to her mother, and both were led back to the enemy's
lines. His love for children was a beautiful part

of his character. Every orphan child he felt was his
special charge. He was devotedly attached to his
own little ones: of his wives we read nothing *;
Eastern gentlemen do not talk of their wives; but
there are many references to his pleasure in his
children. He would not allow them to see deeds of
blood—a precaution natural enough in our eyes, but
very rare in his age. "I do not wish them," said
Saladin, "to become accustomed to bloodshed, young
as they are, or to delight in the taking of life, when
as yet they know not the difference between Moslems
and infidels." He used to teach them himself and
delighted, more perhaps than they did, in instilling
into their infant minds a certain compendium of
theology, which they had to learn by heart.

For above all things Saladin was a devout Moslem.
His religion was all the world to him. In this alone
he was fanatical; and the only act of severity, not
done in war, that can be alleged against him was the
execution of the mystic philosopher es-Suhrawardy,
on the ground of heresy. Saladin hated all eclectic
philosophers, materialists, and free-thinkers, with a

---

* The only one of Saladin's wives whom we know by name is the
princess Asimat-ed-din, daughter of Anar, the celebrated vezir of
Damascus. She married the Sultan Nur-ed-din in 1147, and after
his death she became in 1176 the wife of Saladin, by whom (though
she must have been at least 45) she was recorded to be with child in
1182. No child, however, survived her, when she died in 1185.
Like Saladin's sister, the " Lady of Syria," she was a pious founder
of mosques. At his death, Saladin left seventeen sons and one little
daughter ; and several children died earlier. (Abd-el-Basit, *Description de Damas*, trans. Sauvaire, 198, 248 ; Imad-ed-din in Abu-
Shama, 40.)

holy horror. His own faith was as rigidly orthodox as it was simple, strong, and sincere. Islam, in its essence and as professed by such a man as Saladin, is a religion of noble simplicity and austere self-sacrifice. To say that he was regular in its ceremonious observances is little, except that his determination to make up for the two months of fasting, which he had been forced to omit during the war, probably hastened his end. His frequent illnesses and arduous exertions alike made fasting dangerous to his health ; his doctors warned him in vain, and his persistence in this religious duty whilst at Jerusalem in his last year weakened his constitution and made him less able to resist the fatal fever. No one was more assiduous in the five daily prayers and the weekly attendance at the mosque ; and even when seriously ill, he would send for the Imam and force himself to stand and repeat the fatiguing service of Friday. He delighted in hearing the Koran read to him, but his reader had to be a practised expert. Saladin would listen till his heart melted and the tears rolled down his cheeks. He had this womanish weakness, yet one likes him none the less for his emotional, sensitive nature. " His heart was humble and full of compassion, and tears came readily to his eyes."

It was a grief to him that he was never able to perform the religious duty of pilgrimage ; but at least he was a benefactor to the pilgrims. One of his early acts of sovereignty was to abolish the onerous tolls which had for centuries burdened the Faithful who visited Mecca, and his last public appearance was to welcome the returning Hajj. As the pilgrims greeted him, it was noticed how radiant he looked. He had but a week to live.

In nothing did he show his religious zeal more fervently than in the chief and supreme duty of Moslems, the *Jihad* or Holy War. Naturally averse to bloodshed, even unwarlike, as he was, he was a changed man when it came to fighting the infidels. "I never knew him," says Baha-ed-din, "show any anxiety about the numbers and strength of the enemy. He would listen to plans of all kinds and discuss their consequences without any excitement or loss of composure." He used to ride, as we have seen, between the lines of battle, attended only by a page; and once he sat there on horseback surrounded by his staff and listened calmly whilst the sacred Traditions were read aloud to him in face of the enemy. To wage God's war was a genuine passion with him; his whole heart was wrapped up in it, and to this cause he devoted himself, body and soul. During those last years he could hardly speak or think of anything else, and he sacrificed every pleasure, comfort, and domestic happiness, to its service. He even dreamed of wider battles for the faith: when the Franks should be driven out of Palestine, he told his secretary, he would pursue them over the sea, and conquer them, till there should not remain one unbeliever on the face of the earth. "What is the most glorious death?" he asked his friend, who replied, "To die on the Path of God." "Then I strive for the door of the most glorious of deaths," said Saladin. When he was so prostrated with a painful illness at the siege of Acre that he could not come to table, he would yet sit his horse all day before the enemy; and when men marvelled at his fortitude, he said, " The pain leaves me when I am on horseback. It comes back only when I dismount." So long as he was doing God's work, he felt no pain; but inaction tortured him.

On that Holy War he spent everything, strength, health, one may even say life itself. He emptied his treasury in the cause. But it was natural to him to give, and he gave ungrudgingly, with open-handed, both-handed generosity, as freely when he was poor as when he was rich. Money he compared to mere dust, and he hated to refuse it to him who asked. He would always give more than was expected, and he never said " we have given to him before." He was preyed upon by greedy beggars, and Baha-ed-din was ashamed at the importunity of the petitions that passed through his hands. Had he been left to himself his campaigns would have been ruined for lack of funds—for it was his rule that his commissariat should pay for the provisions they took from the country people. His treasurers used always to keep a secret balance for emergencies, and even then the Sultan would sell his last farm sooner than turn away a poor man. So it happened that when he was dead there was found but one Tyrian dinar and 47 silver dirhems in the treasury. He left neither house, nor goods, nor acres, nor villages, nor any sort of personal property. The great Sultan died almost pennyless. It would be hard to imagine a nature more unselfish, devoted to higher aims, or more wholly lovable. Had he been made of sterner stuff,

or skilled in the prudent economies and saving fore-
sight of mere selfish statesmanship, he might perhaps have founded a more enduring and united
empire, but he would not have been Saladin, the
type of generous chivalry.

The faithful secretary, when he finished his Story
of his Master's life, wrote, " I have ended my record
on the day of his death, God's mercy be on him.
My aim was to deserve the compassion of the Most
High God, and to stir men to pray for Saladin and
to remember his goodness."

CHAPTER XXIII.

SALADIN IN ROMANCE.

THE most celebrated English romance of the Middle Ages relating to Saladin is the "Romance of Richard Cœur de Lion," which appears to have taken its present shape about the beginning of the fourteenth century. In this dreary poem we find Richard, lying sick before Acre, demanding pork with an invalid's persistence. His attendants are in despair, because pork is not easily procured in a Mohammedan country. A crafty old knight hits upon a perfect substitute. He kills a plump young Saracen, and Lionheart finds it excellent "pork." With a refinement of hospitality he tries the new dish on his Saracen prisoners, and bids them to a state banquet, where each man's plate is garnished with the head of a particular friend. Richard himself presides at this Pelopeian feast, and gracefully carves a Saracen's head by way of encouragement. "Friends!" he exclaims, seeing a not unnatural hesitation among the convives:

> Frendes, be nought squoymous!
> This is the maner of my hous,

> To be servyd ferst, God it wot,
> With Sarezynes hedes abouten al hot.

The " Romance of Richard Cœur de Lion" is more than satisfying in regard to its hero, but disappointing in its vague account of Saladin. Like the *Itinerarium Regis Ricardi*, on which its more historical—or less unhistorical—incidents are perhaps distantly founded, it is wholly occupied with the heroic deeds of

> Kyng Rychard, the werryor best
> That men fynde in ony jeste.

When he met Saladin in single combat (which, as we know, he never did) the Sultan was miserably discomfited. At the battle of Arsuf, for example, Richard did not miss the opportunity of personally worsting his " heathen" antagonist as well as routing his army :

> Off a footman a bowe he took,
> He drowgh an arwe up to the hook,
> And sente it to the Sawdon anon,
> And smot hym thorwgh the schuldyr bon.

Whereat Saladin, in great dolour, fled to Cairo:

> The cheff Sawdon off Hethenysse
> To Babyloyne was flowen, I wysse.

He presently plucked up courage, however, to come back and challenge Richard to single combat. Here the true story of the horse which Saladin sent to Richard, when he saw him fighting on foot at Jaffa, is introduced with variations. Saladin sends for his astrologer, "a maytyr Negromacien," who conjures

" twoo stronge feendes off the eyr " into the forms of two chargers. One of these is sent to King Richard, and is warranted to come to the neigh of his mate, the mare whom Saladin was to ride, and thus would the King be snared at the critical moment of the encounter. An angel, it is needless to say, warns Richard of this trick, and instructs him how to manage the strong fiend with a huge pole.

> Ther myghte men see, in a throwe,
> How Kyng Richard, the noble man,
> Encounteryd with the Sawdan
> That cheef was told off Damas.
> Hys trust upon hys mere was.
> Therfoore, as the booke telles,
> Hys crouper heeng al full off belles
> And hys peytrel, and hys arsoun ;
> Three myle myghte men here the soun.

The event of the duel was never doubtful : no man could withstand Richard's arm. He soon

> Gaff the Sawdon a dynt off dede.
> In his blasoun, verrayment,
> Was i-paynted a serpent.
> With the spere that Richard heeld,
> He bar hym thorwgh and undyr the scheelde.
> None off hys armes myghte laste ;
> Brydyl and peytrel al to-brast,
> Hys gerth and hys stiropes alsoo ;

and, to make a long story short, the mighty Sultan, transfixed by his adversary's spears, tumbled over his mare's crupper, and lay in the most undignified attitude, his " feet toward the fyrmament." Yet Saladin challenged Richard again at Jaffa, to whose ambassador the Lionheart made answer:

> God geve the wel evyl pyne !
> And Saladyn yowr lorde,
> The devyl hym hange with a corde.   . . .
> Now go and say to Saladyn,
> In despyte of his god Appolyn
> I wyl abide hym betime.   . . .
> And if the dogge wyl come to me
> My pollax schal hys bane be.

The famous poleaxe, however, the two-handed Danish axe of Ernoul's story, was less baneful to Saladin than to his sons, two of whom Richard slew offhand, according to the Romance.

One finds a much richer store of Saladin legends in the French romances. To take but a thread or two of the mythical skein, the "Tales of a Minstrel of Rheims"* give a good idea of the recitations which used to delight gentle audiences in courts and castles, the Society of the thirteenth century. Indeed, the very same tales were evidently current two centuries later, as anyone may see by a reference to Pierre Cochon. They are much more artistic than the clumsy English romance of Richard, and as their object was by no means to belaud that hero, or the "caudate" Britons—who were supposed (by Frenchmen) to put their tails between their legs and run,— they had to resort to other characters and incidents to excite and retain the interest of their hearers. In matter of history the Minstrel sticks at nothing. He begins Saladin's adventures at a precocious age, and connects him in a discreditable manner with Eleanor of Aquitaine, afterwards the Queen of Henry II. and

---

* *Récits d'un Ménestral de Reims*, edited by M. N. de Wailly for the Société de l'histoire de France, Paris, 1876.

mother of Richard I., but at the time of the story wife of Louis le Jeune of France.

Eleanor, he explains, " qui mout fu male famme," when she went to Palestine on crusade with her husband, was much annoyed at Louis's slothfulness. He stayed at Tyre all winter (1148-9), doing nothing but spend money, while Eleanor became a prey to melancholy. Her wandering thoughts would stray to the gallant person of Saladin, who openly rallied the French king's unwarlike luxury, " sa molesce et sa nicetei," and vainly challenged him to come out and fight. Eleanor was so much impressed with the gossip she heard of Saladin's prowess and generosity, that she fell in love with him *durement*, and, in the good frank medieval way, sent a dragoman to tell him so ; offering to have him for her lord, and to change her religion for his sake. Saladin, of course, could only be delighted, *moult liés*, at such a proposal from so fair a dame, with such a dower— " la plus gentis dame de crestienté et la plus riche." He straightway sent a swift galley from Ascalon to fetch her. In not going himself he showed more prudence, perhaps, than gallantry ; but Saracen lovers, no doubt, had their own canon of etiquette. The galley arrived at Tyre in the dead of night, and the dragoman hastened by a secret passage to the Queen's chamber. When she heard that the galley was waiting she was in ecstasies : " Parfoi," quoth she, " c'est bien fait." Taking two demoiselles, and two coffers well stuffed with gold and silver, she hurried to the strand, when, just as she stood there, " one foot on sea and one on shore," the King her husband laid hands on her and brought her back. A tale-bearing maid of honour had roused the good man, and told him that his Queen was off to Saladin, and Louis had scrambled into his breeches and armour just in time. Restored to a *tête-à-tête* in the castle, he naturally asked her what she did it for. "God's name!" cried the Queen, "because of your poltroonery : you are not worth a rotten apple. And I have heard such fine things of Saladin, that I love him better than you." The enormity of her vice, however, is only fully appreciated when history informs us that, at the date of this amour, Saladin was a good little boy of eleven, going regularly, no doubt, to the mosque school at Baalbekk.*

The Minstrel is not, it will be observed, very careful of chronology, and he thinks nothing of taking us at a leap from 1148 to 1187, in order to tell the story of Count Raymond's treason. When Sibylla had crowned her husband Guy King of Jerusalem, there was great discontent among the old nobility of Palestine ; and Raymond of Tripolis, it seems, took counsel with the Patriarch and the barons, and plotted against the new King. They appointed a secret interview with Saladin, and proposed to surrender the land to him, "car li rois est nices et mauvais, et n'a point de pouoir se par nous non." Saladin had no objection to offer : on the contrary, he promised the conspirators immense rewards. "Tell us what

---

* It is possible, as Mr. Archer has suggested to me, that the romancers have confused our Saladin with an older namesake, Salah-ed-din el-Yaghisiyany, a prominent general in Zengy's campaigns against the Franks. But we do not hear of him at the date of Louis's Crusade, and if he was then alive he must have been a very old man.

pledge you require," said the Count of Tripolis.
" By Mahom my god," cried Saladin, "you say well.
You shall all of you swear by your religion, and
more, for we will be blooded together, and will drink
each other's blood in token of amity and union."
This was done : all swore by their faith and drank
each other's blood, and the plot was settled.   When
the great battle took place "before Acre," three
leagues from the city, on the day of " Sant Jehan
Decollace," the time came for the pledge to be kept.
Saladin called out in the thick of the fight, " Count
of Tripolis, Count of Tripolis, fulfil your oath ! "
Whereupon Count Raymond vailed his banner, and
all the other traitors did the like ; so the Christians
were defeated, and the King and his knights were
sent prisoners to " Babiloine."   But Saladin despised
traitors and treachery, and was moved by Guy's misfortune, finding him indeed to be a " prudhomme
and good knight."   So he shortly set him free, with
twenty of his knights, all well furnished with arms
and provisions, and sent them back to their friends
on the Syrian coast.

We next hear of Saladin in connexion with the
Hospital at Acre.   Ralph de Diceto ascribes the
foundation of this famous house of charity to his
own chaplain, one William, who "on his way to Jerusalem vowed that should he come to Acre harbour
safe and soon, he would there build, as well as he
could afford, a chapel to St. Thomas the Martyr," and
arriving there he did so, and became its prior, and
served the sick.   The Minstrel makes Saladin its pious
benefactor.   His authority is an imaginary uncle of

Saladin, a venerable man of ruddy face (*vermauz en vis*) and a great white beard, which reached half-way to his feet, besides a fine long *tresse* hanging down to his waist. In spite of these eccentricities, he looked the thorough gentleman (*preudons*), and was most courteously communicative about his famous nephew, when questioned as a prisoner at Acre in the days of the merry Bishop of Beauvais.

Saladin, it appears, had heard of the boundless charity of the Hospital, and resolved to test its generosity. So he put on pilgrim's garb, and took a palmer's staff, "*bourdon, escharpe, et esclavine,*" and presented himself in an exhausted condition at the Hospital. They took him in and attended him with assiduous care, but for three days he refused all food. The Master feared he would die, and every means of persuasion was used to tempt him to eat. At last he confessed he had a longing, a sick man's longing, for one special dish. The good brothers gladly promised to gratify his desire. Then he said he must have a dish of the off forefoot of the Grandmaster's horse, and nothing else would he touch. Yet he protested he had rather die, for he knew how choice and rare a steed he was, and how dear to his master, who had given a thousand gold besants for him. But the Grandmaster said the life of a man was worth more than a horse, and at once sent his favourite to the sick man's room. They cast him and tied him down, and a man came with an axe and asked which foot was wanted. "The off forefoot," they said. Then he swung the axe in both his hands and was bringing it down for the stroke, when Saladin cried out:

" Hold ! My wish is satisfied, and now I crave other meat: I would eat sheep's flesh." So the horse was unbound and led back to the stable, and Saladin ate mutton. Four days later he departed with grateful leavetakings, and coming to his own kingdom he caused a charter to be drawn up, granting a thousand besants of gold, charged on the revenues of Babylon, to be paid to the Hospital at Acre each year on St. John Baptist's Day. Whereat the Grandmaster and the brethren rejoiced, " for they knew that Saladin did not lie," and the thousand pieces of gold were duly paid each year, and are so paid to this day.* At least, so said our Minstrel to his thirteenth-century listeners, and very likely they believed his pretty tale.

Another story of the white-haired prisoner has a family likeness to other legends. The Marquess of Cæsarea was a miserly man, who lightened his garrison while he weighted his coffers. Saladin warned him that if he went on in this way, he would lose the city. " Peace ! " quoth the Marquess, " I can make a thousand knights leap out of my coffers when I please ! " In due time Saladin took the city by storm, and the miser was brought a prisoner before him. " Marquess, Marquess," said the conqueror, " where are the thousand knights whom you were to bring out of your chests ? By Mahom, your covetousness has misled you. You were never glutted with gold or silver but I will glut you yet more to-day." Then gold and silver were melted down in an iron pail and

---

* The Minstrel may have got this idea from the fact that Saladin, during his occupation of Acre, did actually endow the hospitals there, but of course as *Moslem* institutions. See above, p. 244.

25

poured down the Marquess's throat, *et maintenant le convint mourir.*

There is an old legend recorded by Vincent de Beauvais and Pippin,* that when Saladin lay dying "he called his standard-bearer to him and charged him, saying: Do thou, who art wont to bear my banner in the wars, carry also the banner of my death. And let it be a vile rag, which thou must bear through all Damascus set upon a lance, crying: 'Lo, at his death the King of the East could take nothing with him save this cloth only.'"

The Minstrel also knows the story, and puts it into the mouth of his confidential prisoner. In this version Saladin is represented as sending a servant through all his cities, with a strip of linen on the point of a lance; the man stood at all the street corners and proclaimed these words: "Of his kingdom and all his treasure, Saladin will carry nothing away, save only these three ells of linen for his shroud." The idea is in perfect keeping with the devout and humble character of the Sultan, and it is a pity that it finds no confirmation in the Arabic records.

The prisoner gave other details of Saladin's last moments. The dying Sultan, he said, called for water, and they brought it in a silver bowl. He took it in his left hand, and with his right he made the sign of the cross over the water, touching the rim of the bowl in four opposite places, saying the

---

* It is quoted in that delightful little volume of English History from Contemporary Writers, *The Crusade of Richard I.*, by Mr. T. A. Archer, a book full of interest and humour, and packed with solid learning. I am much indebted to its author.

while, " As wide is it from here to there as from here to there," to mislead those who were looking on. " Then he poured the water on his head and body, and said three words in French, which we did not catch, but it seemed as if he baptised himself." " So died Saladin," the Minstrel concludes, "the best prince that ever was in pagandom, and was buried in the cemetery of my lord Saint Nicholas of Acre, beside his mother, who was there very sumptuously interred. And there is a beautiful tall dome over them, where burns a lamp of olive oil day and night, furnished and lighted by them of St. John of the Hospital of Acre, who hold large revenues which Saladin and his mother bequeathed them."

Saladin lies buried at Damascus, and assuredly neither gave nor bequeathed a single dirhem to any Christian charity. But the legend of his baptism probably comes from the widely believed story of his having solemnly received the Christian Order of Knighthood. At first sight it seems incredible that a devout Moslem, who carried his religion into his every act, and consecrated the last five years of his life to the Holy War for the faith, could possibly consent to perform the ceremonies involved in the Christian initiation to knighthood, as practised by the Crusaders. Yet the author of the " Itinerary of King Richard " (i., 3) states definitely, and without a syllable of surprise or explanation, that when Saladin came to mature years and was fit for bearing arms, " he came to Humphrey of Toron, the illustrious noble of Palestine, to be mantled, and after the manner of the Franks received from him the

belt of knighthood." If this were a solitary instance, it might perhaps be dismissed as fiction,
since the chronicler was not then present in Palestine. But later on, at a time when the author of the
" Itinerary " was himself probably with the Crusading
army, he records (v., 11), " On Palm Sunday, King
Richard, amid much splendour, girded with the belt
of knighthood the son of Saphadin, who had been
sent to him for that purpose." Thus it appears that
not only did Saladin voluntarily seek knighthood at
the hands of Humphrey of Toron, but he (or his
brother el-Adil, the "Saphadin" of the chronicles)
also voluntarily sent his nephew to be knighted by
Richard himself. There is naturally not a word of
this in the Arabic contemporary histories: if they
knew it, as good Moslems they would feel it their
duty to conceal such painful backsliding in their
hero and master. But if such doings were to be,
Humphrey of Toron was the very man to do them.
He had been bound in brotherly pact (*fraterno
foedere junctus erat*, according to William of Tyre,
xvii., 17) with a powerful Saracen Emir as early as
1152; he spoke Arabic, and his influence was exerted
in 1175 to arrange a truce between the Moslem Sultan and the King of Jerusalem. The friendship may
have begun in 1167, when Saladin was honourably
entertained as guest or hostage in the camp of Amalric before Alexandria. Here he may have acquired
an admiration for the ideals of chivalry, which he
certainly carried into practice. There were also rites
of initiation in the East, which may have prepared
his mind for the ceremony of knighthood ; and the

feudal system of the Turks in which he was brought up, and on which he organised his own empire, may have suggested further assimilation to the military customs of Europe.

The most detailed account of this surprising ceremony is given in the early metrical romance " L'Ordene de Chevalerie." The knighting is here performed by Hugh the son of Raymond, Count of Tripolis and (through his wife) lord of Tiberias, the same Raymond whose supposed treachery on the field of Hittin has been described. The youthful Hugh of Tiberias, for several reasons, was a much less likely actor than Humphrey of Toron ; but the ceremony, and not the officiator, is the point of interest. Hugh of Tiberias had been taken prisoner by Saladin (this actually happened in 1179), and before releasing him on promise of ransom, the Sultan took him aside, and begged him, by his faith towards God and his religion, to show him how knights were made. " Beau Sire," said Hugh stoutly, " I will not ; " and he explained that Saladin being void of baptism and Christianity, it was folly to talk of knighthood, " car mout en seroie blasmés." Saladin, however, urged that he could not be blamed for doing it under compulsion, as a prisoner, and Hugh at length gave way. Then the ceremony began. First he arranged the Sultan's hair and beard.

> Cheveus et barbe et le viaire
> Li fait appareiller mout bel
> Chest droit à Chevalier nouvel.

Then he laved him in a bath ; for, said he, just as the little child comes forth after baptism pure from sin, so must the knight be purified symbolically, and come forth full of courtesy and goodness.

> Sire, tout ensement devés
> Issir sans nulle vilonnie
> Et estre plains de courtoisie,
> Baigner devés en honesté,
> En courtoisie et en bonté,
> Et faire amer à toutes gens.

Saladin, who showed much curiosity to learn the precise meaning of each act in the initiation, was much impressed : "By God most great," he exclaimed, "this beginning is beautiful." Then, after laying him on a bed, the type of the everlasting rest of Paradise, Hugh clothed him in white raiment, to signify purity, and then in scarlet, in token that he must ever serve and honour God and defend Holy Church. Next he shoed him with dark shoes, "to keep you in memory of death, and the earth in which you must lie, whence you came and whither you must go ;" for no knight may cherish pride, but must ever strive after humility. "All this is good hearing," said the Sultan, who was next girt, standing, with a slender white girdle, a sign of chastity and contempt of luxury—

> Car Chevalier doit mout amer
> Son cors a netement tenir
> Qu'il ne se puist en chou honnir.

The gilt spurs were next put on, that he might be spurred to ardour in the service of God—" mout plaisoit bien Salehadin "—and then Hugh girded him with the sword, which stood for Uprightness, Trustiness, and Loyalty, and signified that a knight

must hold his own against the powerful, and succour
the weak, " ch'est œuvre de misericorde." A pure
white coif completed the dress, the symbol of a
white soul, pure of great sins and fleshly follies, fit
to appear before God at the Last Day.

Saladin at each step cheerfully assented, and now
he asked whether there was no more. " Yes, Sire,"
was Hugh's answer, " but I dare not do it." " What
is it then ? " " 'T is the accolade." The prisoner
could not give a blow, even of knighthood, to a king.
But the old French is worth quoting:

> Li Rois très tou chou escouta,
> Et en après li demanda
> S'il falait plus nule cose ?
> " Sire, oil, mais faire ne l'ose."
> " Que chou est dont ? " " Chest li colée."
> " Pourquoi ne le m'avés donnée,
> Et dite la senefianche ? "
> " Sire, chou est li remembranche
> De celui qui l'a adoubé
> À Chevalier et ordonné ;
> Mais mie ne le vous donron,
> Car je suis chi en vo prison,
> Si ne doi faire vilonnie
> Pour cose qu'on me fache et die,
> Si ne vous voel pour chou ferir."

Though too respectful to dub him, Hugh instructs
Saladin in the four devoirs of a true knight. First,
he shall never take part in injustice or treason : if he
cannot turn away wrong, he must at least turn himself away from it. " The next thing is very beautiful : he shall on no account deceive matron or maid,
but if they have need of him, shall aid them to the
utmost of his power, if he would win glory and re-

gard; for women one must honour, and adventure great deeds in their cause." Fasting and hearing Mass were the last duties enjoined upon the new knight. All this much delighted Saladin—" Si en a eu joie mou grant." If he entered upon the cere- mony merely out of curiosity, he was now evidently impressed, and romance and history are at one in the main point, that Saladin became a Knight.

It would be interesting to trace the effect of these medieval tales upon the two great writers who have introduced Saladin among the *dramatis personæ* of European classics. Scott, of course, had read the chronicles and romances, as far as they were readily accessible, and incidents in "The Talisman" may be plausibly traced to the legends of the minstrels. Saladin's visit to Richard's camp in the disguise of a *hakim* may have been suggested by the Minstrel's tale of the equally imaginary visit to the Hospital of St. John at Acre. The quarrel over the banner of Austria is found in the "Romance of Richard Cœur de Lion," published at Edinburgh, in Weber's "Metrical Romances," fifteen years before "The Talisman." But his main source was clearly, not the romances, but the chronicles, which he used as far as they suited him, and very properly threw over whenever they did not fit his scheme. As he wrote himself in the Preface of 1832:

" One of the inferior characters introduced was a sup- posed relation of Richard Cœur de Lion; a violation of the truth of history, which gave offence to Mr. Mills the author of the History of Chivalry and the Crusades, who was not, it may be presumed, aware that romantic fiction naturally includes the power of such invention, which is indeed one of the requisites of the art."

Scott boldly asserts that he "had access to all which antiquity believed, whether of reality or fable," about Richard I.; but he can hardly have gone very thoroughly into the Oriental sources, although some were even then easily accessible in Latin. It is obvious, however, that when he sins against "the truth of history," in regard to his European characters, it is of malice prepense. He admits that he knowingly killed Conrad of Montferrat in the wrong way, and the wrong time, and the wrong place, and his other deviations from history are probably no less intentional. He places the scene of the novel at Jaffa, in the autumn of 1192, as various indications prove; and he must have known that Philip of France and Leopold of Austria had both left the Holy Land after the surrender of Acre more than a year before. He sets "the Diamond of the Desert" close to the Dead Sea, on the road to Jerusalem, half way between the camps of the Crusaders and the Saracens; which would place Saladin's camp, "over against Jaffa," somewhere in Moab on the other side of the *Mare Mortuum.* Nor could Ilderim have been deceived for a moment by the notion that the Knight of the Leopard could possibly find himself beside that inhospitable water if he was riding from Jaffa to Jerusalem, since he must have left the Holy City directly behind him. At that time, moreover, no "pilgrimage to the Holy Sepulchre" was to be thought of. But a crusading tale without a desert, no sand, no oasis, no Dead Sea, no pilgrimage, would lack the essential local colour, and Scott very properly put it in. And so all the quarrelling between the rival nations, which was true enough of the French and English, is infinitely more interesting when the absent King of France himself leads his knights ; no novel-reader would care a rush for the jealousy of a Duke of Burgundy—unless, of course, he were Charles the Bold.

Scott's treatment of the Oriental side of the picture is marked by fewer liberties, because there was less occasion. He has exercised a judicious caution in bringing practically only one Eastern figure, that of Saladin himself, upon his canvas, and avoiding the temptation to dwell upon anything but his personality. He says nothing definite of the Sultan's history, and by substituting him for his brother "Saphadin" in the story of the proposed marriage, he gets rid of the necessity for individualising a second important Moslem character ; but Scott knew very well that it was to be an alliance between "Saphadin," not Saladin, and Joan of Sicily, not Edith. To avoid crowding the canvas with "inferior characters," to say nothing of lowering the dignity of the alliance, a stroke of the pen abolished both Joan and her proposed bridegroom. No one can deny that the story is all the better for it ; and a footnote easily propitiates complaisant history.

But if Saladin was to marry Edith there must be a meeting ; and so the ordeal by battle and the unhistorical slaughter of Conrad and the Master of the Temple (whose name was not "Sir Giles

Amaury ") serve also most conveniently to make
the chief actors acquainted. It is possible that
Scott was really unaware of the fact—somewhat
singular, considering their close relations, both hostile and diplomatic—that Richard and Saladin never
actually met face to face. The King twice proposed
an interview, but in each case Saladin declined. It
was " Saphadin " who really met Richard and exchanged much cordial hospitality, and who conducted all negotiations. Equally fictitious are
Saladin's visit in the disguise of a *hakim*, and his
solitary rides about the plains. The Sultan never
travelled unattended ; he generally had his guard of
mamluks when he was anywhere near the enemy ;
and the chance encounter with Kenneth, the disguise and the talisman belong to the category of
the " Thousand and One Nights." Nor can Scott
honestly be justified in his description of Saladin's
appearance. He says he was " in the very flower of
his age," but Oriental flowers at fifty-four are apt
to be faded ; and he ventures to paint his portrait,
which, to our loss, no contemporary Eastern attempted. All we know definitely about his face is
that at fifty he wore a beard, and we only know this
because he happened to tug at it during the battle of
Hittin. Sir Walter has got the beard right, " a flow-
ing and curled black beard," to boot, " which seemed
trimmed with peculiar care " ; but when he goes on
to work in the nose, eyes, teeth, and forehead, he
trusts to that admirable source, his own invention.

Setting aside these natural licences of the romancer,
the portrait of Saladin is drawn with remarkable

insight and accuracy. His gentleness, courtesy, and nobility of character, his justice, truthfulness, and generosity, which "The Talisman" has made familiar to so many readers who know nothing else in Mohammedan history, are set forth in every contemporary record. His rare bursts of passion, which Scott has finely rendered, were also historically part of his disposition. Unfortunately he seems to have never heard of Saladin's knighthood, and thereby we have probably lost a magnificent chapter. The general manner, dress, and so on are sufficiently Eastern, but show no minute study of the subject. The hatred of the Templars is another true touch. The two Military Orders were the only Christians to whom, as a class, Saladin showed no mercy : and he had his reasons. On the other hand, Scott is altogether wrong when he says that the Sultan "has been ever found" in "the front of battle," "nor is it his wont to turn his horse's head from any brave encounter." Saladin revelled in the sight of battle ; "there was nothing he loved so much as a good knight," says Ernoul—witness his hearty admiration of the Green Knight of Spain—but he did not fight in person. He would fearlessly expose himself between the lines of battle, attended only by a groom with a spare horse, whilst the bolts and arrows whistled about his head ; he would even make his chaplains read prayers under fire ; and he would be seen in all parts of the field. But his duty as general, he conceived, was to lead, encourage, restrain, and order the disposition of the troops, not to engage in personal encounters ; and so far as fighting

went, a marshal's *bâton,* or Gordon's cane, would be
his proper weapon.   Conversing with the Bishop of
Salisbury, after peace was made, he censured the rash-
ness of the " Inkitâr " Richard in mixing personally
in the fray.   That Scott played tricks with history
is really nothing to the point; but that he was able,
through the confused and imperfect records he used,
to see and depict the true character of Saladin with
remarkable accuracy, is but another proof of his
genius.

Lessing, in *Nathan der Weise,* had drawn a portrait
of the chivalrous Sultan half a century before " The
Talisman " was written, and the play shows signs of a
German's serious study of *Quellen.*   Lessing may
have read Marin's *Histoire de Saladin* (1758), or even
Schultens' Latin translation (1732) of the contemporary Arabic biography by Baha-ed-din.   He falls into
historical errors like Scott, but, unlike Scott, he does
not do so on purpose, in deference to the requirements of romantic fiction.   There is no artistic object
served, for instance, in making Saladin's father act as
his treasurer in 1192 in the Lebanon, an inconvenient
centre for the paymaster of an army at Jerusalem ;
besides, the father had been dead nearly twenty
years.   But the very blunder shows that Lessing
had read somewhere that Saladin's father was once
governor of Baalbekk, and was afterwards his son's
treasurer at Cairo, both of which are historical facts.
Again, Lessing adheres to the historical version of
the projected marriage, but adds a wholly unauthen-
tic plan of a marriage between Saladin's sister Sittah
(really Sitt esh-Sham, or " The Lady of Syria ") and

Richard's brother—presumably the bastard William Longsword. The whole story of the marriage is so bizarre, even in the Oriental authorities, that one can hardly wonder at any extravagance in the modern glosses.

> Wenn unserm Bruder Melek
> Dann Richards Schwester wär' zu Theile worden:
> Ha ! welch ein Haus zusammen !

Saladin exclaims to Sittah. What a house indeed! The notion of Richard putting Joan of Sicily into " Saphadin's " harim, and the couple reigning jointly in Palestine, under the affectionate patronage of their Christian and Moslem brothers of England and Egypt, is delightful enough to tempt the poorest imagination to run riot.

There are many true touches, no doubt, in Lessing's portrait of Saladin : such as his love of kindred,

> Der sein Geschwister ingesammt so liebt,

and his generosity and contempt for money ; though

> Ein Kleid, ein Schwert, ein Pferd,—und Einen Gott,
> Was brauch ich mehr ?

gives an impression of knight-errantry, which was not in the real character. The main defect, however, of Lessing's delineation (considered historically), is that it is too European. His Saladin is no real Saracen, as Scott's is. The set purpose of " Nathan the Wise," as a motive-drama, to preach toleration, and to silence the bigoted criticism of worthy pastor Goetze, compels Lessing to hold up Saladin as a type not only of a good Moslem, but a tolerant. The former he was, beyond question ; but tolerance was not his virtue ; his chivalry and clemency were in act, not in thought. He could be kind to Christians, but he never doubted that they must eventually go down into the Pit. He had a holy horror of philosophy, free-thought, "broad views," and all manner of heterodoxy. The only cruel act recorded against him, outside the retaliations of war, was the deliberate execution of a "philosopher"—a mystic Sufi. Like many fanatics, he could better tolerate the flat opposition of other religions than heresy within the pale of his own creed. His chivalry to crusaders was the good-breeding of a gentleman ; it did not touch his intellectual appreciation of their errors. He had a gentle soul and a soft heart, but they did not dispel his conviction that Christians were "fuel for Hell." He is a type of a true Moslem of the purest breed ; but Lessing gives him a theological latitude which he would have indignantly disowned. Of course, all this has nothing to do with the drama as a drama, any more than historical criticism of "The Talisman" touches in any way its merits as a novel. To the student of the widespread Saladin myth, both works have the great interest that they preserve, amidst some historical truth and some romantic legend, the general character which opinion in all times has ascribed to the great Sultan.*

It is singular that the East, the birthplace of Sala-

* The preceding pages originally appeared partly in *Literature*, May 28th, but principally in *Longman's Magazine*, August, 1898.

din, which has been the mother of so many admirable tales, has almost wholly neglected him in its fiction. The " Thousand and One Nights " do not disdain crusading stories, witness the " Tale of King Omar ibn en-Noaman and his sons Sharrkan and Zau el-Mekan "; but Saladin's name is not once introduced. The omission is the more singular when it is remembered that the " Nights " probably received their latest form at Cairo, where the founder of the Citadel has always been a favourite hero. Doubtless he has formed the subject of many popular tales, told in the coffee-houses and in the bazars of Egypt, but so far unpublished. One such romance, indeed, has come to light in an Arabic manuscript at Berlin,* but it is poor stuff. Richard's sister Rumina is brought captive before Saladin. Saphadin falls in love with her on the spot, strikes off her fetters, and leads her to his tent. There she promises to adopt his religion, but only to gain time. Whilst he sleeps, she escapes, dressed in men's clothes. Saphadin writes to Richard to demand her in marriage, but meanwhile is captured by guile. Rumina comes forth on horseback, clad in a knight's coat of mail, to do battle with Saladin. She is again made prisoner, Saphadin is rescued, Rumina embraces Islam—and Saphadin, and the wedding takes place with great pomp. The interest in the story is the repetition of the original idea of a Christian-Moslem marriage between el-Adil and some relation of Richard I., which seems to be the most permanent and universal detail in the Sala-

---

* Published in a German translation by Goergens, *Arabische Quellenbeiträge*, 283 ff.

din myth. It is strange, however, that no better example of Arabic romance should be connected with the subject. The character of the great Sultan, however, appeals more strongly to Europeans than to Moslems, who admire his chivalry less than his warlike triumphs. To us it is the generosity of the character, rather than the success of the career, that makes Saladin a true as well as a romantic hero.

26

INDEX

A

Abak, Atābeg of Damascus, 67
' Abbāsid Caliphs (Khalīfas),
7–9, 38, 52, 109, 116, 142, 164,
191, 268
' Abd-el-Bāsit, 372 n.
' Abd-el-Laṭif, 367, 369, 370
Abū-Bekr, chamberlain of Sala-
din, 337, 350, 356
Abū-Firās, 149
Abū-l-Heyja " the Fat," 340
Abū-Ṣāliḥ, 103
Abū-Shāma, viii., 158, 159, 245,
etc.
Abyssinians' Lake (Birket el-
Ḥabash), 90, 93, 116
Acre (' Akka), 24, 27, 30, 219,
221, 241, 244, 254–299, 334,
337, 344–346, 356, 357, 364,
387; taken by Saladin, 219;
battle of, 261–264; bishop of,
213; description, 259; hospitals, 244, 384, 385; massacre
at, 306, 307; siege by Crusaders, 254–299
Adana, 26
' Āḍid, el-, Fāṭimid Caliph, 86–
88, 96, 108–110
' Ādil, el-, Seyf-ed-dīn (Saphadin), 102, 152, 192, 219, 220 n.,
231, 232, 249, 267, 269, 277,
286, 301, 326–332, 337, 338,
353 n., 355, 356, 364

Afḍal, el-, 201, 213, 261
' Aḳaba, el-, 106, 167, 175
Aḳṣā, mosque of el-, 236
Āḳsunḳur, 17, 35
Aleppo (Ḥalab), 26, 34, 49, 68,
75, 84, 134, 137–141, 143, 144,
146, 147, 164, 165, 170–173,
175, 194, 248
Alexandria, siege by Amalric,
89, 94; by Sicilians, 127, 128
Alliance between Moslems and
Christians, etc., see Treaties
Almeida (meydān, horse-course
or playground), 45 n., see
Meydān
Almohade Caliph, 288
' Aly the clockmaker, 160
Amalric, 81, 83, 85–95, 103–105,
120, 134
Ambassadors and envoys, 42, 86,
112, 191, 192, 364, see Negotia-
tions
Āmid (modern Diyār-Bekr), 33,
36, 56, 172
' Amr, mosque of, 117
Anar (Ainardus), Muʻīn-ed-dīn,
vezīr of Damascus, 52, 53, 55,
69–71
Anar's daughter, wife of (1)
Nūr-ed-dīn and (2) Saladin,
372 n.
Andrew of Brienne, 263
Anṣārīya mountains, 138, 148
Ansel de Pass, 106

403

Index. 405

The Story of the Nations.

MESSRS. G. P. PUTNAM'S SONS take pleasure in announcing that they have in course of publication, in co-operation with Mr. T. Fisher Unwin, of London, a series of historical studies, intended to present in a graphic manner the stories of the different nations that have attained prominence in history.

In the story form the current of each national life is distinctly indicated, and its picturesque and noteworthy periods and episodes are presented for the reader in their philosophical relation to each other as well as to universal history.

It is the plan of the writers of the different volumes to enter into the real life of the peoples, and to bring them before the reader as they actually lived, labored, and struggled—as they studied and wrote, and as they amused themselves. In carrying out this plan, the myths, with which the history of all lands begins, will not be overlooked, though these will be carefully distinguished from the actual history, so far as the labors of the accepted historical authorities have resulted in definite conclusions.

The subjects of the different volumes have been planned to cover connecting and, as far as possible, consecutive epochs or periods, so that the set when completed will present in a comprehensive narrative the chief events in the great STORY OF THE NATIONS; but it is, of course, not always practicable to issue the several volumes in their chronological order.

The "Stories" are printed in good readable type, and in handsome 12mo form. They are adequately illustrated and furnished with maps and indexes. Price, per vol., cloth, $1.50. Half morocco, gilt top, $1.75.

The following are now ready :

GREECE. Prof. Jas. A. Harrison.

ROME. Arthur Gilman.

THE JEWS. Prof. James K. Hosmer.

CHALDEA. Z. A. Ragozin.

GERMANY. S. Baring-Gould.

NORWAY. Hjalmar H. Boyesen.

SPAIN. Rev. E. E. and Susan Hale.

HUNGARY. Prof. A. Vámbéry.

CARTHAGE. Prof. Alfred J. Church.

THE SARACENS. Arthur Gilman.

THE MOORS IN SPAIN. Stanley Lane-Poole.

THE NORMANS. Sarah Orne Jewett.

PERSIA. S. G. W. Benjamin.

ANCIENT EGYPT. Prof. Geo. Rawlinson.

ALEXANDER'S EMPIRE. Prof. J. P. Mahaffy.

ASSYRIA. Z. A. Ragozin.

THE GOTHS. Henry Bradley.

IRELAND. Hon. Emily Lawless.

TURKEY. Stanley Lane-Poole.

MEDIA, BABYLON, AND PERSIA. Z. A. Ragozin.

MEDIÆVAL FRANCE. Prof. Gustave Masson.

HOLLAND. Prof. J. Thorold Rogers.

MEXICO. Susan Hale.

PHŒNICIA. Geo. Rawlinson.

THE HANSA TOWNS. Helen Zimmern.

EARLY BRITAIN. Prof. Alfred J. Church.

THE BARBARY CORSAIRS Stanley Lane-Poole.

RUSSIA. W. R. Morfill.

THE JEWS UNDER ROME. W. D. Morrison.

SCOTLAND. John Mackintosh.

SWITZERLAND. R. Stead and Mrs. A. Hug.

PORTUGAL. H. Morse-Stephens.

THE BYZANTINE EMPIRE. C. W. C. Oman.

SICILY. E. A. Freeman.

THE TUSCAN REPUBLICS. Bella Duffy.

POLAND. W. R. Morfill.

PARTHIA. Geo. Rawlinson.

JAPAN. David Murray.

THE CHRISTIAN RECOVERY OF SPAIN. H. E. Watts.

AUSTRALASIA. Greville Tregarthen.

SOUTHERN AFRICA. Geo. M. Theal.

VENICE. Alethea Wiel.

THE CRUSADES. T. S. Archer and C. L. Kingsford.

VEDIC INDIA. Z. A. Ragozin.

BOHEMIA. C. E. Maurice.

CANADA. J. G. Bourinot.

THE BALKAN STATES. William Miller.

BRITISH RULE IN INDIA. R. W. Frazer.

MODERN FRANCE. André Le Bon.

THE BUILDING OF THE BRITISH EMPIRE. Alfred T. Story.

THE FRANKS. By Lewis Sergeant.